FACING THE FUTURE

FACING THE FUTURE

THE SEVEN FORCES REVOLUTIONIZING OUR LIVES

RICHARD WORZEL

Published in 1994 by
Stoddart Publishing Co. Limited
34 Lesmill Road
Toronto, Canada
M3B 2T6
(416) 445-3333

Canadian Cataloguing in Publication Data
Worzel, Richard, 1950-
      Facing the future: the seven forces revolutionizing
      our lives
Includes bibliographical references and index.
ISBN 0-7737-2830-9
1. Economic forecasting - Canada.   2. Social
prediction - Canada.   3. Canada - Economic
conditions - 1991- . *   4. Canada - Social
conditions - 1971- . *   I. Title

HC115.W67 1994   303.4971   C94-931325-4

Excerpts from David Roberts, "The Brew Crew Takes Over," December 21, 1993, reprinted with permission from The Globe and Mail. Excerpts from Michael Valpy, "The Troubled Children of Families of Convenience," November 3, 1993, reprinted with permission from The Globe and Mail. Excerpts from Reginald W. Bibby, "Who Will Teach Our Children Shared Values?" The Globe and Mail, February 3, 1994, reprinted with permission from Reginald Bibby, University of Lethbridge, Alberta. Shelby Steele, "The New Segregation," Imprimis, August 1992, reprinted by permission from Imprimis, the monthly journal of Hillsdale College.

Cover Design: Bill Douglas/The Bang

Printed and bound in the United States of America

This book is dedicated to
Lord Baden-Powell of Gilwell
founder of the Boy Scouts and Girl Guides,

and to the tens of thousands of men and women in more than 150 countries worldwide who give their time to make Scouting and Guiding two of the largest, most unified, most successful — and best — of global organizations.

Their dedication to teaching children spiritual values, leadership, judgment, self-reliance, compassion, sound ecological practices, teamwork, citizenship, and civic virtue makes Scouting and Guiding two of the few organizations actively working for the future of all humanity.

"Be Prepared"

Contents

Tables and Figures

Many Thanks

"**E**veryone learns how to write in second grade. Most of us go on to better things." So said Bobby Knight, a rather flamboyant basketball coach with little patience for scribes, and there have been many times when I was sure he was right.

This book would not have been possible at all were it not for the many people who helped me. Any errors that have crept in are my doing. So my grateful thanks to these and many others:

- Jacky Simmons, my assistant, chief critic, friend, and wife
- David Lavin, my speaking agent, and Beverley Slopen, my literary agent, for pushing me into writing this book and helping me decide what flavour and texture it should have
- Angel Guerra and Donald G. Bastian of Stoddart Publishing for their help and encouragement along the way
- Rodger Campbell for encouragement and thoughtful commentary
- The Economist, which is, in my opinion, the finest news magazine published in the English language
- Peter Drucker, whose brilliance would be daunting were it not so illuminating
- The librarians at the Mount Pleasant branch of the Toronto Public Library, for their tireless assistance and patience
- The people at on-line services of the North York Public Library for their ability to winkle out needed obscure facts from vague hints
- Statistics Canada, which provided much of the raw data I used
- Dave Killins of Legacy Storage Systems
- John Banka of Argord Industries
- Catherine Swift, Vice-President of Research for the Canadian Federation of Independent Business
- David Pecaut of Canada Consulting/Boston Consulting
- Allan Hughes of the Toronto Waldorf School
- John McFadden, Trustee for Ward 16 of the Toronto Board of Education, who is part of the solution, not part of the problem, with our educational system

- Premier Frank McKenna of the Province of New Brunswick
- Professor Bill Buxton of the University of Toronto and the Ontario Telepresence Project
- Professor Eugene Fiume of the University of Toronto's Computer Science Department
- Bill Worzel of Arroyo Software
- Dr. Ernest Kornelsen, formerly of the Institute for Microstructural Sciences, now retired
- Dr. Hans Kunov of the Institute of Biomedical Engineering at the University of Toronto
- Dr. Al Miller of the Department of Metallurgy and Materials Science at the University of Toronto, and Tony Redpath of the Ontario Centre for Materials Research
- Dr. Ted Munn of the Institute for Environmental Studies at the University of Toronto
- Dr. Ron Worton, Vice-President of the Americas section of the Human Genome Project
- Dr. Silvia Bacchetti, Professor of Molecular Biology at McMaster University, Hamilton, Ontario
- And the World Future Society of Bethesda, Maryland, whose publications, conferences, and book lists have provided so much of my education as a futurist.

O N E

The Path Ahead of Us

The truth waits for eyes unclouded by longing.

— Buddhist saying

A man on a cross-country trip was stopped at a roadblock by a
police officer. When the motorist rolled down his window, the
officer said, "We've had reports of problems farther along this road.
You might want to buy some emergency supplies for your trip or
take another route."

The motorist felt irritated. Up to this point, his journey had
been smooth and enjoyable with only minor problems to deal with.
He was annoyed with the officer for intruding on his pleasure. He
asked, "Are you telling me I can't drive along this road?"

"No, I'm only trying to tell you we've had reports of troubles
ahead. We're recommending that people plan ahead if they take this
route, that's all."

The man thought for a moment. His car was running well, he
felt good, and the day was sunny with a few puffy white clouds
overhead. "I haven't had any problems so far," he said, "so I don't
think the troubles will affect me." And with that, he rolled up his
window and drove on.

I can't tell you whether the future will be easy or hard for you.
No one can do that, no matter what they say. I can tell you, though,
that there are forces at work today that are threatening to make your

life more difficult, with or without your permission. More than this, I can tell you that the near future is going to be very different from the recent past. If you're expecting to drive on without preparing for these problems, I believe you're heading into real trouble and stand to lose much of what you have now. On the other hand, I also believe that turbulent times are times of great opportunity for those who are prepared to meet them. It's up to you whether you simply want to drive on and hope for the best, or are willing to prepare for the future and perhaps profit mightily from it.

As a professional futurist, I get a lot people asking me, half-jokingly, which teams are going to win or which stocks are going to go up. I tell them that whatever I or anyone else says about the future is opinion, no matter how it's presented. The future hasn't happened yet, so whatever is said about it has to be opinion, because no evidence has ever been brought from the future to support one position or another. Accordingly, you should expect to disagree with what I say from time to time — perhaps often.

However, it's less important whether you agree with me than whether I've caused you to think more carefully about what will happen in your future. In fact, I encourage you to think of this book more as a cafeteria than a restaurant: take what you need and leave the rest.

Most of the time, events tend to be shaped by a few major forces. Looking back over the past century, for instance, you can see that the productivity of the Industrial Revolution, coupled with rising levels of international trade and political stability, have created lifestyles that our forebears could only have dreamed of. In agriculture, the green revolution has made farmers so productive that the nature of society and the economy have been completely changed. We have gone from having 45 percent of the population working on the farm a hundred years ago to less than 3 percent today, and the number is still falling. Yet those few farmers produce staggering amounts of food, so much that we can't eat it all and are constantly looking for new export markets.

Technology has produced unbelievable magic. My grandmother, who lived into her nineties, couldn't get over the changes that had taken place in her lifetime. When she was a girl growing up on a farm, entertainment was found in the social events staged by her community church, or in books or in gatherings in the family

2

parlour. Transportation was by horse or on foot. And "store bought-en" food was a rarity and a treat. When she was born, people who talked about heavier-than-air flight were hooted down as fools. "Horseless carriages" were dangerous noisy contraptions that frightened the horses, were found only in major cities, and were eschewed by all God-fearing, right-thinking people.

By the time my grandmother died, entertainment came out of thin air into a box. Transportation was by automobiles moving at speeds of more than "a mile a minute." Food made from scratch was rare enough to be a special treat, while supermarket packaged foods were the rule. Planes took only a few hours to cover distances that the pioneers had taken months to cross. And a human had set foot on the moon — a feat that had been roundly denounced as impossible a mere generation earlier.

Politically, a hundred years ago Great Britain ruled much of the world, and colonial imperialism was the accepted practice. Europe was the centre of the earth, and what happened there shook the foundations of everyone's lives. Canada, although freshly independent, followed the lead of the "Mother Country"; anything else would have been unthinkable. The United States was an immature upstart, a minor power experiencing its great growth phase and still recovering from the political turmoils caused by its Civil War. Japan was a feudal state, only just thinking about machines and modernization. Hardly anyone had even heard of communism.

World population was a fantastic 1.5 billion people, and natural resources were largely untapped, and limitless. The only pollution problems people noticed were the killing yellow fogs of London and the large amount of horse manure in the cities.

Despite all these examples of change clearly set out before us, we have a hard time believing that the future is going to be different from what we see around us now. Indeed, the pace of change has been so great that, emotionally, we believe that things have to slow down, for a while at least. This is wishful thinking and dangerous fantasy. The pace of change is increasing, not diminishing. If we are still around a hundred years from now, we will find the changes even more astonishing than those my grandmother witnessed. Whether we wish to or not, we are rocketing forward into a strange world about which we know very little.

What's propelling us into this brave, new world? I believe there are seven major forces loose today that are carving out much of the scenery and detail of our future lives:

1 The emergence of a **global economy**, which is taking control of Canada's prosperity. This force will dominate our jobs, our lives, and our financial well-being. It is already reducing the power of our governments to intervene for our benefit.
2 **Population pressures**, which fall into two categories: the effects of the postwar baby boom in North America, and the continuing population explosion in underdeveloped and developing countries.
3 **Technology**, which is like the genie from the bottle. It will change how we live, where we work, how we communicate, what we do for fun, how we relate to each other, and much, much more.
4 The **environment**, which is important in two ways. First, its media value affects politics, consumer buying patterns, and the economy. Beyond this, ecological problems affect the real world and hence food production, water quality, health, and so on.
5 **Longer lives**. Medical research is producing startling results that hold the promise of much longer lives — if we can afford them. But longer life is not automatically better life.
6 The **decline of the nation-state**, which could also be called the rise of tribalism. This is changing politics at both national and local levels of government.
7 The **splintering of society and the isolation of the individual**. We are faced with a paradox. Our ability to see and experience so much through travel and communications convinces us that the world is getting smaller. At the same time, our ability to change society and the world is steadily declining, making us feel smaller and less important.

ANTICIPATING VS. FORECASTING

These forces are both big and impersonal. What people really want to know is, What does all this mean to me, and what can I do about it? And how can I have a good life? These questions are the true focus of this book.

Before I start describing the effects that these seven major forces may have on your life, let me give you a couple of warnings about what's to follow. First, there are things happening that I greatly fear and dislike. When I talk about them, people often assume that I am in favour of them; or else they feel that if we talk about these feared and dangerous things, we will somehow cause them to happen. As a result, they get angry with me. Maybe if I would just shut up, they seem to imply, all these problems would go away. In reply, I can only say that these things are likely to happen whether we talk about them or not. I dislike much of what's coming as much as you do, so please don't shoot the messenger.

Second, it's important to understand the difference between fore-casting and anticipating the future. This difference has been clearly expressed by professional futurist Peter Schwartz: "The purpose of scenarios is to help you change your view of reality — to match it up more closely with reality as it is, and reality as it will be. *The end result, however, is not an accurate picture of tomorrow, but better decisions about the future.*"[1]

A forecast is an attempt to produce an accurate picture of tomorrow. Forecasts are almost always wrong and, unless used carefully, they can be misleading and even dangerous. Anticipation, on the other hand, is the step before contingency planning that allows you to make better decisions about the future. This book, then, *anticipates* the future. As such, I hope it will be of value to you.

THE FIRST FORCE

The Global Economy

T W O

How the Rules Have Changed in the Working World

From now on any country — but also any business, especially a large one — that wants to do well economically will have to accept that it is the world economy that leads, and that domestic economic policies will succeed only if they strengthen, or at least not impair, the country's international competitive position.

– Peter Drucker, *The Frontiers of Management*, 1986

Canada is and has always been a trading nation. Today the export sector of our economy represents between one-quarter and one-third of our national income.[1] Canada stands sixth in per capita exports, although our economy ranks no better than eleventh in the world in size.[2] Directly or indirectly, most of our economy relies on companies that are involved in export. If we are to prosper as a nation, we must therefore succeed as global traders. But the rules of the export markets have changed. Indeed, the entire global marketplace has changed.

For centuries, improvements in transportation and communications brought nations closer together and allowed trade to expand and flourish. We are witnessing the climax of this trend, for all the world's countries are now able to trade as efficiently with each other as they can within their own borders. But the world is not homogeneous.

Some places are rich and others are poor. Some are well developed, like Canada, and have a wealth of materials, factories, and skilled workers, while others have little or nothing except cheap labour and a burning desire for a better life. These differences are changing the rules we Canadians must play by if we are to remain prosperous and not slip into poverty.

When Canada emerged as a wealthy country in the nineteenth and twentieth centuries, there were three key factors that allowed a nation to grow and prosper: land (including natural resources), labour, and money. We have abundant land and natural resources, which we have historically used to great advantage. Immigrants have added a continuing flow of willing and eager labour to an already hard-working population. As branch-plant operations were set up here, we imported capital, first from Great Britain and later from the United States, to extract, process, manufacture, and transport the goods we sold. And from our primary industries such as mining, farming, and forestry, and later from our factories, we grew the sophisticated economy of a developed nation.

But a country no longer needs to possess land, labour, and capital to prosper. Consider the rise of Singapore, which seceded from Malaysia in 1965 to form an independent city-state. At the time, Singapore was poor and underdeveloped, with little industry. It had no natural resources to draw upon, and more than half its people had no formal schooling whatever.

Yet since its independence, Singapore has experienced one of the fastest rates of growth in the world. Today this prosperous city-state is richer than New Zealand; 90 percent of its citizens own their homes (a far higher rate of home ownership than ours); and they have a life expectancy of seventy-six years, which is essentially equal to ours.[3] The lesson is clear: the factors of prosperity have changed.

Natural resources are no longer important

"Who has the world's best steel industry?" asked Lester Thurow, dean of the Arthur C. Sloan School of Business at MIT and one of the world's leading economists on international trade and competitiveness. "The Japanese," he prompted. "Who has neither iron nor coal? The Japanese."

Thurow made this point to Canada's federal Liberals when addressing their annual convention in Aylmer, Quebec, in November 1991. He then went on to drive the point home: "Natural resources are no longer important. . . . If you take the price of natural resources (including oil) in 1990 and correct them for inflation, they were 30 percent below where they were in 1980. In 1980, they were ten percent below where they were in 1970. In a two decade period of time, the price of raw materials has fallen 40 percent. The fall will continue. Raw materials prices will fall at least 40 percent in the next twenty years."[4]

This does not mean that we're at a disadvantage because we have natural resources. It does mean, though, that we can no longer rely on having natural resources to guarantee our future prosperity.

There is no shortage of investment capital, for us or for others

What of investment capital? Here again there is good news and bad news. The good news is that investment capital is global. If we in Canada can convince investors (a) that their capital will be safe with us, and (b) that it will produce a satisfying rate of return, we can have all the investment capital we want. I estimate that the money available in the global investment markets exceeds the combined annual GNP of all the nations of the world.

But are we an attractive place to invest? When foreign investors look at us, do they see a stable political situation? Do we have inflation and government finances under control? Do we tax and regulate our industries lightly, giving them the cash flow they need to grow and prosper? And is our economy still growing rapidly compared with other places in the world? Unfortunately, the answer to most of these questions is "no." I'll discuss this further in the next chapter.

Labour and the global job leak

Our unemployment rate testifies to the quantity of labour we have available. But it's no longer the number of workers a country has that is important; it's how skilled they are in the things that count.

The economies of all the developed countries are being pushed through a major transition by two significant trends: automation, and competition from rapidly developing countries (RDCs). The RDCs are the poor countries that are working their way out of poverty. Both these trends are eliminating traditional jobs in developed countries. As a result, Peter Drucker predicts that by 2010 no developed country will employ more than one person in ten in manufacturing.[5]

Work that requires lots of low-skilled labour can be done more cheaply in developing countries, where the wage rates are so much lower. For example, textile workers in Vietnam are paid an average of 18 cents (US) an hour,[6] and they're happy to get the work. Now, if you are a global customer, there's no reason why you would be willing to pay for a garment made in Canada when you could get one of comparable quality far more cheaply from an RDC. This means that jobs that require only low-skilled or unskilled labour will tend to migrate towards the RDCs and away from the rich (and expensive) developed countries. This might be called "the global job leak," since it affects jobs all over the globe.

However, the term "comparable quality" is crucial to our prosperity. Through automation, a manufacturer in Canada may be able to produce higher-quality products at a competitive price. Automation boosts the productivity of our workers to a much higher level than that of our Third World competitors;[7] and if we offer a better product at a competitive price, global consumers will be happy to buy from us. But although this will allow Canadian companies to stay in business, it comes at a price. The automation that boosts Canadian worker productivity also dramatically reduces the number of workers needed. Competition from the RDCs is forcing Canadian manufacturers either to cut the number of people employed or to quit business in Canada.

There's more to the story than this, and I'll deal with much of it in Chapters 4 and 5.

The crucial new factor: knowledge

The very element that makes it difficult for workers in developed countries to compete with those in RDCs — our expensive standard of living — also makes it possible for us to produce jobs that the RDCs can't fill: those requiring a lot of knowledge, experience, and skill. You could, for instance, plunk a biotech laboratory down in a poor country in Africa. But even if you created a complete educational system immediately, you would have to wait many years until you could hire local labour for any but the most menial jobs.

The knowledge structure of a country's industries is like a mountain, with the lowest skills held by the greatest number at the bottom, and the highest, rarest, and most esoteric at the top. It takes time, money, and sustained effort to create and maintain such a mountain, and many of the RDCs have not yet had the time. Note that the vast bulk of the jobs are in lower-skilled tasks — but that the height of the mountain is determined by the those with higher skills. It's this factor that has led to so much palaver about "knowledge workers" being the salvation of jobs in the developed countries. Rarely, though, has the term been explored, even when it has been defined. Knowledge, in this context, has many forms, and each has a different impact on the economy:

• Technology is a highly visible and very important form of knowledge. Indeed, it's so important that I've ranked it as one of the seven forces shaping our future. For now, I'll just make the point that technology plays no favourites: it can be applied by anyone who understands it. The ability to import technology from more developed countries has been a key factor in the explosive growth of the rapidly growing Asian economies. Moreover, being the inventor of a technology doesn't guarantee prosperity. As Lester Thurow has pointed out, three of the most important new products of the last twenty years have been the video camera and recorder, which was invented by the Americans; fax machines, also invented by Americans; and the CD player, which was invented by the Dutch. The production of all three of these products, which result in billions of dollars of annual sales and hundreds of thousands of jobs, are now dominated by the Japanese.[8]

• Equally important to an economy, though not nearly as obvious as technology, is entrepreneurship. This is more than just knowledge. It's a combination of knowledge, experience, motivation, and pure guts. Entrepreneurship will not flourish everywhere. It will take root and grow only in countries where the political and economic climate encourages it, and where the psychology of the people allows it. Even though the Japanese, for example, excel at many things, generally they aren't good entrepreneurs. The successful entrepreneur is the last of the rugged individualists, a free-booting buccaneer — and the Japanese, with some notable exceptions, are highly uncomfortable with this role. In contrast, the Taiwanese seem quite at home with it. We Canadians are very good at it.

• Creativity and innovation are crucial forms of economic knowledge. Whether they concern a complex new invention or simply a better way of tightening lug nuts on the assembly line, your organization had better be fostering both qualities if it intends to survive.

• Sensitivity and responsiveness to the customer's needs and desires — and the ability to anticipate them — can often compensate for higher costs. Coupled with creativity and innovation, sensitivity can be a big enough advantage to allow you to charge more for your products than your competitors do, and still increase your market share.

• Finally, the depth and breadth of a country's knowledge of management skills will play a major role, perhaps the major role, in determining the prosperity of a nation. "The productivity of knowledge," says Peter Drucker, "is going to be the determining factor in the competitive position of a company, an industry, an entire country. No country, industry, or company has any 'natural' advantage or disadvantage. The only advantage it can possess is the ability to exploit universally available knowledge. The only thing that increasingly will matter in national as in international economics is management's performance in making knowledge productive."[9]

THE CHANGING GLOBAL MARKETPLACE

The global marketplace is changing in two principal ways: who is doing the buying, and what is being bought.

Assuming that we can continue to match global competitors for price and quality, many of our traditional customers will continue to buy from us, notably the Americans. But although our principal customers' economies are growing, their growth rate is small beer compared with the real growth markets: the very same RDCs that are causing us so many problems. As their economies grow and prosper, their demand is growing as well. Moreover, their demand for imported goods is rising faster than their overall rate of growth.

To understand this, consider a poor Third World family. How much is it likely to import? Virtually nothing. But if the father gets a job in a factory and his income starts to go up, first he and his family will eat better; next they will start to be clothed and housed better; and then they will start to want luxury goods such as the radios, televisions, and cars that we consider necessities. So when their income gets above a certain level, they start buying imported goods which they could never afford before. Their consumption of imported goods, therefore, doesn't rise slowly. It occurs suddenly. This is the position of many of the RDCs today.

So let's look at the growth expectations of these developing markets:

• According to the International Monetary Fund, developing countries already account for about 46 percent of world economic output. Since they are growing faster than the developed countries, they are almost certain to represent more than one-half of all world production by the year 2001.[10]

• Today, Asia alone (including Japan) accounts for about one-quarter of world production. Without Japan, it still makes up nearly one-fifth. If Asia continues to outperform the rest of the world for the next twenty years, it will have a total output greater than all the OECD[11] nations (i.e., the rich countries) combined, even if you lump Japan in with the OECD and not with the rest of Asia.[12]

• Based on purchasing power parity, China is already the world's second largest economy, and India, Brazil, and Mexico rank somewhere around the eighth, ninth, and tenth — ahead of Canada.[13]

• McKinsey Consulting of Australia believes that China will account for at least 20 percent of world demand for telecom equipment by the year 2000, and may reach as high as 30 percent.[14]

• Asia already accounts for one-half the world market for semiconductors. Motorola, a major producer of semiconductors, expects that semiconductor sales to Asia over the next decade will grow two or three times faster than sales in Europe or America.[15]

• Mexico expects the North American Free Trade Agreement (NAFTA) to stimulate such growth that its economy will double in size in the next fifteen years or so.[16]

Clearly, then, if we want our exports — and our incomes — to grow rapidly, we're going to have to fight for a share of these new, blossoming markets.

New markets, new products

Next, how will the mix of things that we sell change? In the first place, we won't be exporting as much in grain and agricultural products as we have in the past. Not only are many states of the former Soviet Union unable to afford the food we produce, but there is a rising tide of agricultural products being grown and exported in countries that used to be net importers. Peter Drucker noted: "Contrary to all predictions, agricultural output in the world actually rose almost a full third between 1972 and 1985 to reach an all-time high. And it rose the fastest in less developed countries. . . . It is not too fanciful to expect that the true revolution on the farm is still ahead. Vast tracts of land that hitherto were practically barren are being made fertile, either through new methods of cultivation or through adding trace minerals to the soil. . . . Even greater advances are registered in biotechnology, both in preventing diseases of plants and animals and in increasing yields."[17]

The biggest shock in agriculture may still be in store. The fact that the Soviet Union was a net importer of food products may simply have been due to mismanagement of its agricultural policy. In the nineteenth century, Imperial Russia was the world's largest exporter of agricultural products. All that valuable farmland is about to hit the capitalist system again, and the shock could be enormous.[18] It seems a safe bet that the current political and economic upheavals in the former Soviet republics will keep this farmland from bursting onto the world agricultural scene soon. But any prudent planner should bear in mind that in the long run our former biggest customer has the potential to become a major new competitor.

Other raw materials

It also seems likely that exports of forest products and metals will be affected by the declining price of raw materials as well as by the rising production of these materials by developing countries. For example, Chile is in the process of significantly increasing its production of copper — and, ironically, it is doing so under the tutelage of Canadian mining companies. According to Lewis F. Jackson, a professional portfolio manager, who made a research trip to Chile in November 1993, there is intense activity there by such major Canadian companies as Noranda, Placer Dome, American Barrick, Lac Minerals, Teck Corp., Cominco, and Rio Algom, as well as dozens of smaller Canadian companies.[19]

The mines these companies are opening are state-of-the-art facilities. Because they are new and in a developing country, they have more efficient production techniques and lower labour costs, and produce significantly less pollution than comparable mines in Canada. This kind of transfer of technology is happening all over the world and will significantly increase the supplies of all kinds of raw material coming from developing countries.

Earlier, I quoted economist Lester Thurow as saying that he expected that the prices of raw materials would drop by a further 40 percent over the next twenty years. Increased supply is certainly one reason for this. However, diminishing demand is another. This is caused by three distinct but related factors.

First, we are using manufactured products far more efficiently than we used to. A simple example is that when a telephone company lays cable to transmit more phone conversations, instead of using *tonnes* of copper wire, it is using a few *kilograms* of optical-fibre cable. Optical fibre can transmit, kilo for kilo and dollar for dollar, thousands of times more conversations than copper.

Second, the amount of material we use to make existing products — or to achieve specific end results — is falling. A modern radio, for instance, is far smaller than those our parents or grandparents had. Similarly, automobiles are becoming progressively lighter and are using less materials while achieving superior performance. In future, engines may be made of lightweight ceramic composites instead of steel or aluminum. The car body and frame may be made of plastic composites instead of almost a tonne of steel. All of this will mean better, cheaper, safer, and less polluting cars, but it will also mean a decline in the amount and a change in the type of raw materials needed.

Forest products will be affected, too. I expect that in the long run, composite materials from wood scraps, soybeans, plastics, lightweight metals, and other materials will begin to replace high-quality lumber in home building, though wood will continue to be used for decorative finishes and "homeyness." In business, we may at last see the emergence of the oft-ballyhoo'ed, yet seemingly mythical, "paperless office." It will be dragged into existence by the needs of companies to structure themselves around the rapid flow of information. This trend requires virtually instantaneous transmission of orders, costs, specifications, and so on, at speeds that paper simply cannot match. I'll be examining this trend in Chapter 4.

Finally, the world's growth industries mostly sell intellect or knowledge rather than tangible products. Semiconductors, for instance, are the foundation of information technology, which is now the world's largest industry. Yet only 1–3 percent of what this industry sells is in the cost of the raw materials used, compared with 40 percent for cars and 60 percent for pots and pans.[20] The overall result, says Peter Drucker, is that "the amount of raw materials needed for a given unit of economic output has been dropping for the entire century, except in wartime." He adds: "A [1985] study by the International Monetary Fund calculates the decline as being at the rate of one and a quarter percent a year (compounded) ever since 1900. That would mean that the amount of industrial raw materials needed for one unit of industrial production is now no more than two-fifths of what it was in 1900, and the decline is accelerating."[21]

Canada will continue to export significant quantities of unprocessed raw materials — the demand won't disappear overnight — and prices will go up when the economy is strong, just as they always have. Moreover, as the developing economies grow, their demand for raw materials will add significantly to global demand. Nevertheless, since the technology they use in manufacturing will be more modern than we used at their stages of development, Drucker's comments about the decline in the use of raw materials will apply to their economies as well as to our own.

We should expect, then, that supply will grow faster than demand in industries that produce unprocessed commodities. This will put continuing pressure on prices and profits. Consequently, exporters of raw materials will find that the good times, when they occur, won't be as good and won't last as long, and the bad times will get steadily worse.

Manufacturing

As noted above, the low wage rates of the RDCs, coupled with production technology transferred from more advanced countries, are allowing the RDCs to produce manufactured goods at significantly lower prices. A modern VCR, even with a Japanese or South Korean brand name, may well have been made in Malaysia or Indonesia, where wages are distinctly lower. It will also be significantly less expensive than a comparable VCR produced five years ago. Some Canadian clothing companies have been able to turn this trend to their advantage by importing inexpensive but high-quality fabrics from the Asian tigers, then making it into high-quality men's suits, which they sell at very competitive prices in the United States under the Free Trade Agreement.

Another major trend in manufacturing is the steady rise in automation. We are witnessing a revolution in automation that is similar to the revolution that occurred in agriculture. One hundred years ago, 45 percent of Canada's population worked on the farm.[22] Today, that number is less than 3 percent, and falling. Yet agricultural production has risen enormously and continues to do so. This is entirely because of the revolution in farm machinery, fertilizers, and techniques, which has allowed farmers to increase their productivity to heights that would have been unimaginable in our grandparents' time.

Similarly, even as production is rising in manufacturing, employment is falling, not only in Canada but in every industrial country in the world. One estimate is that by 2010, developed countries will employ no more than 10 percent of their workforce in manufacturing.[23] (compared with almost 22 percent in Canada prior to 1980). This represents a massive decline in blue-collar jobs, which in turn will create an enormous political problem for governments.

Products don't vote, but unemployed workers do. Accordingly, there will be tremendous pressure on governments to try to deny the reality and inevitability of what is happening. The dangers are obvious, as Drucker clearly states: "A country, an industry, or a company that puts the preservation of blue-collar manufacturing jobs ahead of being internationally competitive . . . will soon have neither production nor steady jobs. The attempt to preserve industrial blue-collar jobs is actually a prescription for unemployment."[24]

If this was the situation in a single country in isolation, its government might just be able to legislate a halt to automation, though to do so would be stupidity of monumental proportions. But no nation, and certainly no trading nation, can resist the need to automate its industries without risking becoming hopelessly uncompetitive. This is especially true when you consider that without automation, the developed countries would lose these jobs anyway. Any straightforward manufacturing task that was not automated or was only lightly automated would quickly come within reach of an RDC with a much lower pay scale — whereupon the labour-intensive goods produced in the wealthy country would be priced out of the market.

This doesn't mean that Canada will lose its manufacturing sectors. Indeed, I would argue that manufacturing is here to stay; it's only the jobs that are leaving. Manufacturing will, however, be radically transformed. As Drucker states, "the only long-term policy which promises success is for developed countries to convert manufacturing from being labour based into being knowledge based."[25] This will be covered in more detail in Chapter 4.

"PROTECTING" JOBS ACTUALLY DESTROYS THEM

If our jobs are being squeezed out by automation on one side and by low-priced RDCs on the other, couldn't we protect domestic jobs by shutting out both? After all, there's no point in importing low-priced VCRs if no one is earning enough to buy them.

The lure of protecting jobs by trade barriers and artificial restrictions is seductive, and on the surface it appears to make sense. But in fact it doesn't work. There are clear historical examples to show this. For instance: "In the 1890s, Argentina had roughly the same income per person as the United States and seemed to be as well endowed with resources, both human and physical. A century of protectionism, though, left Argentina with hundreds of inefficient industries serving only local markets, and a standard of living roughly one-third as high as that of the colossus to the north."[26]

A more recent example is the Soviet Union. For more than seventy years the Soviet government guaranteed 100 percent employment, markets for all the goods produced in all the factories in the country, and no inflation — all of which sounds like an economist's dream. But the quality of the products was terrible, shortages were more the rule than the exception, and jobs were often little more than make-work projects. "We pretend to work," went one Soviet joke, "and the bosses pretend to pay us." The Soviet Union's ability to prop up this make-believe world failed when it ran out of money to support it, and the collapse of this pretence left their economy in hopelessly uncompetitive ruins.

Clearly, protectionism can do more harm than good. Economic development specialist Sebastian Edwards made the point very clearly when he wrote: "Compare the economies of Asia that stumbled into the 1960s in more or less wretched condition. Those that focused on the expansion of trade (Hong Kong, Malaysia, Singapore, South Korea, Taiwan, Thailand) have done very well. Those that tried to develop by pushing self-sufficiency (India, Burma, North Korea, Vietnam) have done very badly. And those who came late to the open-trade game (China, Indonesia) seem to be on their way to a chicken in every wok."[27]

The problems with protection are that you have to decide whose jobs get protected, which also means deciding whose jobs get sacrificed. In addition, since nothing is ever free, someone has to pay — and it will be those who don't receive protection.

In the developed world, farmers tend to be more protected than anyone else because they are organized and are practised at putting pressure on governments. In France, for example, working farmers represent only 4 percent of the electorate, but the farming lobby controls almost 20 percent of the votes in the National Assembly.[28] Farmers act as a far more cohesive lobby group than consumers, who seldom make the effort to organize. Consequently, it is the consumers who end up bearing the costs of the huge subsidies paid to farmers.

Let's look at what it costs to protect farmers from competition:

• The OECD estimates that in 1992 consumers in developed countries paid $354 billion a year in taxes and higher prices to protect farmers.[29]

• The World Bank estimates that in 1985 government protection of dairy farmers forced up the global price of dairy products to roughly three times what it would have been without protection.[30]

• According to the Australian Bureau of Agricultural and Resource Economics, every $1 of subsidy given to American sugar farmers costs American consumers $2.60.[31]

• The OECD estimates that in 1992 Canadian taxpayers gave Canadian farmers $10 billion in government subsidies; and a GATT study indicates that trade barriers preventing foreign producers from supplying Canadian consumers with dairy, egg, and poultry products in 1990 made chicken prices here 197 percent higher than in the United States, milk prices 221 percent higher, and egg prices 142 percent higher. Yet there are only 33,400 farmers protected by such measures — just over one-tenth of one percent of the total population.[32]

• A study by Purdue University estimated that in 1987 it cost the American economy $107,000 in lost nonfarm output, $80,000 in federal spending, and $14,000 in higher food costs — or $201,000 annually — for each farm job saved through subsidies and protection.[33]

A simple question: When is it worth $201,000 a year to protect a single farm job?

Of course, industry can mount powerful lobbies, too. In 1982 the U.S. government, under pressure from its steel industry, introduced "voluntary" export restraints on steel from the European Community, Japan, South Korea, and others. In order to avoid harassment from the United States, these exporters "voluntarily" restricted the amount of steel they sold into the U.S. As a result, the U.S. government saved the jobs of an estimated 9,000 American steelworkers who couldn't make steel nearly as efficiently as their overseas counterparts. According to the Institute for International Economics, the cost of protecting these inefficient American steelworkers was $750,000 a year for each job saved.[34]

Much the same thing has happened in Canada, where a 1991 study showed that Hydro-Quebec's sale of subsidized power to four aluminum companies cost the province at least $300 million annually. This works out at $190,577 per year per job created over the 24-year period of the power supply contract with the companies involved.[35]

Clearly, no intelligent person can believe that spending $190,577, $201,000, or $750,000 a year to save a job that pays

$30,000 is going to benefit a national economy. That is why the Soviet Union went bankrupt, and why the countries that are growing the fastest are the ones that have, generally speaking, abandoned such measures.

So one of the new rules of the global economy is simple: the more you "protect" domestic jobs with trade barriers and tariffs, the fewer jobs you will have and the more you will hurt your chances of prosperity. This is a luxury that developed countries can no longer afford.

YOU'RE RUNNING A MARATHON, NOT A SPRINT

It seems to me that there is one other way that the rules of the working world are changing, though no one else seems to have noticed. This may mean that I'm wrong, or it may mean that I've stumbled onto something so obvious that others have overlooked it. It is that the economic cycle is getting longer. The North American economy used to rise and fall, going through expansion and recession, about every four years. This was a natural result of the desire of the U.S. president to stage-manage the economy to maximize his chances of re-election. In this four-year cycle, North American recessions typically lasted about nine months.

Today, the process takes much longer because of the steady merging of many diverse national economies into a unified world economy. Not only are the United States and Canada involved, but also all the other developed countries, as well as South Korea, Singapore, Taiwan, India, Chile, Mexico, and the other developing countries. I figure that as a result, the length of the economic cycle has at least doubled, so that a recession that used to last nine months will now last eighteen months or more. A recovery, when it comes, will take a long time to pick up speed because some of the economies will tend to lag behind and slow the expansion of the others. Hence, at the end of the 1990–92 recession, the economies of Germany and Japan were just going into recession so that growth in North America was dragged down. But once the recovery gets under way, the period of economic expansion will last for six years or more. I think this explains the extended expansion that North America experienced in the second half of the 1980s. Similarly, the recovery that started so feebly in 1992 should last beyond 1998.

At the same time, the ups and downs will be harder to live through. Unfortunately for us, with developing countries taking low-skilled jobs from us, more of our workers will be out of work than in previous cycles. This will put a drag on our overall economic performance. Hence, the highs won't be quite as high, and the lows will be lower.

I foresaw this development as long ago as 1976, when I wrote in the Financial Post: "There are going to be bigger booms and more severe recessions as the various economies reinforce each other. . . . Unusually high unemployment in troughs could also result, with all the concomitant social and political problems."[36] What this means is that we need to take advantage of the good times when they're with us — and to be ready to survive long stretches of recession when they come.

In other words, we are running a marathon, not a sprint.

T H R E E

Will Canada Be Rich or Poor?

If the current trajectory continues, the standard of living of Canadians seems destined to fall behind. Yet there is nothing inevitable about this outcome; Canadians have in their own hands the power to change it.

– Michael E. Porter, *Canada at the Crossroads,* 1991

Wishful thinking can be deadly, for it blinds us to dangers that might otherwise be avoided. Right now, we are racing full speed towards the edge of a cliff with our eyes squeezed firmly shut. If we persuade ourselves that everything's fine, we are lost and will fall quickly into poverty. Dr. Porter warned us of this in his 1991 report, but he also noted that there is nothing to prevent us from recognizing our predicament and changing direction.[1]

As a nation, we have many strengths, and many things working in our favour. Right now, they are not enough. On the other hand, if we can pull ourselves together, we have the potential to enjoy a great and prosperous future, for we have a last chance — and a good one — to correct many of our past mistakes.

But first, some hard truths.

THE FIRST HARD TRUTH: OUR GOVERNMENTS RAN OUT OF MONEY YEARS AGO

There is a comforting but very dangerous belief that we can "muddle through" and continue to have much the same life-style that we have now. It's not true. If we keep doing what we've been doing, we are headed for disaster. "The country's real problem as it approaches the next millennium," said the federal government's auditor-general, Denis Desautels, in his January 1994 report to Parliament, "is the accumulated debt threatening the future of social programs and national institutions — the very essence of Canada."[2]

Why is this such a danger? Because we are borrowing from tomorrow's paycheck to pay today's living expenses. You can do that for just so long before you find that you have no money to live on, and your creditors won't lend you any more.

This is precisely what happened to New Zealand. Before 1984, New Zealand not only appeared to be a prosperous country, but it seemed the model of a well-developed social democratic economy. Health care was paid for by the state; the crucial domestic farming industry was heavily subsidized and protected; there were maternity benefits for mothers on leave, and extended unemployment benefits for workers who had been laid off.

It's very easy for us to identify with pre-1984 New Zealand because we are following much the same pattern. Like Canada, New Zealand did not have the money to pay for its social safety net and consequently ran a continual federal deficit. It financed its spending by dipping into the global capital markets and borrowing vast sums of money, just as Canada is doing today. Everything seemed fine — until the fickle herd instincts of the global capital markets turned against New Zealand. Bond buyers who had routinely put New Zealand bonds in their portfolios decided that they didn't like the way New Zealand finances were being managed, and they stopped buying. With no warning, the government of New Zealand was faced with the ultimate crisis: it had less than a week to find money to pay its creditors, or face national bankruptcy.

David Lange, who was prime minister of New Zealand at the time, has since reflected on what caused the crisis: "It was a whole series of pork barrel politics using overseas debt to build up domestic expectations, far ahead of any common sense view of what economic development ought to be."[3] Lange was the leader of the Labour Party, a party dedicated to social democracy, but when New Zealand ran out of money, he had to take drastic action. This hit the people of New Zealand hard:

26

• Their standard of living dropped from third in the world in 1984 to twenty-second in 1993.

• The New Zealand dollar dropped 65 percent in value, from US$1.40 to $0.50, pushing up the price of imported goods enormously.

• VAT (a tax like our GST) was pushed up to 12½ percent.

• Most New Zealanders could no longer afford to buy new cars, and so dealers started importing used cars from Japan.

• Anyone unemployed who turned down two job offers lost all unemployment benefits.

• Single mothers were expected to go back to work when their children were seven years old, at which point their welfare benefits were cut off.

• Unemployed young people were told to move back home with their parents, and their benefits were cut to $125 a week.

• The age at which seniors became eligible for pensions was raised from sixty to sixty-five, and upper-income earners were cut off entirely.

• All farm subsidies were eliminated within three months, and farm incomes and land values dropped by 50 percent.

• Staffing cuts to the government bureaucracy were viciously deep: at TV New Zealand the number of employees was cut in half; the state railway was cut from 22,000 employees to 6,000 (but today actually hauls more freight), and the top 400 bureaucrats in government were put on contract and told: "Deliver, or else."[4]

Could this really happen to us? Simon Upton, who was New Zealand's minister of health in 1993, believes that it could: "The only difference between an African Third World state and Canada or New Zealand is that [the Africans] actually hit the end of their credit limit very quickly; we're given more rope to hang ourselves. . . . [Is] it your birthright to go on borrowing from other, more productive countries to sustain your living standard? No, of course it [isn't]."[5]

If you think that Canada couldn't suffer the same fate, take a look at Table 1, which shows where we are now, compared with where New Zealand was just before the crunch.

TABLE 1   A Comparison of the Indebtedness of Canada and New Zealand

Measure of indebtedness	New Zealand in 1984	Canada in 1993
Foreign debt as a % of GNP	47%	44%
Total government debt as a % of GNP	62%	88%

SOURCE: CTV's "W5" television program, February 28, 1993.

Per capita, Canada is now one of the biggest debtor countries in the developed world; yet as discussed in the last chapter, our growth rate, the key to our ability to pay our debts, is lagging.

So who's been borrowing all this money, and what for? The answer is all our governments, but especially the federal and provincial ones. Since the mid-1970s, they've spent more than they've collected in revenues, and have borrowed the difference. The money has been used to fund welfare, unemployment, equalization to the poorer provinces, support for the arts — in fact, a little bit of everything. And this has been a truly bipartisan effort: the Trudeau Liberals started it, the Mulroney Conservatives, with all their talk of cutting the deficit, were just as flagrantly irresponsible. The federal government is, at the time of writing, spending approximately $45 billion a year more than it receives.

Let me try to put this in perspective. The figure of $45 billion means that every year the federal government borrows almost $1,700 for every man, woman, and child in Canada — say, just under $7,000 for a family of four. Since this is borrowed money, it will have to be paid back, just as it would if you or I continually spent more than we earned and then mortgaged our homes to pay for the groceries. Inevitably, the time would come when the bank would refuse to lend more and would start demanding repayment.

Right now, Canada spends more on interest costs than on anything else — more than on health or welfare or education — and the only way to change this is to pay off some of our debts. But for our governments to do so, they will have to run budget surpluses for many years, which means that they will have to take more money in taxes than they spend providing services.

There are two and only two ways of changing a deficit into a surplus: by major increases in taxes or major cuts in spending (or, obviously, a combination of the two). How much higher would taxes have to be to balance the budget? Well, the typical family of four described above would have to pay $7,000 more in taxes than they do today — and this would be simply to stop piling up more debts. In other words, it would merely allow the Government of Canada to stop borrowing additional money. To actually start paying off our debts, taxes would have to go even higher — much higher, in fact, because we have been considering only one level of government. There are several provincial governments that are in worse shape than the federal government.

Obviously, raising taxes this high is impossible. There are already clear signs that Canadians are fed up and won't pay any more. Ted Carmichael, the senior economist for investment dealer Burns Fry, estimates that Canadians are already dodging almost $20 billion a year in taxes.[6] That's nearly half the current federal deficit. Other estimates place the tax evasion/avoidance figure at twice that amount. Donald Huggett of the accounting firm Coopers & Lybrand believes that while Canadians are basically honest, "any further advances of the underground economy (including smuggling) will surely defeat all efforts towards deficit reduction."[7]

Since it is impossible to raise taxes by enough to solve our governments' financial problems, there remains only one solution: major cuts to spending. The cuts that governments have made so far amount to minor trimming and are nowhere near enough, yet even these have provoked howls of anger. But we don't have a choice whether to cut or not. The choice is whether to make the cuts in a deliberate fashion over a period of years or, like New Zealand, to be forced into them in a period of weeks.

I believe that we have a temporary reprieve. The Canadian economy is prospering again after the horrendous recession of the early 1990s. This will lift our national income, including government revenues, and give us some breathing room. But if we breathe a deep sigh of relief and congratulate ourselves on having weathered the storm, we will be doomed, for there will eventually be another recession, and if we have not put our financial house in order by that time, our deficits will blossom even further, and choices will be far worse than they are now.

What magnitude of cuts will we need to make? This is a complex matter, and one that will have to be solved over a period of four or five years. However, given the size of the problem, I believe we must contemplate such drastic actions as the following:

• Eliminate all business subsidies, trade and tariff barriers, tax breaks, incentive payments, accelerated write-downs, tax credits, subsidies, small-business tax deductions, and R & D write-offs other than the normal ones, such as depreciation, that are used by our major trading partners. One might make a few exceptions for industries or companies whose export sales are growing by at least 10 percent a year, in order to beef up tomorrow's industries. But all the taps should definitely be shut off to industries that survive purely on subsidies or on trade and tariff barriers. They are a drag on the economy, and one we can no longer afford.

• Eliminate all farm subsidies, price supports, export credits, tariffs, import quotas, subsidized loans, and other breaks to farmers. In the words of David Carey, a New Zealand sheep farmer who went through the wringer when government subsidies were cut but now applauds the elimination of subsidies, "We're now getting to the stage where everyone's being treated the same — and why not?"[8]

• Eliminate all regional development grants, all subsidies to politically useful but financially hopeless companies such as Sysco Steel in Nova Scotia, and all PR-inspired government involvement in megaprojects like Hibernia. We no longer have the money to pretend that dying industries and impossible projects in out-of-the-way places can be made profitable if we just wish hard enough.

• Reduce or eliminate government transfer payments and special tax breaks to middle- and upper-income groups. This includes such cherished things as family allowances, child-care allowances, and complete medical coverage. Why should the middle class, which bears the burden of most taxes, pay the government to take away its money and then give it back again? Moreover, social assistance should be for those who truly need it, not for those with the strongest lobby.

• Raise the entitlement age for old-age security and Canada Pension Plan payments, and reduce or eliminate such payments to all those in the top 40 percent of income earners.

This is bitter medicine, and it will undoubtedly be denounced by many. But, to quote Richard Prebble, who was New Zealand's minister of finance when the crisis hit, "Tell all the privileged groups, frankly, to go to hell, and you'll be surprised, you'll get a good response."[9]

Difficult as the above steps are, they will not be enough. As well as slashing spending, we must start to require accountability for the performance of our governments. I suggest we institute two new tests. First, we should assume that governments are guilty of incompetence unless they can prove otherwise. Unless they can show a track record of cost-effective delivery of programs, they should be required to come up with alternatives, such as contracting the delivery of services to private-sector bidders under public tender.

Second, I would change the role of government. Governments have clearly shown that they are not much good at actually doing things, but they are fairly good at supervising, regulating, specifying, inspecting, and informing. Accordingly, I would look for ways of causing governments to change their role from prime mover to watchdog. As Mario Cuomo, Democratic governor of the State of New York, put it, "It is not government's obligation to provide services, but to see that they are provided."

Of course, there are some areas in which governments should continue to be the prime movers. I doubt, for example, whether it would make sense to have Canadian foreign service diplomats provided by a private contractor; or the Canadian Armed Forces, for that matter. But why should schools or health insurance administration or fire departments or the processing of welfare payments be run by government instead of being contracted out to private suppliers on fixed-price contracts? I believe that changes of this type would not only achieve better performance but would provide government workers with improved working conditions and opportunities for advancement.[10] Here's Peter Drucker on the productivity of government workers:

> The lowest level of productivity [in developed economies] occurs in
> government employment. And yet governments everyplace are the largest

31

employers of service workers. In the United States, for instance, one fifth of the entire work force is employed by federal, state, and local governments, predominantly in routine clerical work. In the United Kingdom, the proportion is roughly one third. In all developed countries, government employees account for a similar share of the total work force.[11]

If we made all these reforms, would it be worth it? It's turning out that way for New Zealand. The 1993 World Competitiveness Report of the World Economic Forum (a Swiss conference group) ranked New Zealand first out of twenty-two countries for the quality of its government policies; and the *Economist* reported that "exports are booming and foreign direct investment is flowing in. In the two years to June [of 1993], New Zealand's GDP rose by an average of 3.8 percent, faster than any of its rich-country rivals."[12]

But if we want the same success as New Zealand, we have no time to waste. If we don't start to solve our problems within the next three to five years, we will find ourselves living in poverty, and our country declining rapidly towards Third World status.

OUR EDUCATIONAL SYSTEM IS A FAILURE

While studying successful countries and reading the works of thoughtful people, I've noticed one theme emerges over and over again: education is crucial to the future success of every country, every business, and every individual. Moreover, it's not just education in school; it's lifelong education, both on the job and by individuals on their own. Time and again, commentators, economists, and politicians have emphasized "knowledge workers" and "knowledge industries" as the key to future prosperity. "Increasingly, nations compete on the quality of their human capital,"[13] says the *Economist*.

If this is so, how is our educational system doing? Here's what professor Michael Porter of the Harvard Business School had to say:

> Canada's overall illiteracy rate stands at 24 percent, [and] more than 30 percent of young people drop out of school before receiving high school diplomas. The level of advanced skills in Canada — critical to sustaining and upgrading sources of competitive advantage for Canadian industry — is inadequate. There are shortages of skilled labour in a variety of occupational sectors that require advanced training, especially in technology-related

occupations. Post-secondary enrollment in science and engineering disciplines has been declining in recent years. . . . Occupational standards for skilled trades are poorly developed [and] technical and vocational schools — extensively used in many other countries to provide intensive skills training — are widely perceived to be "second best" in Canada.[14]

Nor is this view held only by foreign critics. Consider, for example, this comment from the federal government discussion paper, *Learning Well . . . Living Well*:

Nearly half our workforce has not graduated from high school; 40 per cent of adults cannot read well enough to deal with written material encountered in daily life; nearly one-third of our children drop out before completing high school. Yet 60 per cent of all new jobs created in the next 10 years will demand at least a high-school education.

We are a long way behind the leading industrial countries in our commitment to public education, and in on-the-job training we appear even worse. The World Economic Forum of Geneva ranks Canada 20th among 24 industrialized countries in corporate-training programs. For Canadians, the culture of lifelong learning is still remote.[15]

Professional educators can argue until they are blue in the face about the wonderful things they're doing or the terrible problems they have to cope with, but the fact remains that the job is not getting done. Why? What's wrong with our educational system?

The most common response is to blame the teachers, because they are the most active and visible people in the picture. But the reality is that although there are far too many bad teachers, teachers as a whole have been doing a better job than most of the other people involved. I reckon that there are eight groups who have varying degrees of responsibility for the educational system: politicians, administrators, parents, faculties of education, students, taxpayers/voters, corporations, and teachers. All eight groups are failing in their responsibilities to at least some degree. Let's take them one by one.

Politicians

Politicians are responsible for ensuring that standards are set and maintained, that schools get good value for the money spent, and that nothing gets in the way of learning. They are not, in general, doing any of these things. In fact, I would contend that many school board trustees and provincial ministers of education are actually preventing teachers from doing as good a job as they might.

In my home province of Ontario, teachers tell me that the provincial Ministry of Education has written a curriculum that is so vague as to be almost useless. The ministry decides which books and which educational methods can be used, yet the people in the ministry don't appear in the classrooms and don't have to teach; they tend to be big on theory and short on reality.

Next, let's look at the way school boards run things. Mark Twain once remarked that the Almighty first made an idiot for practice, then He made a school board.

Early in the winter of 1991–92, a storm blew down some phone lines at my son's school. The principal called the school board, which sent out an electrician. The electrician took one look, noted that the wooden board to which the lines had been attached had come loose, called a carpenter, and left. The carpenter showed up, noted that the board was fastened to sheet metal on the outside of the building, called a metalworker, and left. The metalworker came, fixed the sheet metal, called the carpenter, and left. The carpenter returned, fixed the wooden board, called the electrician, and left. The electrician fixed the phone lines. Total elapsed time — almost two weeks. Total cost — who knows? But you can bet it wasn't cheap.

Perhaps this is an isolated case, peculiar to the Toronto school board. Then again, perhaps not. A 1992 study by the Economic Council of Canada noted that of all the people employed by the educational system in Canada, only 43 percent were full-time teachers.[16] Can somebody please explain why we need almost four other people on the payroll to assist three full-time teachers?

Then there's the matter of petty politics interfering with education. I once asked my trustee if he could provide me with the Toronto Board of Education's statement of purpose, or mission statement. He kindly sent me a publication entitled *Partnerships: Working Together for Excellence and Equity*, published, I think, in 1990 (the document was undated). The report is written in classic edu-babble, a peculiar dialect of bureaucratic bafflegab adopted by pedagogues to ensure that no outsider can understand or argue with what they say.

If I can paraphrase statements spread over three paragraphs into a single sentence, the mission statement of the Toronto Board of Education is as follows: "The Toronto Board is committed to excellence and equity in opportunities and outcomes for our students and our employees, regardless of race, ethnicity, culture, class, gender, or disability."

I have some real problems with this. First, nowhere does it say anything about anybody learning anything, though I'm sure the board believes that somebody ought to. Next, it talks about "equity in outcomes," which I think means that the trustees want to ensure that everyone gets the same result. This happens too often right now — and it ain't often excellence. "Equity in outcomes" is a misguided and destructive fantasy. The trustees modify this later when they acknowledge that there will always be a wide variation in results, but they also state that they don't intend to let the backgrounds, attitudes, or abilities of students interfere with the final results of their education. But life isn't like this — and the world they are releasing their graduates into doesn't help people along through the tough bits. Employers won't make allowances for the fact that English or French isn't your first language. What they want to know is whether you are the best person to do the job.

At best, this mission statement is politics thinly disguised as education. At worst, it guarantees that capable or hard-working students are being denied the extra resources devoted to others, including those who aren't trying to learn.

Next, when was the last time you heard of a private company whose reason for existing was to provide "excellence and equity of outcomes" for its *employees*, regardless of their ability or initiative? Rely on them, certainly; encourage and support them, absolutely; assist them in attaining their career goals, indubitably. But make one of your reasons for existence the outcome of your employees' careers? I don't think so.

All told, this is a fine example of muddled thinking, lack of focus, and a desire to pervert the purpose of the educational system in order to re-engineer society. This problem is not, of course, unique to Toronto; and, in fairness to the Toronto board, it is now starting to change some of the boneheaded policies it adopted in the past. But I suspect that if you check with almost any school board in any part of Canada, you will find similar forms of idiocy.

Administrators (excluding school principals)

Here I'm talking mainly about the bureaucracies at the provincial and municipal levels. I believe they are actively interfering with education by overregulating principals and teachers, and overloading them with meaningless paperwork. Studies have repeatedly shown that the single most important variable in the results that a school produces is the experience of the teachers. Yet educational bureaucracies seem determined to tell teachers what and how to teach, even though teaching is something that happens between two individuals, teacher and pupil, and cannot be controlled by memo.

The Economic Council of Canada had some provocative comments on this subject:

> In the United States, there is evidence that those schools which have the most freedom and least bureaucratic interference (namely, private and religious schools) do best in increasing student achievement. Similarly, in Quebec — where private school enrollment as a proportion of total enrollment is the highest in Canada — the achievement of students in private schools has consistently been higher than that of students in the public sector. In Ontario, Grade 8 private school students . . . were, at the beginning of the school year, more than a full year ahead of their public school counterparts.
>
> This does not mean that all schools must be privatized. Rather, it suggests that achievement can be improved in the public school system by reducing interference, increasing the principal's freedom, disseminating the results of assessments, and increasing parental freedom of choice among schools.[17]

It is the job of administrators to hand the tools to the teachers. They have no other function. Yet they have been building empires for their own glory and to pad their own paychecks. It needs to stop.

Parents

In September 1992, I wrote: "We parents hold more responsibility for the ills of the system, and are doing less about it, than anyone else. Specifically, the children we are delivering to school are, as a group, ill-mannered, over-stimulated, violent, undisciplined brats, addicted to television and video games, ill-disposed to learning, and unreceptive to the efforts of their teachers."[18] If you, as a parent, are unhappy with the educational system, you'd better check what kind of children you are sending to school before you sound off about what the schools need to do. Are you part of the problem or part of the solution?

You'd also better be involved in your children's education by speaking regularly with their teachers and monitoring your children's progress and their homework status. Studies have repeatedly shown that parental involvement makes a big difference in the scholastic success of children.

It is absolutely the case that we, as parents and taxpayers, should be storming the offices of our trustees and ministries of education, demanding that they take some responsibility for the mess our system is in. We've been asleep at the switch for too long, and many (most?) of the incumbent bureaucrats and politicians couldn't organize a weenie roast, let alone an educational system that spends billions of your dollars a year.

So by all means get involved. Get militant! Scream and fight to fix the problems of our system.

But start at home.

Faculties of education

Those who teach teachers how to teach seem to spend their time focused on the theories of education, when what is needed is practical knowledge of how to reach the spirit of the student and raise it to understanding and exaltation. In my conversations with teachers, student teachers, and school board trustees, there has been a persistent frustration with the pedantic, hypothetical gobbledygook fobbed off by most education faculties as "teacher training."

"I don't need the newest theories on how we should teach children," one student teacher told me. "What I really need is practical advice on how to keep them quiet in class, get their interest so that they pay attention, and then step-by-step instructions on how to get material across to them. Education faculties are so Mickey Mouse. The hard part is getting in. Once you're in, there's no challenge at all — and there's precious little information of any practical value."

But education faculties are entities unto themselves and seem to be answerable to no one. Perhaps it's time that ministries of education (if someone could rouse them) took a look at how proto-teachers are being taught.

Students

If it seems odd to hold students responsible for their own education (after all, they're only kids), let me point out that education is impossible without their active cooperation. On the occasions when I give talks in schools, I find that many of the students are interested in their future, though they often can't see what it has to do with their schoolwork (which is a fault of the system, not the students). But too many students are choosing to sleepwalk through school, and the schools are baby-sitting them, with the result that the students are wasting their opportunity to prepare, and taxpayers are wasting their money.

It's time we told our kids that if they screw up, they're the ones who are going to pay for it. And any children who show no interest in working, or who interfere with the education of other kids, should be barred from schools until they start behaving. Education is too expensive to be a form of glorified baby-sitting.

Taxpayers

Taxpayers write the cheques and, as voters, have ultimate control over the system, but for years they haven't bothered to see how the money was spent, or what was being done in their name. Indeed, until very recently, school board trustees were often elected by acclamation because there was only one candidate. This left the educational system open for ivory-tower theorists, petty bureaucrats, and incompetent wastrels who could plunder the system for their own private gain — all because the public did not get involved. As the Economic Council of Canada noted, "It is not just a question of paying our taxes and waiting for the system to produce. For sound investment, we must be more demanding, and we must also be active participants."[19]

I believe that of all the representatives we vote for — federal, provincial, and local — school board trustees are the most important. If we get the school system right, we can correct many of the other problems. If we get it wrong, in the long run it won't matter what else we do.

Corporations

After the students themselves, Canadian companies have the most to gain or lose from the results of the educational system. Despite this, they have been curiously inactive. Note that I say "inactive" rather than "quiet." Our corporations love to complain about the failure of the school system. But with a few exceptions, they hardly lift a finger to help, even though Statistics Canada says they spend somewhere between $1 billion and $7 billion a year on re-educating their workers. (As you can tell, this is not an exact science.) In contrast, companies in the United States have exploded on the education scene, adopting schools, contributing employee time for tutoring, offering financial sponsorship and support for needy high school and college students, and coming up with a wide range of innovative ways of providing assistance.

So what could Canadian companies do? Let me offer two or three suggestions that would cost virtually nothing yet could have a revolutionary effect on the educational system if done by enough companies, preferably through their industry associations.

First, your company or industry association should announce that you will only hire students who have a high school diploma. You may already be doing this, but it's the announcement that's crucial. If there's publicity every September that a student without a diploma can forget about a career with most of the companies in Canada, this will be something specific that teachers can point to as a reason for students to stay in school.

Next, the educational system has shied away from setting standards. "Canada is virtually alone among advanced countries in having no national educational standards of any kind," said Michael Porter.[20] There are valid pedagogical reasons why standardized testing is not always a good idea, but this doesn't mean that it's never a good idea. Part of the reason for having such tests is to test not only the students (for diagnostic and corrective purposes) but also their teachers and schools. How can you correct a system when you don't know who is doing good work and who isn't?

Accordingly, I suggest that, perhaps through your industry association, you announce that all candidates who want to be considered for a job must take the Scholastic Aptitude Test (the SATs), and have the scores available at the interview. The SATs are the college entrance exams — the famous American "college boards," administered by the Educational Testing Service of Princeton, New Jersey. These tests have a long history of withstanding attack from the educational establishment, and provide an off-the-shelf, standardized test that measures literacy and numeracy.

Of course, by requiring such exams, you'll lay yourself open to charges of being elitist. To this you can answer, "Yes, indeed. We want to hire only the best people, regardless of race, ethnicity, culture, class, gender, or disability." Until there is a reliable, made-in-Canada yardstick of performance, the SATs will do just fine.

The third step that industry can take is to publicize what it expects its workers to know and be able to do. This should give educators some idea of what they should be teaching. Remember that most teachers become teachers straight out of college and have never had to run a business. They can't be expected to know what you need unless you tell them.

I would love to see a permanent Canadian Education Forum, where industry and educators worked together on a continuing basis to make sure that students learned what would be most valuable to them — and so that teachers could tell them why the knowledge was relevant.

I don't mean that industry should dictate the curriculum or that our schools should teach only vocationally oriented material. Education is much too important to be nothing more than job training. As Allan Hughes, a Waldorf School teacher, pointed out to me, schools must not only teach skills, but they should give students "as many perspectives as possible on what it means to be human, and how to re-create themselves as well as to be self-realized." He added, "The ability to think creatively and clearly and act in a moral context is what I think we should be aiming for."[21]

Even so, the vocational value of education is also important, so it would certainly help if industry and educators allied themselves and spoke to each other from time to time.

Teachers

Teachers, including school principals, are the only reason the system works at all. In Ontario, for instance, the geniuses at the Ministry of

Education have decreed that high school students are to be de-streamed starting in grade nine. This means that students of all levels of ability, including those with behavioural problems and learning disabilities, are required to be placed in the same classes as students capable of doing advanced study. The result, teachers have told me, is that they spend a disproportionate amount of time dealing with problem children and children with problems, and much less time teaching.

Worse, the more advanced students get bored and create problems, and the students needing more assistance get lost and create problems. As a result, many Ontario high schools, while officially de-streamed, are unofficially streaming again in defiance of the regulations and regulators. Real teachers and principals are doing whatever is necessary, as they always have.

Of course, there are also some lousy teachers and principals in the system — far too many, in fact. This is largely because there is no way of getting rid of them, partly because of tenure and partly because of teachers' unions. Undoubtedly, individual union members have great concern for their students, but their unions will fight for everything they can get, regardless of whether it benefits the students or not. The inability to fire incompetents is a perfect example.

Another example is the unions' rearguard (and ultimately fruitless) action to ward off the extensive use of computers in the classroom. I've had principals tell me that if they could make proper use of computers, they could cut staff (by getting rid of the bad teachers, I trust) and reduce costs yet improve results. But they say it will never happen because the unions won't let it.

The educational system of the future

All the above proposals are aimed at solving existing problems, but we must also look to the future. The educational system of the future has to produce citizens who are relative superbeings compared with today. If knowledge is the currency of the future, and knowledge workers are the crucial members of society, we will have to gear our educational system to produce these knowledge workers.

What would such a system look like? First, it would not be restricted to children. From now on, you will be "in school" for the rest of your life, whether or not you ever walk into another school building. To put it bluntly, if you are not relearning your profession

from the ground up every four to five years, then you are either in a
dead-end job or are risking obsolescence and unemployment. Much
of this "lifelong learning" will have to be initiated by the individual,
though our corporations and our educational systems will have to support and assist the process unless they want to have obsolete workers.
(I'll be saying more about this when discussing jobs in Chapter 4.)

Next, children who finish their first schooling (say, at the end
of Grades 12 or 13) will have to have a grounding in basics which
goes well beyond current levels. In particular, they will require
eleven things the educational system does not currently supply:

1 First and foremost, they will need to think innovatively and
   creatively, to be able to perform independent research (even
   to defining their own goals and objectives), and reason
   logically and rationally. This is absolutely essential. The
   Japanese know it and are trying to remake their whole
   system, which today produces conforming "know-bots" but
   not independent thinkers. It is one of the highest priorities
   of both their government and their industry. It must also be
   one of ours.

2 School leavers will have to be able to read complex manuals
   and books, and identify, select, extract, distill, and absorb
   crucial information from them.

3 They will need to be able to communicate well, both verbally
   and in writing. This communication will have to be more
   than clear and understandable; it will have to convey
   conviction and authority, and be persuasive.

4 They will have to be competent at a distinctly higher level of
   mathematics than at present. I've been told, for example, that
   Mitsubishi of Japan requires the workers on its car assembly
   lines to have the equivalent of first-year college level
   operations research, which is a branch of statistics. Why?
   Because global manufacturing standards are already pushing
   defects down to one in a thousand or even one in a million.
   Further, manufacturers are now talking about zero defects —
   no mistakes, ever, for any reason. To achieve this requires
   militant quality control every step of the way, and this
   requires that all workers understand the applied statistics that

go into modern quality control. Anyone who wants a job in tomorrow's factory had better be able to do high-level math.

5 The graduating student will need to be able both to lead and to follow. Tomorrow's workers are much more likely to be self-employed than today's. This means that to make a living, they must be prepared to work on their own, initiating their own projects, carrying them through to completion, and assembling teams of other free-lancers to complement their skills for a given project. When the shoe is on the other foot, they will need to be good team players, or people won't include them in their projects.

6 Self-employment also implies other kinds of skills, such as business math, familiarity with compound interest calculations, a rudimentary understanding of tax and employment regulations, and promotion, marketing, and sales techniques.

7 Tomorrow's workers will need at least an elementary understanding of economics. We can no longer afford the luxury of making unwise choices in government policies, and if we voters don't understand what the costs and trade-offs of such policies are, how will we be able to decide? Politics has become too important to leave to the politicians.

8 We will also need to have an understanding of different cultures as well as our own, and an appreciation for people who are different from us. We will be working in a global marketplace, so we must be able to understand and appreciate our customers and competitors.

9 Everyone who wishes to prosper in future should be able to speak another language conversationally (as opposed to learning it academically). If I had to suggest useful languages for the future, they would be Chinese and Spanish, and possibly Hindi.

10 Students should have an understanding of global history, non-European as well as European and our own, in order to put current events in perspective. Remember George Santayana's dictum that a people who do not study history are condemned to repeat its mistakes.

11 They will need an appreciation for their own — and others' — humanity, as well as the resources to grow as human beings. This would include an appreciation of the arts, an understanding of the philosophy of science, and an active pursuit of their own talents and skills as human beings beyond the commercial needs of the working world. I'll return to this much later, in Chapter 13.

Is all this possible? I don't see why not. After all, the people we are competing with are no more than human. Anything they can do, we can do too — if we are willing to work at it. But first, we must stop treating students as if they were widgets to be run through a stamping mill, and must start trying to reach their humanity and get them excited about their own education. Here's Peter Drucker again:

> Actually, we *do* know what to do. In fact, for hundreds, if not thousands, of years we have been creating both the motivation for continuing learning and the needed discipline. The good teachers of artists do it; the good coaches of athletes do it; so do the good "mentors" in the business organizations of which we hear so much these days in the literature of management development. They lead their students to achievements so great that it surprises the achiever and creates excitement and motivation — especially the motivation for rigorous, disciplined, persistent work and practice which continued learning requires. . . . *Achievement is addictive*.[22]

Finally, there is one crucial fact to bear in mind. Canada ranks among the top two or three nations in how much it spends on education per person, so we already have the money. We just need to start spending it wisely.

COOPERATION WILL REPLACE CONFLICT

The old ways of confrontation and conflict between sectors, between government and business, between business and unions, and between employer and employee, must go. In a world of ever-rising competition, the companies and, indeed, nations that work best as teams will prevail over those that struggle with internal conflict. People who argue over who gets a bigger piece of the economic pie are going to see the total size of the pie shrink as a direct result of their selfishness. Ultimately, this will lead to disaster for everyone — there will be no winners.

The Province of New Brunswick, realizing that its traditional resource-based industries would not provide enough employment for future generations, has made tremendous efforts to revitalize its industries. As Premier Frank McKenna recently said, "Governments must strive to minimize the bureaucracy and red tape that businesses must often wade through to get themselves established. They want to know that they are dealing with a responsive, enthusiastic and helpful bureaucracy who will spare no effort to see them successfully established. We must also ensure that government regulations, often required to safeguard other social and economic objectives, do not become barriers to progress. It is a delicate balance that must be maintained, and governments must be constantly vigilant in this area."[23]

There are some very obvious steps that governments can take to encourage growth, employment, and prosperity. For instance, they have to stop making it unprofitable for businesses to hire people. Some governments are moving in this direction by changing, reforming, or eliminating such things as payroll taxes, which penalize employers for having employees. One manufacturer told me that on top of every dollar he pays in wages, he has to pay 36 cents for unemployment insurance, provincial health insurance, the employer's portion of Canada Pension Plan contributions, and so on. As a result, over the next ten years he expects to automate virtually the whole of his operation. It just doesn't make sense for him to hire people for 136 percent of what they are worth.

However, not all such problems have yet been recognized. Employment laws, intended to protect employees from being abused and discriminated against by their employers, are having the unintended effect of causing employers to eliminate people from their payrolls. One small-business owner, obviously fed up with such laws, wrote: "There are the troublemakers and problem employees; even one is too many in a small company with no legal or human-resources department to fall back on. And so decidedly one-sided is current labour law in favour of employees that owners of small businesses are virtually defenceless, another disincentive to job creation."[24]

From these comments, and from my earlier comments on the poor performance of the public sector in government finances and the school system, some might infer that I am against governments, politicians, and civil servants. They would be wrong. In any country experiencing extraordinary growth, including and especially the so-called Asian tigers, governments have played a vital role in fostering that growth. Indeed, I believe that any country that hopes for growth and prosperity must have the active participation and support of its governments.

However, all those who study the role that governments play are quick to comment that what does *not* work is for bureaucrats to pick winning industries (although protectionist policies try to do just that). It is businesses and workers who know what the marketplace is demanding, and they are in the best position to tell governments what policies will work and what won't. If they can pass on this information, and if governments get used to working with the private sector to fashion policies that will encourage growth and employment, we will all benefit.

The same principle applies between employer and employee. The employee on the factory floor is more likely to know how to improve the way things are done than the president sitting at his desk. But if there is no communication between the two, things are unlikely to change. This may best be illustrated by some of the companies that are partly or wholly owned by the workers themselves, such as Great Western Brewing Company of Saskatchewan. When Molson's decided to close the old Carling O'Keefe brewery in Saskatoon, the employees pooled their resources and bought it. They then went out and hired professional managers to work for them in coordinating the company's marketing and operations.

One result was that they very quickly found that they didn't need as many middle managers. "We knew there were ways to do things more efficiently," says Don Ebelher, Great Western's president and CEO, and a former maintenance chief. "We knew from the guys on the line there were ways to eliminate dead spots."[25] As a result, Great Western has four managers instead of twelve, one warehouse foreman instead of five, and the total staff is down from sixty-five to fifty-five.

More than just saving money on salaries, the involvement of the workforce in owning their own company, combined with a flatter management structure, has dramatically improved internal communications. "In the old days," says Ebelher, "if you had an idea, you went to your foreman, who'd go to the first foreman and then up to management, and then it would get kicked to Toronto and by that time it was too late. Now we can react very quickly." The shared ownership and responsibilities also improve cooperation. The *Globe and Mail*, commenting on the change, said, "Veteran employees notice that people on the plant floor work differently when they work for themselves — especially when they know how and why management decisions are made."[26]

WE DON'T SAVE ENOUGH MONEY

Earlier I talked about how access to the global capital markets is open to any concern that can make itself attractive to investors. However, domestic savings prime the investment pump and provide a more consistent and less fickle source of capital for domestic industry than the hot money of global investors. Unfortunately, we Canadians are not very good at saving money compared with our hungrier competitors. About the only good thing we can say about our rate of savings is that it's better than the Americans'.

Our economic policy has largely encouraged consumption and discouraged investment, the reverse of what would be to our long-term benefit. If we Canadians were less conservative by nature, we would be in deep trouble. As it is, we save on average about one-sixth of what our counterparts in Singapore do. Compared with the rapidly developing countries, we are spendthrift wastrels, and we may yet come to rue our folly. Were it not for RRSPs and our attachment to life insurance and pensions, we would be in a bad way indeed, and yet we are eroding even these pools of capital.

If we are to be competitive as a country and prosperous as a people, we have no choice but to increase the rate at which we save money. Some of this can be done by government policy, such as the tax policy that has produced the prodigious RRSP flows. And policies should be reviewed to see what more might be done to encourage further savings. For instance, the overall savings rate might perhaps be increased by something as simple as telling home owners that one of the best things they can do with their money — if not the best — is to pay off their mortgage. Nevertheless, the official policy of our governments must be that consumption can wait; investment is more important. Without savings and investment, consumption will wither away.

QUEBEC SEPARATISTS ARE DESTRUCTIVE FOOLS

My concern in this section is the collective ability of Canadians to compete in a global economy, and it is from this perspective that I say that Quebec separatists are fools. The nation of Canada has more influence in the world than it is entitled to. It has this influence by virtue of accidents of history and geography, first as a colony of the British Empire and its subsequent ties to the "Mother Country," and then as neighbour of the United States. Our voice is listened to in the councils of the world, and we have influence far beyond that appropriate to a country with a mere one-half of one percent of the world's population.

We are a member of the G7 countries (the Group of Seven) and as such, we are considered to be one of the seven wealthiest and most influential countries in the world. We don't deserve to be there. By accurate measure, we are no better than eleventh or twelfth.[27] More importantly, the world's greatest economic and military power is our closest friend. When we negotiated the FTA and NAFTA, we negotiated, if not as an equal, then at least as a partner to be taken seriously.

An independent Quebec would have none of this influence. It would be a brash young upstart, and a small one. It would have no more influence in world affairs than, say, Austria or Turkey, and this lack of influence would cost it — and us — dearly in matters of trade. How much attention would U.S. senators from Wisconsin pay to the trade concerns of Quebec farmers? How much consideration would American trade negotiators give to a newly formed, breakaway country that has only 3 percent of the population of the United States, is more socialist than Canada, protects its farmers and industries more heavily than the rest of North America, and doesn't even speak English? Why would the Americans care what Quebec thinks any more than they care what Jamaica or Surinam thinks?

If Quebec wanted a free trade agreement with the Americans, what terms and conditions would the United States dictate as the price? Trade is a game played by one rule: might makes right. An independent Quebec would have less power and less influence than it does as a province of Canada. That would guarantee that it would be a loser in comparison with today. Moreover, the transition period, when foreigners were adjusting their thinking about Canada and Quebec, would be disastrously expensive. The Canadian dollar would plummet, perhaps to less than 50 cents American. Foreign investors would find ample reason to buy the bonds of less troubled countries of the world rather than ours. Foreign companies would find reasons to locate their factories elsewhere. And many knowledge workers with exportable skills would find more hospitable places in which to practise their professions.

I suspect that within ten years of independence, Quebec would find itself impoverished, its farms and industries decimated. It might well be able to stage a comeback, but that would be from a very low base.

And the rest of Canada? I suspect that the degree of our importance would come into question, and we would be excused from the major discussions and decisions. Foreign leaders would be confused about how to regard this poor, divided country, and their only lasting impression would be that we were less than we used to be.

The day may come when national boundaries will mean little more than postal codes, and this issue won't matter to Quebec or Canada, but that day is not yet here. In the meantime, separation will cost Quebec and Canada dearly. As Benjamin Franklin said on a different occasion, "We must all hang together, or assuredly we shall all hang separately." Even so, I believe that any prudent person laying plans for the future would be wise to make contingency plans for the separation of Quebec (as I shall describe in Chapter 12, "The Fate of Canada"). Quebec separatists may yet prove to be the single-minded fools they appear.

ARE THESE OBSTACLES INSURMOUNTABLE?

Are we, then, condemned to becoming poor while watching poor countries become rich? The answer is no. If we think about global competition as a race, with today as the starting line and everyone starting even, we have enormous advantages over most of the 200 countries in the world. However, our attitude will determine how successful we are. If our aim is to do well compared with the other countries, we should do very well indeed. But we won't do as well if instead of getting down to work, we stand around and complain because we aren't guaranteed the standard of living we enjoyed in the past. Lester Thurow made this point when commenting on the American response to the increased level of global competition: "The United States' answer is to have a temper tantrum, yell, kick, scream, shout and say 'They cheat!'"[28] Clearly, this kind of attitude won't get us anywhere.

What have we got going for us? First, we are aware of the problems. When I first started speaking to conferences and seminars about these subjects, there was a general feeling that they were somebody else's problems. Today, my audiences don't need to be convinced, but are looking for solutions. This is equally true whether I'm addressing groups of civil servants, teachers, business executives, or workers in large or small corporations. I won't say that there is agreement on what to do about the problems. The stifling federal deficit, the faults of the educational system, the aspirations of Quebec separatists — none of these have been resolved. But we are at least working on them.

Next, our industries and our workers are responding rapidly to the changing world conditions. More companies are stripping away layers of middle management, are putting top management in contact with the people doing the work, and are getting leaner, more productive, more responsive — and more competitive. We are exporting more and are finding niche markets in which we excel, even in such supposedly hopeless industries as furniture manufacturing and automobiles.

In addition, we have some structural things working in our favour. We are right in the midst of the biggest boom of savings and investment in our history, and one that should last for twenty years. If we use these funds well, we can benefit mightily. (I'll talk more about this in Chapter 6.)

Another advantage is that the current economic expansion will be prolonged, lasting until into the late 1990s, perhaps even to the turn of the century. It should give shaky companies time to get their operations and finances in order, and it will give strong companies opportunities to find new markets and exploit them while beefing up their balance sheets.

Then, too, Canada is still a much-sought-after destination for immigrants, who have historically been a vital force in the development of nations. If we are selective in admitting people who have skills (not just money) and allow them to enter in large numbers, they will provide vitality and a tough-minded work ethic that will enrich us all.

Finally, Canadians are seen, virtually worldwide, as the good guys, an image we can exploit. As a nation, we are regarded as having the virtues of the Americans without their arrogance or gun-slinging mentality. I've been told by Canadian high-tech companies that when a global customer from, say, Japan has a choice of whether to deal with an American or Canadian supplier, and all other factors are equal, it is the Canadian who gets the business. I don't believe most Canadians understand what an advantage this is. It won't allow us to sell shoddy goods or goods that are overpriced, but if we can justify this faith and deliver good value for money, it gives us an enormous edge.

Canada can be rich. We can do well. But we can only do so by being as good or better than the world's best. To do this, we must become the world's best. Any other choice will leave us in poverty.

FOUR

Tomorrow's Business

The fastest growing and most profitable businesses today are those that tailor products or services to the particular needs of "small-grained" markets. Customers are willing to pay a premium for products that can meet their specific needs, and these products are not being supplied by the mass-manufacturers. Advantage comes from *customization*.

– Robert Ferchat, Chairman, Atomic Energy of Canada, 1991

It's very tempting to pick an industry or set of industries and say, "This is where the best businesses of the future will be found." But the reality is that the successful business of tomorrow can be in any industry if the company is managed properly. This is the point made by two Englishmen, Charles Baden-Fuller and John Stopford in their book, *Rejuvenating the Mature Business*.[1] One example they give that particularly stands out is the hamburger stand. Thirty years ago, nobody would have thought that hamburgers would be fertile ground for a growth industry. Yet over the last thirty years, McDonald's has become one of the classic success stories of all time by revolutionizing the management and marketing of a mature, dull business.

Having said this, let's see which industries, as a whole, are most likely to grow and prosper beyond the average. I'll approach this from a couple of different directions, starting with a broad, general view.

THE BEST INDUSTRIES FOR THE FUTURE

Economists often identify three major classifications of business: primary industries, such as farming, forestry, and mining; secondary industries, essentially manufacturing and processing; and service industries. Bearing in mind the points made in Chapters 2 and 3, the general outlook for these three sectors will be as follows:

• **Primary industries** are going to be under continuing pressure, especially from competitors in emerging countries such as Chile. In general, any individual (especially a farmer) or company that produces an undifferentiated commodity will have a tough time staying in business. Salvation in this sector must come from innovation in production techniques that will allow a distinct edge in costs; or, more likely, using the raw commodity as the basis for producing a niche product that can command a premium price.

One example is certified pure foods — a small but rapidly growing niche. Wal-Mart Stores, the giant American retailer, makes its house brand, "Sam's Corn Chips," from a particular brand and strain of corn that is grown without artificial fertilizers or pesticides. Farmers who supply Wal-Mart must be able to certify that they have followed the requirements to the letter, so that the retailer can advertise that it is selling environmentally healthy corn chips. Although this means taking extra trouble in order to meet the retailer's demands, it gives the farmers who supply Wal-Mart a niche that cannot be touched by the vast majority of farmers, who grow ordinary corn, and it leaves the specialty farmers less prone to the boom-bust cycle typical of agricultural products.[2]

• **Manufacturing**'s future will be more mixed than that of the primary industries, because ever-rising levels of competition create many significant successes as well as lots of fatalities. Markets will be increasingly fragmented as customers start demanding customized products rather than off-the-rack look-a-likes. This trend, coupled with the dynamic new markets of the rapidly developing countries, will produce major new opportunities for smart and nimble players. But as with the primary industries, producing undifferentiated commodity-type products will be a prescription for disaster.

• **Service industries** will continue to grow, and the range and type of services will broaden. More to the point, services are, by their very nature, primarily local and hence not as subject to foreign competition. But competition will increase nevertheless, because there will be fewer jobs available in the primary and secondary industries, and this will cause more people to look for opportunities in the service sector. Because of the vigorous competition, service providers who want to stay in business will have to work hard at finding ways of delighting their customers. The days of mediocre service are passing. Mere customer satisfaction will no longer be enough.

One segment of the service industries that will not expand is administration, particularly in government. Deficits and taxpayer revolts are going to prevent governments from increasing the number of their employees and may even result in significant cuts. In business, "administration" has come to mean "overhead," which is both a dirty word and something that slows a company's ability to adapt to change and respond to customer demands. Much of the "downsizing" that is being done in corporations is in middle management, leaving top-level policy makers and front-line workers, with very little in between.

The seven vital industries

In his speech to the Liberal Party in 1991, Lester Thurow listed seven industries that will be vital for the future.[3] He obtained that list from a Japanese government publication called *Vision for the Nineties* and later saw the same list printed in a publication put out by the Deutsche Bank of Germany. Since Deutsche Bank is a privately owned bank that controls about one-third of German industry through its investments, it is in an excellent position to know what's going on in the German economy.

Both groups agreed on the following seven industries that developed countries should be aiming for: microelectronics, biotechnology, telecommunications, civil aviation, materials sciences, robotics (plus machine tools), and computers (plus software). All seven offer three things that a developed country wants: high wages for workers, high rates of growth in wages, and lots of high-paying jobs.

Companies tend to do best when they are part of a cluster of companies working in and around a specific industry, because they then have local resources on which to draw, and they find it easier to experiment with potential clients and to source new ideas and suppliers. For instance, anyone thinking of going into competition with Boeing in civil aviation would want to check how many related industries there were nearby that might be of value as suppliers.

In some of Thurow's seven industries, Canada is well represented. We have Northern Telecom in telecommunications, Canadair (owned by Bombardier) in civil aviation, and a clutch of small and medium-sized companies such as Corel Graphics, Alias, and Hummingbird in computers and software. There are also a few Canadian companies involved in biotechnology, such as Quadra Logic Technologies of Vancouver and Ortho of Toronto. However, in microelectronics, robotics, and materials science, I know of no major Canadian companies, though some Canadian universities are doing interesting work in these areas.

As well as the seven key industries that are going to grow so rapidly, there are several others that will grow faster than average. While doing the research on the seven major forces that are the subject of this book, I developed a list of these growth industries (see Table 2). I've grouped them in three categories: those driven primarily by developments in the global economy; those driven primarily by demographics (population factors); and those driven primarily by technological developments. This grouping is somewhat arbitrary because it is possible, for instance, for a health-care company to be driven by both medical technology and demographic factors. Also, it should be noted that not all sectors of these industries will grow faster than average. For example, although the demand for energy will expand, it doesn't follow that the demand for traditional petroleum products will do likewise.

TABLE 2   Above-Average Growth Industries

DRIVEN PRIMARILY BY THE GLOBAL ECONOMY
Management, business, and administration
    (a) Human resources (especially maximization of productivity)
    (b) Management consulting (however, the field will be crowded)
    (c) Industrial and wholesale sales
    (d) Streamlining corporate information flows

(e) Accounting/auditing/financial controls and performance measurement (especially for entrepreneurial and fast-changing businesses, and especially across jurisdictions)

(f) Tax management (especially across jurisdictional boundaries)

(g) Temporary-help service organizations

    (i) Temporary professionals, including legal, executives, accounting

    (ii) Leasing of non-core employees

II. Manufacturing

(a) Civil aviation

(b) Telecommunications

(c) Robotics, plus machine tools

(d) Instrumentation

III. Energy

(a) Offshore petroleum industry

    (i) Geophysical services

(b) Alternative energy sources

    (i) Fuel cells

    (ii) Hydrogen

    (iii) Wind power

    (iv) Solar power (from space as well as on earth)

(c) Energy transmission (from where it is to where it's needed)

(d) Energy storage (including, but not limited to, battery technology)

IV. Education

(a) English as a second language

(b) Foreign-language translation and training for business applications

(c) Adult education/training/skills upgrading

V. Marketing

(a) Compiling and interpreting computer data about consumer purchases

(b) Identifying new niche markets

(c) Direct marketing

    (i) Direct appeals based on detailed knowledge of the actual purchases of specific individuals

---

DRIVEN PRIMARILY BY DEMOGRAPHICS

I. Health care

(a) Fitness/wellness

    (i) Clubs: the "third home" concept

    (ii) Sports

        (iii) Dietetics/nutrition

   (b) Most medical specialties, especially

        (i) Anesthesiology

        (ii) Geriatrics

        (iii) Oncology

        (iv) Osteopathy

        (v) Dentistry

        (vi) Ophthalmology/optometry

        (vii) Gynecology (but not obstetrics)

   (c) Veterinary services

   (d) Medical supplies and instruments

   (e) Private medical insurance

   (f) Nutri-ceuticals (i.e., food as medical therapy)

II. Finance

   (a) Personal financial planning

   (b) Investing and investment banking

   (c) Savings/trust services

III. Personal services

   (a) Home services, especially for the elderly

        (i) Companions, housekeeping, physiotherapy, paramedical and nursing, shopping, house maintenance

   (b) Child care (until the baby-boom children mature)

   (c) Funeral homes

   (d) Direct sales

   (e) Retail sales

   (f) Repair services

   (g) Home renovation

   (h) Second home/vacation home construction

IV. Entertainment

   (a) Fine arts

   (b) Graphic arts

   (c) Magazines and newspapers (electronic and print)

   (d) Performing arts

   (e) Films and videos

        (i) Multimedia

   (f) Music

   (g) Computer games/virtual reality

   (h) Spectator sports

V. Hospitality industry

(a) Travel

(b) Hotels

(c) Restaurants

VI. Office equipment

(a) Home office suppliers

DRIVEN PRIMARILY BY TECHNOLOGY

I. Information technology

(a) Computer software

(b) Communications/computer networks

(c) Database compilation and management

    (i) Data entry, classification, and management

    (ii) Sales of databases, including films, music, art works, newspaper and magazine files, stock market databases, vacation destinations, etc.

(d) Systems analysis

(e) Systems integration

(f) Information science

(g) Artificial intelligence

(h) Applications of computer technology, especially

    (i) Medical diagnosis

    (ii) Robotics in surgical procedures

    (iii) Voice programming of computers

    (iv) Applications of computers in personal appliances

II. Science and technology

(a) Environment

    (i) Hazardous waste management and disposal

    (ii) Reducing waste and pollution

    (iii) Energy management and conservation

(b) Molecular chemistry

(c) Biotechnology/genetic engineering

(d) Nanotechnology

(e) Robotics

(f) Materials science

(g) Agricultural research and development (both biotech and mechanical)

(h) Food/nutrition

(i) Lasers and optical technology

(j) Consulting engineering services

Driven by the global economy

Most of the forces driving these industries have already been discussed: the leaching of low-wage, low-skilled jobs from developed countries to RDCs; the steadily rising level of competition; the increased emphasis on "knowledge work"; and the lessening of importance of the traditional factors of competitive advantage: natural resources, labour, and capital.

Driven by demographics

In this category, most of the industries will grow because of the aging of the population and the shifts in the kind of services and products that this will produce. The demographic forces include the baby boom, which I'll deal with in detail in Chapter 6.

Driven by technology

Technology is the subject of the third force, which I'll describe in that section. These sectors of industry will grow because it will become possible to do new things, or to do old things in a more economical way. For example, there will be video channels on demand. Another example might be ethical drugs, or pharmaceuticals, that are custom designed to your unique genetic pattern to solve your specific condition or disease. We are not near this yet, but the computer design of molecules, coupled with the explosion in understanding genetics and its implications for medicine, may make this possible in the future — always assuming that we can afford it.

WHAT WILL MAKE COMPANIES SUCCESSFUL IN THE FUTURE?

The steadily rising level of competition and the need to place ever-increasing emphasis on knowledge, innovation, and creativity in business is forcing rapid change on the successful corporation. Let's look at some of the factors that are changing the way business operates.

Mass production is giving way to mass customization

In many ways, the company of the future will be patterned on Toyota of Japan. Toyota has had as revolutionary an impact on business as Henry Ford did. Whereas Ford demonstrated the power and worth of the assembly line, Toyota introduced the concept of "lean production," and along with other Japanese car makers it is now moving to "agile production."

Toyota developed lean production in the 1950s because it couldn't afford to keep large stockpiles of parts around until they were needed; nor could it afford to waste quantities of materials through poor production practices. To deal with the first problem, it developed a strong relationship with a small number of suppliers and invented the "just in time" (JIT) method of parts shipment and delivery, by which parts would arrive at its factories just as they were needed. This eliminated the need to finance large inventories of parts. A couple of things were necessary for JIT management to work: the assembly line had to operate reliably, so that the exact time the parts would be needed could be reliably predicted and agreed upon; and Toyota had to develop exceptional communications with its suppliers in order to coordinate the arrival of parts at the right moment.

To eliminate excessive wastage, Toyota developed a system that emphasized high quality, so that it got production right the first time rather than having to go back and repair, correct, and explain mistakes later. It accomplished this by encouraging its assembly workers to use their wits to improve results. Any worker who saw a major problem developing could slow or shut down production for the entire factory. When this happened, management would hurry out to learn about the problem; then management and line workers would try to find solutions to ensure that it never occurred again. The end result was that bugs, problems, and glitches were rapidly eliminated from the production line, and everything happened just as it should at every stage of the process. Note that this couldn't have happened if management and workers had not cooperated well and relied on each others' judgment.

A side result of this emphasis on quality was that Japanese cars were soon seen to be better than North American cars. Toyota (and the other Japanese car makers) had a double win: lower costs *and* better products. In fact, one could argue that the quest for lower costs actually produced better quality as a by-product. Keep this point in mind, for I shall come back to it in Chapter 10. Incidentally, if all this sounds familiar, it's because these concepts have come to be accepted as the best way of doing things. "Total quality management" (TQM in business-speak) and "lean production" are now everyday buzz-words in North American business.

Agile production goes one step further. As automation became more sophisticated and computers more capable, smart manufacturers started introducing "mass customization" into their factories. Mass customization means being able to produce the exact product the customer wants, but at a speed and cost equal to or better than mass-produced items. It, too, seems to have started with Toyota.

Because the Japanese market of the 1950s was so much smaller than the American market and thus couldn't support long production runs of identical cars, Toyota wanted to be able to make relatively small numbers of cars at competitive prices. This meant being able to produce more than one body type on a single assembly line. The main drawback was that in order to change to a different body type, all production had to stop for several hours while the molds used to stamp out the steel car parts were changed. By the mid-1950s, Toyota had reduced the time to one hour; it was down to fifteen minutes by 1962, and three minutes by 1971.[4] As a result, Toyota was able to produce a greater variety of models and put new models into production more quickly. Add this to JIT, teamwork, and relentless attention to lean quality production, and it has led to a new way of making cars. Today, Toyota can manufacture more than 45,000 variations of body type and features for its domestic market alone, with little, if any, halt in the flow of production.[5] Similarly, Mazda's plant in Hofu can manufacture eighteen different body types on a single assembly line.[6]

Agile production isn't restricted to the car industry or to Japan. Motorola's plant at Boynton Beach, Florida, receives custom orders for radio pagers by computer and then manufactures and tests the end product within two hours. Moreover, the results are often cheaper than the mass-produced pagers made by many of its competitors.[7]

Badger Meter, Inc., of Milwaukee, which makes flow-measurement and control equipment (gas meters and the like) recently switched to a "continuous flow manufacturing" system that allows it to make more than a hundred different types of meter from a variety of materials. It used to take Badger twelve weeks to change over its plant to produce a different kind of meter. It now takes six minutes, and when used with a computer-aided design (CAD) system, it can make mass-customized products with a high added-value that accommodate its customers' specific needs. As a result, Badger Meter increased its sales by 33 percent over the five years from 1986 to 1991 — an astonishing increase in a mature industry.[8]

There are several important implications of mass customization. First, its flexibility will lead to a world in which customers can have exactly what they want, and at no greater cost than if they bought it "off the rack." Moreover, they will come to expect this. It also means that companies will have to be able to accept change as a normal part of a day's orders.

In such an environment, quality control will be vital. No longer will it be sufficient to do spot checks, as in mass production, where a defective item can be replaced with any other item from the assembly line. If each order is custom made, replacing a defective item means repeating the whole order/production/delivery cycle. Thus, management and workers will have to be alert and intelligent, sharing ideas, seeking solutions together, and acknowledging each others' contributions. In tomorrow's company, the atmosphere is more likely to be collegial than hierarchical.

Finally, mass customization means that the days of looking inward for product ideas are over. It will be customers' needs that drive production.

Everything starts with the customer

Toyota knows that each year 30 percent of the cars it builds for the Japanese market will be white, but it doesn't make a single white car until a customer orders one. Toyota wants to maintain the discipline of responding to the wishes of the customer. The whole organization is oriented around this, and to change part of it by guessing what customers will want would be damaging. (Of course, this only works if the production plant is near the customers. If a car had to be shipped from Japan to North America, it's unlikely that customers would be willing to wait from four to six months just to get the car they want.)

By comparison, North American car companies seem to follow a strategy that might be called "pile 'em deep, then sell 'em cheap." They produce the cars they guess customers will buy, based on previous years' purchasing patterns. The cars that don't sell have to be discounted to get them out the door. Lean production manufacturing despises such wastage, and agile production techniques make it unnecessary.

Letting everything start with the customer might produce a radically different kind of car company in the future. Imagine, for instance, that you go to your local car representative and, using what amounts to a CAD system, perhaps in conjunction with virtual reality, you design exactly the car you want. This design is then transmitted to the nearest car factory, which may not be owned or even related to the company that sold you the car. The car factory, which is able to take unique designs and build customized cars at mass-production prices, makes your car under contract with the designer, and delivers it to your door two days later.

In this kind of scenario, the car business has split into two parts: design and production. With mass customization, there is no need for the two to belong to the same company. An interesting sidelight is that the design of cars, which was classified as manufacturing when it was performed by a car manufacturer, becomes a service-industry job now that it is performed by a car-design company.

The most important and potentially most difficult transition that many companies will have to make will be doing what the customer wants and only what the customer wants. Every company in the last fifty years has paid lip service to serving the customer, but in fact the vast majority have done what they think they're good at and have then left it to their sales and marketing people to shove the result down the consumer's throat. This is called "stimulating market demand."

Wal-Mart Stores, however, chose another approach. It has become North America's biggest and most successful retailer by its single-minded pursuit of what the customer wants: "The starting point was a relentless focus on satisfying customer needs. Wal-Mart's goals were simple to define but hard to execute: to provide customers access to quality goods, to make these goods available when and where customers want them, to develop a cost structure that enables competitive pricing, and to build and maintain a reputation for absolute trustworthiness."[9]

Let's talk, then, about what the customer wants.

The value equation

If you ask competent salespeople how they get a reluctant customer to buy something, they'll tell you that they make sure the customer believes that the value of the product is greater than the apparent cost. But what is "value"? I've thought about this a lot and have finally settled on a very simple definition:

Value = Quality – Price

Price is more than what the customer actually pays for the product. It includes such things as how reliable the product is, how usable, how much time was involved in its selection, and how much it costs to get hold of it. Hence, a cheap car that is always in the shop, isn't available when the driver wants it, and costs a lot to repair isn't really cheap. Similarly, a PC clone microcomputer running a Macintosh look-a-like program may have a lower sticker price than an Apple Macintosh, but if it takes a lot longer to learn how to use and is more difficult to use even when learned, it will eventually be seen as more expensive. This is why the product with the lowest sticker price isn't always the cheapest, and why the lowest sticker price doesn't always sweep the market.

However, the question of quality is more complex than the question of price. Indeed, people have become so tangled up in different concepts of "quality," charging off on crusades for "total quality management," that they've lost sight of what quality really is.

What is quality?

The best definition I've seen of quality in business is the one given in Peter Drucker's book, *Managing for Results*:[10] "What a producer thinks of as the 'quality' of a product is often unimportant to the customer. The producer's idea of 'quality' is likely to be what is hard, difficult, and expensive to make. But the customer is uninterested in the manufacturer's troubles. His only question is — and should be — 'What does this do for me?'" In other words, quality resides in the mind of the customer, and anything else is self-deception on the part of the producer. This, of course, tracks right back to the idea that the whole process begins with the customer, and it applies to services as well as manufacturing.

Simple though Drucker's definition is, it has many implications and not all of them are reassuring. The first is that improved quality means improved customer satisfaction. You may huff and puff, and spend millions on R & D to change your product, but if your customers don't care about the change, you've wasted your money. So you'd better know an awful lot about what your customers want — today and tomorrow — before you start running the R & D taps.

Of course, if you're working on a new product for which there isn't a significant market at present, inevitably it will be a gamble, so make sure you're aware of the risk you're taking. Also, remember that what the customer wants is results. The fax machine exploded on the scene not because people had a tremendous desire to own fax machines but because it let them send documents and information much more quickly and reliably than before.

The second implication is that higher quality is often produced at less cost than poorer quality because the whole process of delivery has been improved. (I'm tempted to say that higher quality is *almost always* less expensive to produce than lower quality.) We saw this with regard to Toyota and lean production. Another example is Motorola, which cut $700 million from its manufacturing costs between 1987 and 1992 by using "total quality management" (TQM) techniques.[11]

However, many companies have embarked on a quality crusade only to find that it did very little for them. A survey of 500 American companies by consulting firm Arthur D. Little showed that only one-third felt that their TQM programs were having a significant impact on their operations, and I venture to say that Canadian firms have had much the same experience.[12]

I think there are two main reasons for this. The first, which I've already touched on, is that companies lose sight of what their customers want. Many companies seem to think that talking about quality, attending seminars, and reading books about quality will somehow do the trick — as if TQM is a mantra that will bring results if it's mumbled often enough. But the customer is not impressed by such piety. As the master said about the customer, "His only question is — and should be — 'What does this do for me?'"

The second reason is even tougher. Although quality will increase customer satisfaction and may also cut your costs, it's difficult! Quality requires careful, creative, systematic thought, combined with great patience and persistence. It's not something that can be done in a week, a month, or a year. It takes many years of steady pushing and hard work. How many years? The greatest Japanese disciples of quality — for example, Honda, Nissan, and the auto parts maker Nippondenso — have been pursuing quality with great single-mindedness for thirty years. There are no "ten easy steps" to quality. It's a way of thought and a way of life.

Quality is more than an absence of defects

As noted above, quality not only means high standards; it's closely tied to customer desire. The experience of David Pecaut, vice-president of Canada Consulting/Boston Consulting, provides a good example of this.[13] On behalf of a client, Pecaut looked into the manufacture of porcelain tableware (plates, cups, and so on), checking out wage rates and the level of automation in Japan, South Korea, and China. The biggest threat came from a Chinese company, which paid its workers 28 cents an hour and was introducing automation that would result in a high-quality product.

This seemed an unbeatable combination — low costs and high quality — but when Pecaut returned to North America, he found a porcelain company that was experiencing great success in marketing its products despite paying its workers $10 an hour. This company had redesigned its business around the concepts of speed and innovation, while working with its retailing clients to respond to consumer demand for fashion-oriented tableware. Whereas most of its competitors changed their designs no more than once every twelve months, this company changed its designs every twelve weeks. And because of its proximity to its customers, it could respond to their needs far more quickly than its overseas competitors.

In other words, the company had redefined the concept of quality to mean "what the customer wants *right now*." This kind of strategy of sensitivity, responsiveness, and innovation can make it tougher for RDC competitors to break into developed markets. Low wages, state-of-the-art automation, and long production runs can be defeated by playing to knowledge-based advantages.

Companies can compete in mature, commodity-type industries if they add value

It follows from the above example that Canadian businesses employing minimum-wage workers can compete with low-wage RDCs if they can add value in other ways. This is the case with Argord Industries of Toronto. Argord manufactures electric motors for household appliances such as blenders and mixers, and is one of the principal suppliers of motors to Weed-Eater, the gardening appliances company.

Argord pays most of its largely immigrant workforce something close to the minimum wage for what is essentially repetitive, assembly-line work. Even though the workers in such countries as Mexico and Taiwan are paid far less, Argord has beaten off potential competitors and has gradually increased the amount of business it does with Weed-Eater. John Banka, president and CEO of Argord Industries, explains how the company achieved this:

> A couple of years ago, Weed-Eater wanted to change the design of their product. This meant that we had to redesign and re-tool our production line to accommodate their new model, so we used it as an opportunity to completely re-work the product we were supplying.
>
> We used several different design criteria, working through the problems on a CAD system over a period of weeks. We came up with a design that let us cut down the number of steps necessary to assemble the motors, which reduced a lot of the labour out of the product and lowered the cost, while simultaneously improving the reliability of the end product. This meant we were able to cut our price to the client, reduce the warranty claims of their end customers, while improving our margins. We also sourced a new industrial plastic that had just appeared six months earlier out of Germany that further improved reliability and also let us use the motor for new kinds of applications.
>
> In a very real sense, we've kept Weed-Eater's business with a better designed motor. And that's happening all over; with automation crunching so much of the labour out of manufactured products, it takes something like a good design to rocket you to the top of your field.[14]

Even in a mature manufacturing industry and in a company that relies on minimum-wage labour, it is the application of knowledge that enables them to make a superior product. Companies that sit still and produce the same old commodity product will not survive. If Argord hadn't made the changes Banka described, it would have lost out to a Mexican *maquiladora* factory years ago. Instead, it is aggressively pursuing business from other brand-name appliance manufacturers and is turning out product as fast as its capacity allows.

Rising quality can erode brand loyalty

The final implication of quality seems to be perverse. Steadily rising standards of quality may erode brand loyalty. J. M. Juran, one of the grandfathers of quality management, explained it this way: "When 30 percent of U.S. products were failures, vs. 3 percent for Japan, that was an enormous difference. But at failures of 0.3 percent and 0.03 percent, it'll be difficult for anyone to tell."[15] In other words, even if Honda's product defects were one-tenth of Ford's, when competition has pushed the level of quality high enough, the difference becomes so small that it is unimportant to the customer. This is one reason, though not the only one, why North American car manufacturers are taking market share back from the Japanese. Although the Japanese still build better cars, theirs are now only slightly better than North American cars. As a result, other factors, such as price, are more important in the customer's buying decision, and this is eroding customer loyalty to Japanese automakers.

On the other hand, if the North American automakers had not worked hard on improving their offerings, the Japanese might have completely buried them by now. Quality, then, is not an option in a competitive situation. It's essential for survival. And this brings me to the next factor, a relatively new concept called "clientship."

Clientship

I'm indebted to David Killins, president of Legacy Storage Systems of Markham, Ontario, for introducing me to the concept of clientship. It makes plain common sense, but like most common sense, it requires someone to express it well before it gains credence.

Clientship means anticipating your client's needs so well that the client never bothers to look for an alternative supplier. After all, most people don't really want to be bothered changing suppliers — provided they feel they are getting good value and good service. Clientship therefore involves competitive pricing, meeting or

exceeding the reliability and desirability of your competitors' offerings, and making it easy for your customers to get what they want
when they want it. More than anything else, clientship means being
in tune with what's going on in your customer's head and, even
harder, anticipating what's going to go through the customer's mind
in the future.

The long-term implications of this trend are significant. As
Forbes Magazine put it in a special report on the corporation of the
future (which it called the "virtual" corporation): "[In future] losing a customer will mean trying to find a replacement from a
picked-over population that has been reduced to the disenchanted
ex-customers of one's most incompetent competitors."[16]

Downsizing is not necessarily the answer to cost cutting

If labour costs are a major problem for a company that wants to stay
competitive, it won't necessarily improve its position by firing some
of its workers — so-called downsizing, or rightsizing. In 1992 Right
Associates of Philadelphia released a five-year survey of 1,204
American companies. This survey showed that almost 75 percent
of the downsized firms reported no improvement in financial performance, and two-thirds said that they had seen no increase in productivity! In other words, the companies had gone from being big
mediocre companies to being medium-sized mediocre companies.

In probing these results, Right Associates found that only 18
percent of the companies had bothered to explain why they were
cutting jobs or how they expected the cuts to produce better results.
Consequently, three-quarters of the workers covered in the survey
felt insecure about their jobs, and morale fell. Worse still, management had no goals — just a vague hope that somehow having fewer
employees would make them "more competitive."[17]

As John Diebold, considered by many to be the father and architect of modern automation, said in a recent speech, "If people are
our principal resource, why are we so eager to downsize?"[18]

Survival requires that management change its attitude towards
its workers. Companies must now consider that their principal asset is
what the company's management and its employees collectively carry
between their ears, and the business must be managed accordingly.

This is leading many companies to re-examine exactly what "management" means. No longer does it mean "control"; it is now much more likely to mean "coordination" or "encouragement." "The present managerial attitude that executives know all the answers and workers know very little will be replaced by a mutual respect for the important contributions of each,"[19] says Carol Kleiman, business columnist for the *Chicago Tribune*.

This is leading to new ideas of how to manage an organization. For instance, instead of a manager being the "boss," she or he is now more likely to be the "servant leader" whose responsibility it is to make sure that there are no roadblocks stopping the team from being productive (and so that there are no excuses for them not producing). In a very direct sense, managers of this type serve their employees by solving the problems that interfere with the employees' ability to achieve excellent results. A description of this management style can be found in Max DePree's *Management Is an Art*.[20]

How effective is this new wave of management compared with traditional methods? Professors Kathleen Eisenhardt of Stanford University and Jay Bourgeois of the University of Virginia made a study of eight small high-tech firms in the computer industry — the sort of firms that ought to be long on networking and collaboration and short on hierarchy. They found that the firms whose executives employed "authoritarian" management methods had difficulty making strategic decisions compared with those who had more participatory management styles. The authoritarian companies were also the poorest performers, getting bogged down in internal power struggles, which made it difficult for them to adapt swiftly and decisively to rapid changes in the marketplace.[21]

Creative work and an entrepreneurial approach to work cannot be closely supervised, and cannot be produced by shouting. They are most likely to appear in an environment that encourages the participation of employees and acknowledges the value of their contribution, both with recognition and with a portion of the profits.

Finally, there's one more reason why decision making should be spread around the corporation. There is now far more information to deal with than any one person can absorb. It is literally only with more brains that we can cope with the greater flow of information.

Tomorrow's company knows the competition and knows itself

Some 2,500 years ago, in *The Art of War*, the Chinese scholar Sun Tsu wrote: "If you know the enemy and know yourself, you need not fear the result of a hundred battles. If you know yourself but not the enemy, for every victory gained you will also suffer defeat. If you know neither the enemy nor yourself, you will succumb in every battle." These remarks apply to business as well as military strategy. In our world of ever-rising competition, a company needs to know what it does well and how it does so; and it needs to know who the competition is and what harm it might cause.

The first idea has worked its way into business jargon in the phrase "core competency," which means focusing on the things you do best and eliminating everything else from your company's activities. A good example is SEI Corporation of Philadelphia, a company in the investment counselling business. It has some 1,400 employees, all of whom are professionals who deliver services to the client. There are no secretaries, no clerks, no accountants, no maintenance people — no *anything* except people who serve customers. They "outsource" (another new buzzword) everything else through personnel agencies and the like. This allows them to focus on their central business without distractions.[22]

SEI believes that outsourcing is the wave of the future, and undoubtedly the practice can cut costs by using service bureaus for accounting, data processing, and the like. But there are also disadvantages. Outsourcing means that you lose the ability to manage some of the company's significant costs, and you may lose technical workers who might help develop the next steps in new customer services. Banks, for example, might be at a disadvantage if they outsourced their data processing just when computers are starting to become of major significance in delivering new banking services.

The second part of Sun Tsu's prescription — "know your competition" — is tougher, because it might spring up next door, or it might come from the other side of the globe. The important thing is to assume that there will be new competitors and to keep a watch for them. This may mean travelling to other countries to see what's happening there, or it could mean working through your industry association to keep track of more trends than you can see for yourself. It will certainly mean reading more widely than most people normally do. The main thing is to keep scanning the horizon for potential competitors, and be prepared to consider preemptive actions. You might, for instance, consider invading a potential competitor's home market in order to disrupt its business before it enters Canada.

WHAT WILL TOMORROW'S BUSINESS LOOK LIKE?

Tomorrow's company will likely have a specific niche in which it excels. This niche may be global, or it may be regionally based in an industry that doesn't allow national or international competition because of shipping costs, or it may be a local service industry. What will be true is that the company will be competing to be the best in its niche. It will emphasize flexibility, innovation, and experimentation. Rather than spending years developing and testing new products or services, it will be in a state of constant development, and the marketplace itself will test the results while the company refines them based on customer reactions.

These two trends — niche marketing and greater flexibility — coupled with mass customization and automation, will negate most of the advantages of being big. Accordingly, with a few notable exceptions, more and more market share of most industries will be taken up by small or medium-sized companies that will carve out niches in which they excel — a reversal of the postwar trend of big companies putting small companies out of business through economies of scale.

Access to investment capital, though, will be a continuing problem for these smaller corporations. Whereas big companies have clout and can get the attention of senior personnel in banking and investment companies, small and medium-sized companies have little or no influence. Their top management often spends a disproportionate amount of time looking for suitable financing rather than working to make the business successful. Indeed, one of the most important things that Canadian governments at all levels could do to help the economy is to look for ways to help businesses find capital.

Canadian banks are going to be forced to choose between financing big, well-established companies with traditional assets, or much smaller, unknown companies with few tangible assets. This will be a dilemma for the banks, because the big companies are going to shrink and come under financial strain, and their assets will decline in value. Meanwhile, virtually all the growth will be in the small, assetless companies that offer knowledge and market niches.

More and more companies will sell as much knowledge as possible and deliberately cut back on the amount of materials or products sold. A good example is Legacy Storage Systems of Markham, Ontario, a world leader in highly sophisticated computer storage systems for computer networks. In the computer hardware and software products it markets, Legacy makes none of the hardware, and it produces only a fraction of the software. Instead, it sells its knowledge of sourcing and buying sophisticated hardware and software, of assembling and integrating diverse equipment into a smoothly operating system, and then supports the final assembled end product. It calls itself a "hardware publisher" rather than a hardware manufacturer, because it is, in a very direct sense, selling knowledge rather than products.[23]

In the company of tomorrow, the relationship with suppliers and customers will be much closer and more carefully selected than before — more like "shared destiny" than the traditional supplier/customer relationship. Forbes Magazine, in an extensive article on the "virtual corporation," talked about this change in relationships:

> The virtual corporation is in many ways a metacorporation. That is, its sphere of influence extends upward through its suppliers and downward through its distribution and retail channels and even to end-users. The most descriptive term for this new relationship is co-destiny.
>
> For example, take suppliers. A manufacturer cannot move fast enough to create and maintain virtual products unless its suppliers can not only meet its needs, but anticipate them. This can occur only if the suppliers are privy to the manufacturer's future product plans, market strategies, even financials — a degree of outside access that would dry the throat of most modern executives. Furthermore, to be properly responsive, the supplier will nearly have to dedicate its production to that one supplier, perhaps (as some aircraft equipment suppliers have done) move into physical proximity to that customer, and even aid that customer in market research. In return for those sacrifices, the supplier will expect sole sourcing.[24]

This is already happening in the computer field, where the product gestation time has fallen from over two and a half years to under one year. In their quest for speed, flexibility, and concentration on core capabilities, companies will cooperate with suppliers and customers to create a process or a product that might have been made by a single company in the past. A perfect example is the car industry, where individual parts, such as bumpers or body trim, are being sourced from independent suppliers, whereas in the past they might have been made by company-owned parts divisions.

Costs will be managed with an eye towards total cost, not just sticker price. An example of this is Hyundai, which in 1992 shut down its personal computer manufacturing plant in South Korea and opened a new plant in Silicon Valley, California. Although the wages in California are much higher, the transportation costs to Hyundai's major market — the United States — are lower, its responsiveness to the market is much greater, and the amount of inventory it needs to keep on hand has declined. Hence, Hyundai expects to trim manufacturing costs despite higher labour costs.[25]

Finally, the corporate organization chart will essentially be flat instead of pyramidical. Managers involved in strategic planning, market and technical research, and advertising and marketing will act as advisers and coordinators to their fellow employees, and may actually be hired by those employees and report to them. Ownership and profits may well be spread throughout the — not very large — organization, and entrepreneurial talents will be as highly prized and carefully studied as technical skills.

The service company

Earlier I talked about how the rising level of quality is eroding brand loyalty. It's having other effects as well. As product quality differences diminish, more and more customers are going to make buying decisions based on their total experience with a company. This effectively puts a manufacturer in the service business, with its product merely being the vehicle by which it delivers service to the customer.

In the traditional service sectors, the rising level of competition, coupled with the steadily improving quality of manufactured products and the aging of the all-important baby-boom consumer, is pushing up customers' expectations of service quality as well as product quality. What would have been acceptable levels of service five or ten years ago is no longer good enough.

I believe that anyone who wants to see the near-term future of service quality need go no farther than the Walt Disney Company. Its aim goes well beyond "customer satisfaction." Indeed, the idea behind customer satisfaction is to give service that is just barely good enough. Instead, Disney aims for customer delight — to leave customers thrilled with the service they've received and to make them enthusiastic supporters of Disney.

As for the long-term future of service, that too is very much in evidence, and once again it is the Japanese who lead the field. This was expressed very well in a powerful article by Robert Hicks, a Canadian who teaches English in a Japanese high school:

> In many [Canadian] stores I visited the staff ignored me. Clerks who did offer to serve me had only the vaguest idea of what merchandise their store carried. Few saw their job as involving more than making change. In contrast, businesses in Japan value their customers. They try to please them. . . . I like the role of *okyakusama*, the Japanese word for customer that is formed by combining the words for "honourable," "guest," and "lord." Here [in Japan] I am never referred to as "a guy at your cash." I never leave a Japanese store without feeling like I have been treated well. . . . In Japan I rarely visit my bank at all. Three times a week a teller comes to the school where I teach to see if there is anything I need.[26]

Can you imagine a bank teller in Canada coming to your workplace just in case you might need something done? Neither can I. Nevertheless, this kind of attention is the way the service economy is moving. There will, of course, be those who deliberately choose to go in the opposite direction: no frills, no service, and rock-bottom prices. Price Club, a retailer that sells in bulk from warehouse stores, is a perfect example. Then there are companies such as Wal-Mart that are trying to do both — provide attentive, friendly service along with no-frills pricing.

What is bound to fail will be mediocre service at moderately expensive prices.

WHAT DO I DO NEXT?

Clearly, all these changes aren't going to happen immediately. Nor will all of them happen to every company or every industry. Nevertheless, these will be the major trends, and companies should be deciding which apply to them and start thinking about how to adapt to them. To assist in this transition, I suggest you consider three things.

First, recognize that in future your principal resource is going to be brainpower — the collective brains of yourself and your employees. Accordingly, ask yourself how you are going to maximize the return on this asset. This will probably cause you to place much more emphasis on recruiting and on human resource management, as well as on training and continuing-education programs. It may also lead you to change your management style.

Next, expect that the level of competition will rise steadily and rapidly for the rest of your life. This means that every day when you come into work, you will face the same questions: What will our customers want today that's different from what they bought yesterday? How can we deliver it faster, cheaper, better, and more conveniently? What could our competition do today to steal our market share? Where might new competition occur, and how can we respond?

Tomorrow's battles are going to be tougher than yesterday's. This may lead you into a much more dedicated effort to research trends around the world to unearth new technologies, new ideas, new tastes, and new competitors. The day you say, "Well, we've done all we can," is the day you surrender to your competitors.

Finally, you should look at ways to improve relationships with both customers and suppliers. This may mean giving up some freedom of action, but the purpose is to become closer to your customers and more responsive to their needs.

The future belongs to the nimble, the smart, the well educated, the attentive, and the entrepreneurial. If this doesn't describe you, you'd better start changing, for the times most certainly are.

F I V E

Where Will the Jobs Be?

Garbage collectors will need computer skills because one-person garbage trucks will be completely automated.

– George Vander Velde, Vice-President of Science and Technology, Waste Management Inc.

The best description I've heard of how careers are changing comes from Richard L. Knowdell, president of Career Research & Testing of San Jose, California.[1] He said that in the 1950s employment was like a train. You chose your profession, then got on that train and stayed on it for your entire career. You didn't set the direction or speed of the train. That was done by the profession you chose, and the track was fixed, unmovable.

In the 1960s and 1970s careers were more like a bus. You hopped on a particular bus, which was the company you worked for, and stayed on it until you decided that you wanted to change direction. Then you left that bus and boarded one going in another direction. You still weren't the driver, and you still didn't control the direction or speed, which were determined by the company, but you had more control because you could change routes.

In the 1990s jobs are like all-terrain vehicles. You are the driver, and there are no roads. You determine the direction, the speed, the state of repair of the vehicle, and you're responsible for everything good or bad that happens along the way.

So how do you choose the direction to go? Let's start with the obvious: it's clearly an advantage to get a good education. As Table 3 shows, during the three years from 1990 to 1993, Canadian workers saw their prospects of employment go up or down according to their level of education:

TABLE 3   The Relationship between Education and Employment, 1990–93

Level of education	Change in no. of jobs	% change
University degree	+308,000	+17.0%
College diploma or trade certificate	+170,000	+5.0
High school diploma	−16,000	−0.4
Less than a high school diploma	−651,000	−19.0
Total	189,000	−1.5

SOURCE: Statistics Canada, quoted in "Why It Pays to Stay in School," *Globe and Mail*, January 17, 1994.

And as Table 4 below shows, the better-educated people also tend to make more money:

TABLE 4   The Relationship of Education to Income in U.S. Workers, 1986

Level of education	Average income	Average unemployment rate
4+ years of college	$33,443	2.1%
1–3 years of college	23,400	2.3
High school graduate	19,844	4.8
Less than a high school diploma	16,606	6.8

SOURCE: 1986 study by the U.S. government, as quoted in Carol Kleiman,
The 100 Best Jobs for the 1990s & Beyond (Chicago: Dearborn Financial Publishing, 1992), p. 35.

However, education or training on its own may not be enough. To a large extent, the results will depend on what you have studied or have trained to do. There's little point in training for a career that is disappearing, such as stenography, any more than you would study how to make buttonhooks or apprentice yourself to a blacksmith.

When I'm invited to speak to high school students, and after I've told them that they face a world that is tougher and more competitive than the one their parents or teachers experienced, they often ask what they ought to be studying in order to prepare themselves for it. As well as listing the skills I discussed in Chapter 3, I give the students much the same advice as that offered by Premier Frank McKenna of New Brunswick, a politician who seems to be trying to lead his province in the right direction:

> It is essential that young people achieve higher levels of schooling, that will equip them with an understanding of technology, computer literacy, numeracy, problem-solving abilities, and good analytic communications skills. We must increase the numbers of students taking maths and science in school, not merely to provide more engineers, but to prepare them for the labour market of the next century.
>
> More students need to pursue employment-related college training. Increasingly people will create their own jobs, acquiring shorter-term skills as needed.[2]

The last two points — creating your own job and acquiring shorter-term skills — are particularly important. There's an excellent chance that your next job won't be a job at all; it may be your own business — one of the many entrepreneurial companies I described in the previous chapter. If all the self-employed people in Canada were counted in a single industry, I believe it would be the third largest and the fastest growing in the country. This is partly due to the downsizing of major corporations, and partly due to the frustration of baby boomers who can't see much hope for advancement in their current jobs. In any event, we are experiencing the greatest boom in entrepreneurship in our history. As I explained in my last book, *From Employee to Entrepreneur*,[3] the skills of an entrepreneur are very different from those of an employee.

The other point Premier McKenna makes is also worth considering: the ability to pick up new skills. Just as corporations will have to be flexible and change direction quickly in response to the needs of their clients, so will the employee (or entrepreneur) have to be prepared to learn new things, whether it's a new language, computer proficiency, public speaking, leadership, selling skills, or something else.

Even the greatest hunter finds no game
in an empty field

When looking for a job, you'll have to do some digging to find out
where the best opportunities are. In the last chapter, in Table 2, I listed the industries that I expected would experience above-average
rates of growth. Remember, though, that even in growing industries,
jobs may be hard to find because of the downsizing caused by
automation. Here are two more lists: occupations that are hot, and
those that are not.

What's hot: amusement and recreational services; arrangement of
passenger transportation; computer and data-processing services; day
care; electronic computing equipment; electronic home entertainment equipment; human resources management; management consulting services; medical instruments and supplies; nursing; office
furniture and fixtures; offices of physicians and osteopaths; oil and
gas field services; optical and ophthalmic products; out-patient and
health services and facilities; partitions and fixtures; pharmaceuticals;
radio and television communication equipment; residential care;
retail; semiconductors and related devices; telephone apparatus; temporary personnel services; x-ray and other electromedical apparatus.

What's not: blast furnaces and basic steel products; crude petroleum;
electrical and electronic assemblers; footwear except rubber and plastic; iron and steel foundries; silverware and plated wear; new non-
building facilities; luggage; handbags and leather products; metal mining; mobile homes; natural gas and gas liquids; new farm housing
alterations and additions; new gas utility and pipeline facilities; new
local transit facilities; new nonfarm housing; new conservation and
development facilities; private households; railroad equipment; ship
and boat building and repairing; tobacco manufacturing; watch,
clock, jewelry, and furniture repair.

These lists were compiled by Valerie A. Personick, an economist
with the U.S. Labor Department's Office of Economic Growth and
Employment Projections.[4] There are also several books that deal
extensively with this subject. Two that I found most helpful were The
100 Best Jobs for the 1990s & Beyond, by Carol Kleiman;[5] and Emerging
Careers: New Occupations for the Year 2000 and Beyond, by S. Norman Feingold

and Norma Reno Miller.[6] Virtually all the books agree that someone who has a degree in engineering in a growing field will never have to worry about finding a job. The same is usually said of scientists, particularly those specializing in fields that are in demand, such as materials, electronics, and the environment. A degree in computer science is widely considered to be a job guarantee, although I have my own doubts about this, as you'll see in the section on technology.

Honing your workplace skills

To this point, I may have given the impression that if you stay in school and pick a "hot" industry, you should be able to have a nice safe career. It ain't necessarily so. Unfortunately, an education guarantees neither a job nor a career. All it does is improve the odds of getting a job, for there are other factors involved, such as individual creativity, initiative, and presentation skills; what's going on in other parts of the world; and just plain luck.

Job competition is creeping up on us in novel ways, too. Not long ago, I spoke to a conference in Tallahassee, Florida. Afterwards, I was chatting with a Florida architect, who told me of the competition he was getting from some local companies. Instead of employing a team of local architects, these competitors were using just one, plus a fax machine. When there was a call for proposals, these firms faxed the specifications to their architect partners in Mexico. They were able to produce significantly lower bids by using educated professionals in an RDC who were paid about one-quarter of the salary of an American architect.

This pattern holds true in other areas. One of my clients, an engineering firm, told me that it had been offered drafting and other support services by a firm in India at a small fraction of what the services would cost in Canada. Indeed, India has become a hub for software programmers and systems analysts, who charge much less than their developed-world counterparts. In a slightly different vein, New York Life Insurance now sends all its claims by overnight courier to a small town in Ireland, where they are keypunched into a computer. The data is then transmitted back to New York over a computer network by the afternoon of the next day.[7]

In other words, it's not just low-skilled and manufacturing jobs that are disappearing to the developing countries. White-collar jobs, including those requiring high levels of education, are also starting to migrate. What this means for you, as an individual, is that you can't make a couple of career decisions and then go to sleep. Every day is a challenge, and you'll need to stay on your toes, just as businesses must be constantly on the lookout for higher levels of competition.

This is difficult, to be sure. But I see one great advantage: people find that more challenging jobs are more fulfilling as well. With routine jobs disappearing, we have no choice but to seek challenging occupations.

THE FUTURE OF WORK

I want to end this chapter with some thoughts on the long-term future of work, because it's something that worries me.

I am not concerned that we are losing jobs to RDCs. As the RDCs develop, they become better customers as well as tougher competitors, and the demand for everything rises. As a result, everybody winds up better off, except for those who cannot or will not adapt to the new reality. No, my concern is not global competition; it's an overall decline in the need for work, brought about by the increasing capabilities and sophistication of computers.

I seem to be very much in the minority on this view, and I may be dead wrong. The conventional view is that as jobs disappear from manufacturing and clerical work, for instance, the steadily rising productivity of workers using increasingly sophisticated automation will create a new prosperity that will increase demand and create new jobs. This is certainly reasonable, because it is precisely what has happened throughout history. But where, I wonder, will the new jobs appear? The conventional view is that new services will spring up and that higher living standards will allow people to spend money on things they could never afford before, and much of this will be for personal and personalized services.

I can see logic in this. New services do appear. There were no aerobic instructors, for example, in my grandfather's day. But how much personal service can we use? Moreover, generally speaking, service jobs pay less than manufacturing jobs. As for being able to buy things that we couldn't afford before, since manufacturing will increasingly be automated, the higher demand for manufactured goods won't necessarily generate more jobs.

This is not a problem that will burst on the scene in the next five to ten years. Humans are still capable of offering a flexibility, initiative, and creativity that machines cannot duplicate. But at some point, whether it's twenty years away or one hundred, I'm afraid that the time will come when there will be very few jobs that computers can't do better, faster, cheaper, and more reliably than humans. As that day approaches, we will be confronted with several problems.

In the first place, we will need a new economic system. Much as it grieves me to say so, free market capitalism may be dying, for it pays only those who are part of the production process. If virtually no one is part of this process, all the fruits of production will belong to those who own the machines — a recipe for the peon-and-aristocracy patterns of Third World economies. But where will the machine owners find their customers? People can't be consumers unless they have money to spend.

I believe that the appearance of large numbers of homeless people in the major cities of the developed world are the leading edge of this process. In Toronto alone, it's been estimated that there are 47,000 homeless people.[8] The same homelessness is evident in New York, in Paris, in London — and, I suspect, in every major city in the world.

An even more significant problem will be finding a purpose in life. Even if we have money, if we do not need to work, what will we do? Will we be a burden to ourselves, with time hanging heavy on our hands? Will we all turn to the arts and become painters, poets, and dancers? I doubt it. Few of us are capable of being good artists, and I think most of us would find art as a livelihood unfulfilling.[9]

Lest you think that this is all overblown nonsense, let me finish the chapter with two quotations. The first is from Richard Barnet, an expert on international affairs, as quoted in the *Globe and Mail*:

> Across the planet, the shrinking of opportunity to work for a decent pay is a crisis yet to be faced. The problem is starkly simple: an astonishingly large and increasing number of human beings are not needed or wanted to make the goods or to provide the services that the paying customers of the world can afford. Since most people in the world depend on having a job just to eat, the unemployed, the unemployable, the underemployed . . . have neither the money nor the state of mind to keep the global mass consumption system humming. Their ranks are growing so fast that the job crisis threatens not only global economic growth but the capitalist system itself.[10]

The second quotation is by W. W. Leontief, winner of the Nobel Prize in Economics:

> Adam and Eve enjoyed, before they were expelled from Paradise, a high standard of living without working. After their expulsion, they and their successors were condemned to eke out a miserable existence, working from dawn to dusk. The history of technological progress over the past 200 years is essentially the story of the human species working its way slowly and steadily back into Paradise. What would happen, however, if we suddenly found ourselves in it? With all the goods and services provided without work, no one would be gainfully employed. Being unemployed means receiving no wages. As a result, until appropriate new income policies were formulated to fit the changed technological conditions, everyone would starve in Paradise.[11]

THE SECOND FORCE

Population

SIX

The Time Boom

Throughout history, most social phenomena have repeated over and over again. We have had political movements shift from the left to the right, good leaders and bad; social behaviors have become more liberal, and then conservative again. But we have never before had a mass population of middle-aged and older men and women. . . . It's no wonder we're all so baffled by what to make of it. Just think of all the problems! . . . But just think of all the opportunities!

– Larry Tisch, Chairman, CBS

We are in uncharted waters. Never before has there been such a one-two punch as we are experiencing today — a substantially increased life span, and too many people concentrated in one relatively narrow age bracket: the baby boom.

WE'RE LIVING LONGER LIVES — MUCH LONGER

Longevity is the fifth force, and I shall be dealing with it in more detail in Chapter 11. Here I shall simply point out that our life span has increased enormously, so we don't conveniently die off and leave the world to our children as our forebears did.

Two centuries ago the average life expectancy of Canadians was around thirty-five years, and the median age of the population was about sixteen. This was largely because so many people died of typhoid, tuberculosis, tetanus, cholera, smallpox, and other diseases, and because of the many women and children who died in childbirth. That was one reason why people had such large families — it was the only way they could ensure that some of their children survived.

As recently as a hundred years ago, the situation wasn't much better: average life expectancy was forty years, and the median age of the population was twenty-one. Since 1901, life expectancy has risen almost thirty years — an increase of almost four months per year. This is astonishing, and it means that today we have more middle-aged and elderly people (both in absolute terms and as a percentage of the total population) than at any time in history. Moreover, these groups are growing far more rapidly than the population as a whole. This is one of the reasons why we need to re-examine what we consider "old."

In our cultural mythology, we still cling to the belief that people become old at sixty-five, even though there is no longer any good reason to think so. The pension age of sixty-five was fixed by the German statesman Otto von Bismarck more than a hundred years ago, at a time when people lived to an average age of less than forty-five years. This was Bismarck's way of keeping pension costs down. Today, when many Canadians are hale and active in their late sixties and well into their seventies, the sixty-five benchmark no longer makes sense. We must redefine "old."

And now let's look at the other significant development — the baby boom.

HOW THE BABY BOOM IS DISTORTING
OUR SOCIAL STRUCTURES

Why is there so much fuss about a group of people born just after World War II? Why do they make such a difference?

In fact, the baby boomers weren't all born immediately after the war. Although the boom started around 1947, it went on for more than twenty years, until about 1967. As a result, this one generation of people makes up almost 35 percent of the Canadian population, or about the same percentage as the province of Ontario. The major difference is that unlike the people of Ontario, the baby boomers tend to think and act in much the same way. So what the baby boom wants, the baby boom takes.

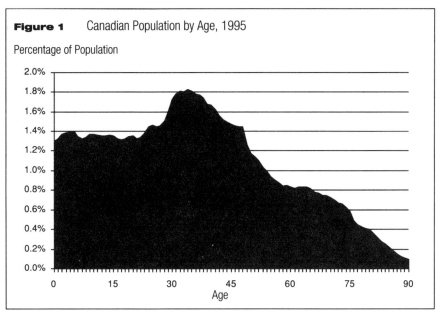

Figure 1 Canadian Population by Age, 1995

Source: IF Research, based on Statistics Canada data[1]

Figure 1 above shows how the Canadian population is distributed by age — in other words, what percentage of Canadians fall into each age group. As you can see, about 1.3 percent of Canadians will be under

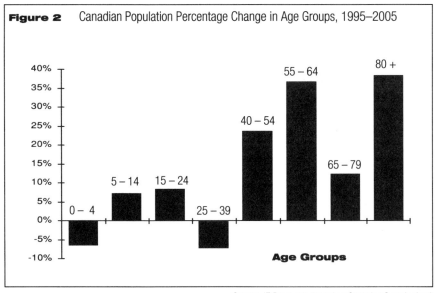

Figure 2 Canadian Population Percentage Change in Age Groups, 1995–2005

Source: IF Research, based on Statistics Canada data[2]

89

one year old in June 1995, and about 0.1 percent will be over ninety. If the baby-boom generation had been no more numerous than the generations around it, this graph would have been shaped roughly like a triangle, sloping downhill from left-to-right as the members of each age group gradually died off. Instead, there is a tremendous lump in the middle. That lump — representing Canadians between approximately twenty-eight and forty-eight years old in 1995 — is the baby boom.

Figure 2 divides the Canadian population into eight different age groups and shows how each is expected to change in size over the next ten years. Thus, there will be about a 7 percent decline in the number of children under five, and a 38 percent increase in the number of people over eighty. Of course, there are more children under five than elders over eighty, but the percentage of elderly is growing much more rapidly because people are living longer.

How will this affect society? Let's look at each age group in turn and see what kinds of change can be expected in the next ten years.

Preschool children (born 2001-2005, who will be aged 0-4 in 2005)

The women of the baby boom are now leaving their prime child-bearing years, and consequently the number of children born each year is falling. This will have great significance for the industries oriented to young children (for example, baby food, parenting magazines, and infants' toys) as well as for obstetricians and neonatal and obstetrical wards in hospitals.

Even more significant will be the effect on the school system. Since it takes about five years from birth for a child to begin school, school systems should keep an eye on the declining number of births and realize that they must resist the temptation to build additional school facilities. Overspending on facilities could exacerbate school closings and teacher layoffs, much as happened in the 1970s.

School-age children (born 1991-2000, who will be aged 5-14 in 2005)

This group, and the next older one, are the children of the baby boom (sometimes called the "baby-boom echo" or "mini-boom"). They are currently giving the school systems fits, because each year sees more children entering school than the one before it.

90

To cope with this mini-boom, I reckon that every school in Canada will, on average, need at least one extra classroom along with the staff to support it. But as I've just pointed out, the school systems should be trying not to build additional facilities (though new buildings could be feasible if schools worked in cooperation with their municipalities to make sure that the facilities would be used for other purposes after the mini-boom has passed). In any case, the school systems will not be getting enough money from their own tax base to allow them to build extra schools or hire extra teachers. So they will have to stretch current facilities to fit, which means poorer student-teacher ratios; fewer specialty teachers for subjects like science, music, art, and gym; the widespread use of portable classrooms; and so on.

Subject to local variations, kindergarten classes will continue to grow in size every year until about 1998. This means that primary schools will see enrollments grow steadily until 1998; junior high schools (Grades 7 and 8) will continue to grow in size until about 2005; and high schools will keep expanding until about 2007. Colleges and universities will see their enrollments swell until about 2011. Meanwhile, companies that supply products for kids will enjoy a steadily growing market for toys, clothes, bicycles, textbooks, candy, pop, video and computer games, popular music, and so on. Theme parks will have an increasingly large clientele, as will TV shows for kids and movie theatres showing kids' films.

Of course, there will be problems too. In most baby-boom families, both parents work, which means they have less time and energy to devote to raising their kids. As a result, these children will be less disciplined than earlier generations and will create more problems in school and in their neighbourhoods. Coupled with school overcrowding and overburdened teachers, this is a potentially explosive mixture. I'll come back to this in Chapter 13.

Labour force entrants (born 1981-1990, who will be aged 15-24 in 2005)

Reversing a trend of the last fifteen years, there will be more young adults making the transition from school to college or employment. Depending on the state of the economy, this may be a blessing or a curse. There are going to be more service jobs, many of which will be entry-level or minimum-wage jobs. The leading edge of the echo-boom kids will be available to fill these jobs — if times are good.

If you are in this age group, you will be competing with the two age groups above you and will be at a disadvantage if they haven't settled into permanent and better-paying careers. Professionally, your best strategy will be to look for a skilled occupation in which workers are already scarce, and then be patient. As the baby boomers age, the scarcities will increase and your prospects will improve. On the other hand, if you're not patient or don't have the necessary skills, you should seriously consider starting your own business.

Meanwhile, as your age group enters the labour force, you will need all the things that people starting a career usually need: working clothes, housewares, cars, and so on. You and your contemporaries will also have social lives, which will involve going to restaurants, taverns, movies, and other forms of entertainment. That your group is smaller than your baby-boom parents often overshadows the fact that you will nevertheless be a significant buying group, and marketers would do well to take note of your presence.

Your best housing strategy will be to hang back and wait until the boomers find they need more space for their growing families and sell their starter homes, thereby creating a glut on the market.

Note that all this won't happen at once. In fact, the effect of your group won't be felt in a big way until the late 1990s.

Lower- to middle-level workers (born 1966-1980, who will be aged 25-39 in 2005)

This is the so-called baby-bust generation, or Generation X. If you belong in this group, you are in the unenviable position of having to follow along behind the baby-boom parade, and as with all parades, quite a lot of mess has been left behind.

Your group has had to struggle with this all your life: schools were being closed and teachers let go when you were in school, and you had to cope with funding crises in college. Now that you are in the labour force, you're probably finding that you're competing with the older, more experienced, and usually better educated tail end of the baby boom, who also have struggled and consequently are willing to take jobs for which they are overqualified. You, too, will often wind up settling for jobs beneath your abilities and qualifications.

Ironically, businesses are going to find that after two decades of having too many middle managers, there won't be enough when top management needs them to fill senior positions. This will further spur companies' efforts to create horizontally structured organizations and to use computers to replace white-collar workers.

There's also a certain amount of irony in the fact that it will be from your group that the next crop of health-care professionals should come, the ones the baby boomers will look to first as they get older. Since there are fewer of you and since the budget crisis in health care means that a smaller percentage of you will be motivated to enter this field, the baby boomers will have difficulty finding all the doctors and nurses they need (though the government will likely import health-care professionals — probably from RDCs). The baby boomers, especially in ex-urban areas, may well wind up being served by doctors and nurses whose first language is not English (or French) and whose culture and attitudes towards health care are quite different from ours. Obviously, the details will depend on where we recruit such immigrants at that time.

All this will be quite a contrast from today's picture, for health-service professionals of the baby-boom generation have flooded the system so that we have too many professionals. But when these professionals start retiring, the picture will change.

Like the group following you, your best strategy will be either to look for an occupation that requires a high level of skills (and thus has a relative shortage of qualified labour) or to create your own opportunities as an entrepreneur. In housing, you will continue to have problems resulting from the enormous demand created by the baby boomers. In many ways, you would be best off not buying a house. Alternatively, you could buy a vacation property in the hope of selling it to the boomers at a profit in about ten years' time, when you could use the proceeds as down-payment for a smaller house vacated by a boomer with an expanding family.

More senior workers (born 1951–1965, who will be aged 40–54 in 2005)

This group represents the core of the baby boom. Because of its size, the baby-boom generation dictates what is happening in the economy, in advertising and marketing, and in politics, and it will continue to do so until its members start to die off in significant numbers in the second quarter of the next century. Since the boomers will be entering middle age over the next ten years, middle-aged issues will be in the ascendant, especially fitness and "wellness." Health clubs will see a bull market, and less rigorous exercise, such as low-contact aerobics, yoga, tennis, and Tai Chi, will enjoy wide popularity.

Medicine and health will become hot topics, both for marketing purposes and in politics. Grocery stores will experience a revolution as food comes to be viewed as "nutri-ceuticals" — natural drugs and remedies to sustain health and vitality. "Pollution-free" food, grown without insecticides, artificial fertilizers, or pesticides, will be in great demand, as will water filters and bottled water.

Waiting lists for surgery and other medical treatments will become a hot potato for politicians as boomers encounter the financial problems of the Canadian health-care system. Because of their numbers and political activism, the boomers will continue to be of huge importance in elections, yet their demands may be impossible to finance. Preventive medicine and preventive dentistry should flourish. As well, dentists and optometrists (who are not affected by the financing problems of the health-care system) will see their practices continue to expand.

Saving will become *au fait*, and the demand for financial instruments and services of all kinds will be enormous. People even vaguely associated with the financial industry will try to elbow their way into the market, which will lead to crowding, confusion, conflicting claims, and the occasional financial fiasco.

Movies, videos, and television programs will develop more mature themes, turning from the crash-bang of adventure films to more thoughtful and thought-provoking plots. Recycled material from the 1950s, 1960s, and 1970s, such as "The Flintstones" and "Maverick," will continue to be mined as a safe investment by film and television production companies. The Beatles will continue to sell, and the Stones will stay on tour and in demand, contrary to all common sense and decency. Advertising will raise the age of the sex symbol in order to keep in step with the aging boomers. "You're not getting older, you're getting better," said Clairol to a generation wanting to believe. Indeed, the cosmetics and personal-care industries — including hair salons and facial and skin-care products — will enjoy new and lucrative challenges, especially as the boomers approach fifty.

Despite all this dominance of trend, style, and politics, if you are a boomer you will have problems that earlier generations did not. You have had heavier competition from your contemporaries than your parents did. Consequently, you and your spouse have both had to earn, unlike your mother, who stayed home while your father worked. Despite this, you still don't have as comfortable a life-style as they did.

A major problem is and will be housing. When you moved into the housing market, the prices sky-rocketed because your generation created such a massive demand. When the time comes to sell, you'll be facing a similar problem; there will be too many sellers and not enough buyers, so the prices will drop. Most people view their house as their greatest financial asset, their retirement nest egg; but you may find that you can't finance a comfortable retirement from the sale of your house.

If you were at the tail end of the baby boom, you will have an especially tough time because you are competing with the early boomers as well as your contemporaries. When you entered the job market, the early baby boomers had already overloaded the system with workers, so your group has often failed to find decently paid, fulfilling work. Your parents and older siblings tend to blame you for not trying hard enough (though they rarely say so), but the truth is that the cards were stacked against you, as they will be for the rest of your life. Worse, if you are a white male in this group, you will already be finding that governments are actively discriminating against you in favour of minorities and women, thereby compounding your problems. In a very real sense, you are paying for the sins of the generations ahead of you. Many of you have turned to entrepreneurship as a way of side-stepping the normal corporate ladder towards advancement, reasoning that if you are the president of the company, your age won't matter as much.

People preparing for retirement (born 1941-1950, who will be aged 55-64 in 2005)

If you are in this group, you are riding on the crest of the wave created by the baby boom and will be helped by it for the rest of your life. Many of you consider yourselves boomers. By and large, jobs and advancement haven't been a problem for you, and you are now reaching the upper echelons of your organizations. You are, however, quite worried by the downsizing that has hit corporate Canada and are hoping you can ride out the storm until you reach retirement. You will suffer higher taxes and the same kinds of problem with the health-care system as the boomers themselves, but these problems will come later in life and so will have to be endured for a shorter length of time.

Your group should expect the stock market to be good to you, though the days of high interest rates are past. Nevertheless, driven by the saving surge of the boomers, the stock market will help your investments perform well. You should plan on selling your home before the baby boomers start selling theirs, but this shouldn't be much of a problem unless you want to hold on until the very end.

Active retirees (born 1926-1940, who will be aged 65-79 in 2005)

If you are in this group, you probably had a generally prosperous career and face a long and generally prosperous retirement. You may be outraged at the level of taxation and the deterioration in health-care services, but the truth is that you are much better off than your children and those that follow you will be at your age. While your investments won't bring in as much as they used to, you needn't worry about your house. It won't appreciate more than it already has (with local variations), so keep it or sell it as you like.

Your group will do a lot of travelling for pleasure and will become involved in many different types of education of more and less formality. You will spend a lot of time looking for alternatives to the high interest rates of the last twenty years for your investments, and will probably never be really comfortable with these alternatives. You will, in fact, probably be annoyed that you can't just get a high, regular, and predictable income any more.

Socially, you face a real problem. Advertisers will be attempting to persuade the baby boomers that they're not old, and in the process they will probably make you look bad. Yours may be the last generation to suffer significant discrimination because of age. People will be patronizing and will treat you as senile, even though you are hale and vigorous. As a result, you will probably spend more time in the company of your peers than with younger people.

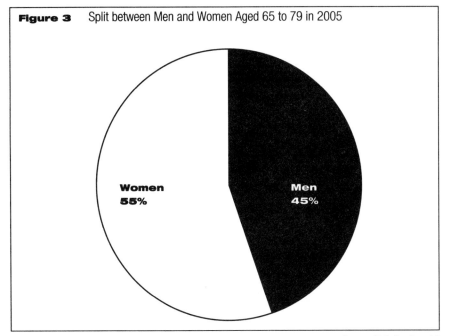

Figure 3   Split between Men and Women Aged 65 to 79 in 2005

Women
55%

Men
45%

Source: Statistics Canada[3]

Another problem is that the men of your age group have been dying off faster than the women. There are now only 100 men for every 123 women, yet you and your contemporaries are still active and fully functional human beings with the same needs for intimacy (not necessarily sex) and human contact as your juniors. This may lead to conflicts between women over men — albeit discreetly. Some futurists have gone so far as to suggest the emergence of *de facto* polygamous relationships (with more than one woman sharing a single man), as well as the blossoming of elderly lesbian relationships. Whatever you do, though, it will be discreet, so as not to frighten your children — who wouldn't believe what you were up to if you told them.

The elderly (born 1925 or earlier, who will be aged 80+ in 2005)

If you are in this group, you are the oldest yet healthiest elders in human history. Somehow, the honour of the position seems to escape you, especially considering the demeaning attitudes of the young — coupled with your own real, and growing, physical indignities. Advertisers seem to delight in pointing out those of your faculties that are less than they were, with ads for grown-up diapers, dentures, retirement homes, walkers, and so on.

Like the age group directly behind you, you are not greatly affected by the baby boom, save that you benefited from it economically through your working life. If you did well in your career, you should now be well off financially. But you are beginning to be truly concerned about your physical limitations — such things as opening doors and jars, and reaching the top shelf of the cupboard or the bottom of your bathtub. Home renovators are encouraging you to make alterations in your house so that you can stay there longer, and you keep getting ads through the mail about retirement facilities. The winters seem to be colder, and many of your peers fly south — and worry about the American health system as well as the financial limitations of the Canadian one. Meanwhile, the male-female imbalance of your age group has become worse. Among people over eighty, there are 209 women for every 100 men. Women's relative longevity is proving to be both a blessing and a curse.

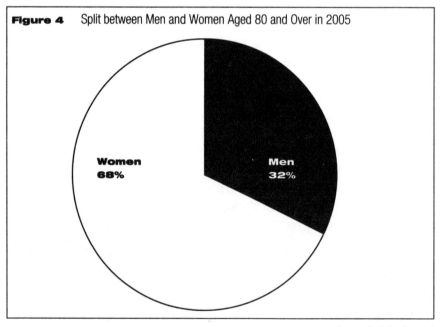

Figure 4   Split between Men and Women Aged 80 and Over in 2005

Women
68%

Men
32%

Source: Statistics Canada[4]

No age group gets off free — but some will find the future harder than others, and none will admit that others have it worse than they do. Unfortunately, this will lead to political conflicts that will make the Quebec separatist movement look like a discussion about the art collection of the National Gallery. It is only with compassion and understanding that Canadians can weather the storms ahead — so let's cultivate friendships with other age groups and try to understand their challenges as well as our own.

HOW DEMOGRAPHICS WILL AFFECT INDUSTRY AND SOCIETY

As we have seen, different groups will have different experiences because of the numbers of people around them and before and after them. These demographic forces will also have differing effects on different industries, governments, and sectors of society. Accordingly, let's look at some of the broad changes that we can expect during the next ten years or so.

The stock and bond markets

The typical financial life cycle of an adult goes something like this:

• During your early working life, you buy all the things you need to establish a household and set up life on your own: dishes, working clothes, a car, furniture, and so on. Since you aren't making much money at this stage, you borrow to make your major purchases, and you are therefore a borrower on an incremental basis.

• As you approach and then enter your thirties, you begin to think about owning a house, and when you eventually buy one, you go heavily into debt. You may later increase this debt as you trade up to a bigger house, especially if you start a family.

• As you enter your forties, your borrowing slows down as you stop making major purchases (though you replace things that wear out, especially your car). Your income is rising, and as you make your monthly car and mortgage payments, pay your pension plan contributions, and start putting money into RRSPs and insurance plans, you switch over from borrowing more money from year to year into saving money from year to year. So although you still have significant debts (and may even have new costs, such as your children's education), you have become an incremental saver rather than an incremental borrower.

• The drive to save money accelerates as you enter your fifties and early sixties. You are now in your peak earning years. The spur of saving for retirement increases your desire to save, and your higher income gives you more room to do so. You will typically finish paying off your mortgage during these years and will then own your house free and clear.

• Once you reach retirement, you will start cashing in your investments — or will at least live off the income they generate. Your income will drop (often by as much as 50 percent) but so will your spending requirements, since you no longer have the clothing and travel expenses of a working life. You may seek to sell your house at this stage in order to realize on your single biggest asset or to enable you to live somewhere that is more convenient, less expensive, or warmer. On balance, then, you start dissaving — drawing money out of the financial markets to live on. This stage continues for the balance of your life.

Over the next twenty years, the baby boomers will be moving into the period of life when their incomes will be rising, their borrowing falling, and their saving rate increasing. At the same time, the size of the age group that tends to borrow most — people in their twenties and thirties — will fall sharply. As a result, there will be a flood of money into savings while only a trickle will be going out in borrowing.

As with any other commodity, when demand for money dries up and the supply of money blossoms, the price of money — interest rates — falls. This is precisely what we are seeing today, and it is a trend that will continue until the baby boomers start hitting retirement age. As interest rates fall and as money floods into investments of all kinds, stocks will inevitably be forced up in price. Accordingly, the next twenty years should see the biggest investment boom in the history of securities trading in North America.

This does not mean that all investments will do well all the time. I expect that all this money washing around the system will create unprecedented volatility, making for dramatic market surges — and frightening market crashes. Moreover, not all the money the baby boomers save will go into the North American stock markets.

Many people will invest in the rapidly developing countries (RDCs). You're more likely to make money in a rapidly growing economy than in a slowly growing economy.

Here in North America, a two-tiered market will develop. Small, innovative, rapidly growing companies will attract the same kind of attention as investments in the RDCs. Meanwhile, mature, stodgy companies will trade at a discount, since their appeal will be modest in comparison. All of this will undoubtedly lead to abuses, and even fraud.

I also expect that some investments made in RDCs will end in disaster. These markets are young, their political stability is still relatively new, and the accounting standards and so on are flimsy. So although this will be a boom time for investments, not every investment will be a boon. More than ever, it will pay to investigate before you invest.

Housing

For the next ten years or so, the demand for housing will persist, but at a steadily declining rate compared with the past two decades. Most of the baby boomers have already bought their houses, though many of the tail-end boomers are still looking to get into the market, as are the baby busters. As noted earlier, there will be some trading up by the boomers as families grow in number and as children grow in size. At the same time, the renovation market will blossom as the boomers seek to make their homes more comfortable for their growing families. Over the next few years, the boomers will continue to buy vacation homes such as cottages or ski chalets, thereby boosting the demand for such properties.

Younger retirees — those in their sixties and seventies — will, by and large, want to stay in their homes, although, as mentioned earlier, some will sell up for more convenient or more comfortable locations. There will be a renewed interest in renovations in this group, too, as homes are adapted to make them more livable for older people.

As our population of elderly people swells, the demand for seniors' housing will rise. Much of it will be "lifecare" housing, as opposed to old folks' homes. Lifecare allows seniors to live in their own self-contained apartments or cottages in a housing development that offers various services, including a restaurant. There are usually medical facilities and staff on site for emergencies, with arrangements with a local hospital for major or chronic problems.

101

Retailing

Buying stuff is very much on the agenda for baby boomers — and hence for retailers. Yet because of the trends I described earlier, consumers will expect better quality plus lower prices plus great service. At the same time, they will be prepared to shop in a warehouse store with minimal service — but only if the bargains are irresistible compared with the alternatives. This expectation of more for less has been called "breaking the compromise,"[5] and companies that can manage it, such as Wal-Mart, the world's largest retailer, will gobble up market share at the expense of those that can't.

Once, when I was speaking at a planning conference for Canada's largest office supply company, someone in the audience questioned whether this was in fact new. Haven't price and service always been the keys to successful retailing? Yes, of course they have. The difference is a matter of degree and the amount at stake. The rising level of competition worldwide is creating much higher expectations and offering consumers better alternatives.

At the same time, niche specialists will flourish as the boomers become more decisive about what they want and as their incomes rise to allow them to experiment. However, sensitivity to market whims and a keen understanding of the customer's mind are absolutely essential for survival. This is why inventory control will be vital. Not only will it allow companies to keep their working capital needs slim, but the up-to-the-instant information that can be gleaned by the intelligent retailer about what's hot and what's not can make the difference between success and bankruptcy.

Meanwhile, there are three retailing appeals that will continue to grow and command market share: (1) make me younger; (2) entertain me; and (3) make it easy for me. All three are related to the changing tastes of the aging boomer.

"Make me younger" comes from the obvious boomer reluctance to accept that they are aging. They want flattering clothes, flattering hair styles, and settings and surroundings that make them look good and feel strong and healthy. Health spas, beauty salons, and fitness centres all fit this prescription, especially if they can help the boomers believe they are holding back the clock.

"Entertain me" means that consumers are more interested in buying experiences than in owning things. If this means a car with wicked styling, or cowboy boots, or a trench coat like the one Bogey wore, so be it. If you put up a sign in your office saying, "Boomers just want to have fun," you won't be far off the mark.

"Make it easy for me" is a continuation of the trend towards convenience. This is especially true as stress levels rise and people want to simplify their daily chores. Since one secret of managing stress is to cut down the number of decisions you make, the successful retailer will find ways of relieving customers of small decisions.

If, for example, you are a travel agent with a client who has booked a trip to Barbados, you might offer to make all the travel arrangements door-to-door, rather than just mailing out the plane tickets. If you're selling an appliance, you could arrange not only to have it delivered but to have someone install it and then give lessons on how best to use it. Remember, you're selling an experience, not things, and the experience starts with being comfortable with what they've bought. But remember, when making decisions for your customers, that you must let them disagree with you if they wish. For instance, if you suggest that a limo will pick them up two hours before their flight, but they want to wait until one and a half hours, do it their way.

Education and training

In a world in which everybody agrees that knowledge workers and knowledge industries are crucial, education becomes the strategic industry. When I say education, I include adult education and training, which I believe will be one of the fastest-growing industries in the developed world. Remember what Peter Drucker said: "In the post-capitalist society, it is safe to assume that anyone with any knowledge will have to acquire new knowledge every four or five years, or else become obsolete."[6]

For this reason, companies and individuals will continually want to upgrade their knowledge and skills and to broaden their understanding of the things that affect their field. This is, frankly, why companies and industry associations hire me to speak at their conferences: to sensitize their people to what's happening and what's going to happen in the world, and to broaden their outlook on what they are doing. Fortunately for me, I thoroughly enjoy this kind of work, especially as it challenges me to stay on the leading edge of things.

However, there will be a change in the way people acquire this knowledge. As technology opens up new ways of conveying information, and as the cost of accessing it drops, technological solutions to the need to stay up to date will come into vogue.

Leisure activities and the arts

As consumers age, their tastes mature as well. Not everybody will become fans of Mozart and Monet, but there will be enough people doing so to produce a boom in the arts. Indeed, there will be a boom in all things related to leisure activities as the baby boomers broaden and deepen their tastes beyond the Beatles, bowling, beer, and pizza. I fully expect that ballet, theatre, symphony concerts, musicals, and art galleries will enjoy much increased prosperity over the next couple of decades — always assuming that they are perceived as offering good value for money and that they make their works accessible to boomers who are cultivating new tastes.

Boomers are no longer in their courtship years, so the frequency with which they go to restaurants will decline. But when they do dine out, it will be as a form of entertainment, so they will want it to be not just a meal but an experience. This increases the emphasis on the quality of service, and it opens the door to new kinds of cuisine and new dining experiences. Meanwhile, their demands will change at fast-food restaurants, too. A "burger to go" will give way to table service and a broader range of menu alternatives. Healthier food will be preferred — if it's palatable.

Theme parks will do well, though the rough and raucous rides of the boomers' younger years will be reserved for their children. More cerebral, or at least less painful, attractions will appeal to the adventure-oriented mentality of the boomers, and places such as the EPCOT and MGM theme parks in Disney World will flourish.

The type of travel that is combined with education, or at least offers new experiences, will grow in popularity compared with the fly-to-the-beach travel of the past. Exotic locations, such as Antarctica, and transpacific sailing voyages and the like will become more popular as the boomers start giving the "Been there, done that" response to plain-vanilla vacations.

Speciality magazines will flourish, both in traditional printed forms and in new electronic forms. The economics of magazine production rather than demand will be responsible for a publication's success, for there will be a demand for almost every conceivable kind of publication. "Narrowcasting," the idea of appealing to a very carefully targeted audience (as opposed to broadcasting, which attempts to appeal to everybody) will continue to develop as an advertising art form, focusing on smaller and smaller groups.

This trend towards appealing to ever more focused groups will be complemented by developments in communications technology that offer an explosion of alternatives, especially in electronic media. People who are talking about 500-channel television systems are missing the point. They should be considering the implications of 50,000-channel systems.

Health services

As people get older, they tend to use more medical services — doctors, hospitals, nurses, pharmaceuticals, and so on. Indeed, the Ontario Economic Council reports that the per capita costs of health care for those over sixty-five are at least seven times higher than those under eighteen.[7] Consequently, as the baby boomers age, the demands on the health-care system will increase. Our so-called health-care crisis is not a one-year or short-term phenomenon; it is a problem that politicians, voters, and health-services workers will face until the middle of the next century, when the baby boomers die off. This will inevitably lead to the rationing of all types of health-care services. Every country in the world that had a baby boom after World War II will be in the same situation; it's only the kind of rationing that will be different.

Here in Canada, where we have a universal health-care system of which we are justly proud, rationing will show up as long waiting lists for treatment. Many of us may die as a result of these waiting lists, and this could create enough political friction, as the boomers age, to cause us to change the rationing system. Wherever possible, we will try to maximize the capacity of the system by making better use of the resources we already have. For instance, an Ontario cardiac patient waiting for an operation will be directed to the province's next available surgical slot, regardless of location. Hence, a Toronto resident might have to fly to Thunder Bay to get the next surgical procedure available in the province — or vice versa.

Of course, this also means that we will have less choice over who performs our medical care. It may even be that the general practitioner we see for our routine ailments will be selected from who's available on a given day rather than being the person we want. Many won't like this lack of choice — but it is one of the implications of maximizing the use of our resources and ensuring that as many people as possible get the best health care available.

In the United States, the rationing system will continue to be money. Those who have money (or have insurance companies that have money) get treated; those who haven't, don't. Of course, well-to-do and desperate Canadians will travel to the States to receive treatment, thereby switching their rationing system.

I suspect that other rationing systems will come under consideration, too. One possibility is that used in Oregon, where the state-run medicare system drew up a list of medical procedures and then ranked them in order of importance to the commonwealth of the state as a whole. (For instance, the vaccination of children has a much higher priority than triple-bypass heart surgery for an elderly smoker, because it represents a more cost-effective way of improving the health of the largest number of people.) Oregon's next step was to draw a line as far down the list as its health-care budget could afford. The procedures above the line get paid for; those below it must be paid for by the individual, because the state will not foot the bill.

Another possibility is for a person's life-style to determine what proportion of health-care costs the government will pick up. In this case, if you're a smoker, you'll pay a bigger percentage of your health-services costs than someone who doesn't smoke. If you're fit, you'll have more of your health-care costs picked up than if you are fat and flabby.

Yet another alternative that has been proposed is to cut off all health-care treatment to people over a particular age. This has a cruel logic that is so lacking in humanity that I suspect it will not be widely considered. However, variations of the idea will be included in rationing systems. One commentator reports that in the United Kingdom, for example, certain kinds of major surgery and certain treatments (for example, kidney dialysis) are denied to people over seventy.[8]

Regardless of what kind of rationing system is used, the entire process is a political minefield. Our knowledge of medicine, nutrition, fitness, and the care of the human machine is producing a steadily rising life expectancy, and the medical techniques for doing so are becoming steadily more expensive. Both these factors — longer lives, and more expensive treatments — will push up the health-care bill. But if a procedure is available that can save your life or the life of a parent or child, are you prepared to see it denied because the state can't afford to pay for it? Rationally and logically, we may come to one answer. Emotionally, our answers may be very different.

There is no simple solution to this problem; there can only be a range of unsatisfactory measures. Yet there is a big difference between bad solutions and terrible solutions. Accordingly, the first step must be to assemble the three principal groups involved — politicians (and the civil servants who work with them), the health-care providers, and the health-care users (who are also voters). They need to sit down together to discuss the issues, and find the best possible solutions in view of the fact that we cannot afford all the health care we will want.

Right now, there is no significant dialogue between the politicians and health-care users. The implied message is that our health-care system will go on functioning as it has — which is not possible. Most of the discussion, such as it is, has been between health-care professionals and civil servants, and much of it has been less than fruitful, with both sides feeling that they are being victimized by the other. Doctors, for example, feel that because they are such a small proportion of the electorate, they are being taken advantage of. Meanwhile, health ministry bureaucrats believe that doctors are whining and dragging their feet over finding solutions. Indeed, health ministries across the country believe that our current over-supply of doctors is a major part of the problem because each new doctor needs to build a stable of patients in order to make a living. The civil servants feel that if the ministries of health could just limit the number of doctors, we would be able to solve — or at least manage — a large part of the problem.

This lack of discussion cannot last. At best, these are band-aid solutions for a situation that is going to get steadily worse for about the next fifty years. It's time that the public was told the unvarnished truth, and it's high time that the health-care professionals, politicians, and bureaucrats began to work together to come up with some rational, long-term solutions that everyone would be prepared to live by.

Outside the public health-care system, there is going to be a boom market for all sorts of health-related products and services. Indeed, health services generally are one of the fastest-growing sectors of the economy, accounting for a significant fraction of all new jobs created. This includes certain sectors of pharmaceuticals, dentistry, optometry, physiotherapy, and so on, as well as such related fields as nutrition, fitness, and rehabilitation. Everyone in and associated with these fields, as well as their suppliers, will enjoy the biggest bull market this sector has ever known.

Politics and government

The fastest-growing demographic influence over governance and politics is the seniors juggernaut. As discussed earlier in this chapter, there are more people moving into the ranks of the seniors than at any time in history, and this trend will continue to gather momentum well into the next century. The increasing number of seniors is particularly important politically, because a larger percentage of them vote than the younger groups. They also have the time and the inclination to work as political volunteers in election campaigns, and this further multiplies their influence.

Perhaps even more important is that regardless of their inclination to right- or left-wing political views, seniors, and especially the retired, tend to vote as a block on issues that concern them, such as pensions and other age-related benefits. This became evident when the Mulroney Tories tried to reduce the cost-of-living increases in pensions as a cost-cutting move, and were met with such a firestorm of protest from seniors' groups that the government hastily backed down.

Imagine what will happen with this kind of political power as the size and political importance of seniors continues to grow. Today, about one voter in every five and a half is over sixty. By 2005, it will be one out of every four; and by 2015, when the baby boomers start to pile into the seniors category in massive numbers, it will be one in three, rising fast, and the seniors' lobby will be unstoppable. This is not hopeful for Canada as a country. It means that our political agenda will be dominated by the aged. It means that the country's finances will be dominated by the demands and expectations of seniors — and not all of these expectations will be financially possible.

This one issue on its own carries the potential to tear the country apart. Younger age groups, the ones that will be asked to foot the bill for retirement and senior benefits, will find that their taxes will be dramatically higher than those of earlier generations, yet they won't be able to muster the votes necessary to turn back the demands of the seniors. One of the potential effects of this trend is that the number of poor young people — which is already high relative to our historical levels — could well balloon as the issues of the young get neglected in favour of the issues of the elderly. Schools may suffer, day care could languish, street kids may be neglected, and low-income couples with children could find life progressively more difficult.

Does it have to be this way? Not if seniors are sensitive to the problems of the young and, more importantly, if they are willing either to pay higher taxes, sharing some of their comparative affluence with the young, or to accept a lower level of benefits so that the needs of children can be met. Whether or not this will happen, I don't know. What I do know is that in most jurisdictions the elderly have tended to be very selfish, voting with their pocketbooks and ignoring the needs of children. School bonds have been defeated, though desperately needed, because seniors' groups have rallied against them. Monies have been denied to programs for day care, for school lunches, for young people living in poverty. Indeed, young Canadians of the future run the risk of being impoverished by those over sixty.

However, our seniors can't entirely be blamed for their attitudes, for they worked hard during their careers and regularly made contributions to government-sponsored health-care programs, the Canada/Quebec Pension Plans, and old-age security. They believe, not unreasonably, that having paid for these programs, they should be entitled to receive them. But in fact they did not pay for the programs. With the exception of the Quebec Pension Plan, the monies taken as "contributions" were spent on other programs, and those monies are long gone. For today's seniors to receive the benefits they were promised, they should have been asked to make significantly higher contributions, and those contributions should have been invested in assets that made a return to the investment fund. Instead, the cupboard is bare.

It's a pretty problem. Do we tell those over sixty that their long-promised rewards have not been paid for, or do we beggar future generations to pay for the unrealistic benefits that have been promised? With either course, we break faith. And what should the politicians do? Their best hope is to state the plain truth and seek the cooperation and understanding of all concerned — and then institute means tests for all age groups to ensure that benefits go to those who truly need them. Will they do it, or will they meekly cave in to the powerful and even dominant lobby group of the future — our elderly selves?

Pensions

Most Canadians expect to rely on public and private pensions in their old age, but the baby boom creates problems for both types of pension. Let's look at the Canada Pension Plan (CPP) to start with. When it was implemented in 1966, it was to be a "partly funded" pension system. This takes some explaining, so bear with me.

A fully funded pension system is one that collects enough in contributions so that these monies, combined with the investment income they earn, can pay for each person's pension. It is thus the individuals themselves, by contributing throughout their working lives, who pay for their entire pension benefits (based on actuarial assumptions about life expectancy and the investment return earned on pension investments).

At the other end of the spectrum is the pay-as-you-go pension system, which collects from current workers only enough money to pay for the pensions of those who are retired at that time. If the number of workers is high relative to the number of retirees, this has the advantage of keeping the level of contributions low and deducting less of the workers' take-home pay. Clearly, pay-as-you-go schemes work only if the ratio of workers to retirees is high and stays high. If the number of retirees rises relative to the number of workers, the contributions that the workers have to pay will go up too. In our present situation, longer life expectancy means that there will be more retirees collecting benefits for longer periods of time, and there will be a rising number of retirees relative to the number of workers. This is putting pay-as-you-go systems into financial danger.

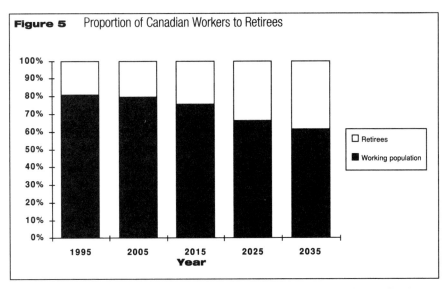

Figure 5   Proportion of Canadian Workers to Retirees

Source: IF Research estimates, based on Statistics Canada data[10]

A partly funded system is a compromise between these two extremes. At the outset of the plan, more money is collected than is needed to pay the pensions of those currently retired, and the monies are invested to help defray the costs of future pensions. But not enough money is collected from each worker to pay the entire cost of that worker's pension. Under this kind of system, as the proportion of retirees rises, not only do the contributions by workers go up, but some of the investments have to be sold to help keep the contributions from rising too quickly.

Now, in theory the CPP is a partly funded plan. To be fully funded, with our future pensions completely financed and secured by us instead of relying on future taxpayers, it would need an estimated $656 billion — more than half a trillion dollars — more than it has.[9] In fact, though, the situation is even worse than that. CPP contributions in excess of requirements in the early years of the plan were supposed to be invested, and the investments used later to help defray the cost of pensions as the ratio of workers to retirees declined. But this is an illusion created by politicians, who deliberately and cold-bloodedly deceived the public.

In reality, although the funds have supposedly been "invested" in the bonds of the provincial governments of nine of the ten provinces

(Quebec being a partial exception), they have in fact merely been spent, and the money is gone.[11] Instead of investing the money when it was received, in order to secure it against the day when the monies would be needed, the provincial governments spent it as if it was revenue and simply ignored the need to pay it back later. That, after all, would be a problem for some other group of politicians.

For the CPP to get its money back from these "investments" (or, more technically, for the CPP to call the bonds), the provincial governments would have to do one of three things: borrow more money in the bond markets; cut expenditures; or raise taxes.

But based on what I've said in Chapter 3 about the state of government finances, I cannot imagine that any of the nine provincial governments would want to take any of the three steps necessary to repay their debts to the CPP. Accordingly, I suspect that what they will do instead will be to quietly lobby the federal government not to demand repayment. The Canadian Society of Actuaries has released a report to this effect, calling the CPP a pay-as-you-go pension scheme — thereby ignoring the funds that were supposed to have been invested, and side-stepping the necessity of provincial repayments. So the CPP is now a *de facto* pay-as-you-go scheme, whether we thought that was what we were getting for our money or not. This means that we are in real trouble, for we are walking into both of the booby traps of such a scheme: longer life expectancy, and a much higher proportion of retirees.

What does this mean, and what are the alternatives? First, it means that CPP contributions will inevitably increase in order to pay for the rising tide of pensions. Policy could be changed to increase contributions faster than is currently needed with the intention that the excess could then be invested against future need. But if the excess is "invested" in provincial bonds in the same way as past surpluses were, this will simply increase the current tax bite (in the guise of CPP "contributions") of present taxpayers without solving any of the long-term problems.

The second alternative is to keep raising the contribution rate to match the steadily growing pension payments as the number of retirees grows. This, in effect, will leave the problem squarely on the shoulders of later generations — our children and grandchildren. We already know that their taxes will have to be significantly higher than ours are. Will they be willing to shoulder the obligation to pay our pensions, simply because we could not be bothered to finance them properly? How cheerful will they be about this (especially as the political dominance of the baby boomers will force these younger groups to pay, no matter how they vote)?

In 1984, the Ontario Economic Council issued a set of reports on pensions, old-age supplements, and the health-care system. One of these reports concluded that for governments to maintain 1983 levels of payments and service, taxes and CPP contributions would have to rise by between 50 and 65 percent from 1983 levels.[12] This would set the highest marginal rate somewhat above 85 percent. In other words, for every incremental dollar of income a taxpayer in the highest brackets earned, 85 cents of it would go to the government in taxes.

The other alternative is for governments to cheat. The pensions promised to the baby boomers (which they mistakenly believe they have paid for) will be denied them. Pensions will be cut, either in the amount paid or by raising the age of eligibility; or by debasing the dollar through inflation. Regardless of how it is done, the baby boomers, and perhaps the generation before them as well, will not receive what they were promised by politicians who are now long gone. I suspect that all three of the above measures will be taken to some degree. This will spell further trouble between generations, along with further political pressure on governments to deliver on unrealistic promises.

Private pensions
Unlike the CPP, most private pension schemes are run on a fully funded basis. The funds are invested in private-sector companies, which for the most part are profitable and increase the value of the pension assets. This would be well and good if it were the whole story. But consider this: just as the current flood of money from the maturing workers of the baby boom is pushing stock markets up to record levels, so too, when the time comes for pensions to be paid to the boomers, will the selling pressure on the assets of the various funds reduce the prices of these assets, making them less valuable. Consequently, more assets will have to be sold to meet pension obligations, putting further pressure on prices. This could lead to a downward spiral, significantly reducing the

monies available to pay pensions, despite the careful calculations of the actuaries who guard the funds. Their calculations do not, to the best of my knowledge, include the potential effects of this selling pressure when the time comes to pay.

Ironically, the Quebec Pension Plan, far more soundly managed than the CPP funds, will suffer the same selling pressure as the private-sector funds. More, the selling pressure will have significant political ramifications, because the Caisse de dépôt et placements du Québec, which manages the funds, has invested heavily in Quebec industry. It will therefore be forced to put extreme selling pressure on Quebec stocks, making it even harder for such companies to raise operating funds. This could be a severe blow to the Quebec economy — an ironical outcome considering that the indirect cause would be Quebec's own careful planning and prudence. But of course, Quebec, too, could cheat on pension payments like the rest of the provinces.

POSSIBLE SOLUTIONS TO THE TIME BOOM

Although all these problems seem insoluble, we are not necessarily headed for disaster. But we can't afford to wait until the problems are on us. We must start working on the solutions now.

First, it's time our politicians told us the truth — that we cannot afford the pensions Canadians have been promised. Once this horrible truth has been told, it will become possible to discuss the alternatives. But as long as our politicians pretend that everything is okay and that, with just a little fine tuning, the money will be there, we can't even start to tackle the problem. So far, the politicians I've asked about this will only reply, if it's on the record, that contribution rates will have to rise. Off the record, they are much more frank.

Next, there are only two humane ways of dealing with a generation of people that is much too big: either we must all have a lot more children or we must let a large number of immigrants into Canada. Since our birth rate isn't likely to shoot up suddenly, let's talk about immigration policy. High levels of immigration often produce a political backlash, especially during difficult economic times when people feel that immigrants are taking jobs from them. In truth, Canada has a very generous immigration and refugee policy, especially when compared with other developed countries.

The United States set its 1993 immigrant quota at 700,000 people, which sounds like a lot. But as they have roughly ten times as many people as we do, a comparable immigrant quota for Canada would be 70,000, and in fact our federal government's policy was to allow 250,000 immigrants into the country in 1993 — about three and a half times as many per capita as the U.S. quota. Frankly, we have it right and they have it wrong. The graphs and long-range demographic projections that I have given in this chapter are based on this 250,000 gross immigration quota. If we allowed fewer immigrants than we are doing, our situation would be much worse later on.

Today, we have more than four workers for every person over the age of sixty-five. Based on our current rate of immigration, when my son is my age and part of the middle-class tax base, there will be about two people working (1.9 to be precise) for every one over the age of sixty-five. If we were to drop our immigration rate from 250,000 per year to 140,000, that ratio would be less than 1.7 workers for every person over the age of sixty-five. In other words, high levels of immigration will make our long-term situation better.

Of course, there is a price to be paid for large-scale immigration in the form of cultural friction and transitional unemployment as immigrants try to find their niche in the Canadian economy. We are seeing evidence of both of these today. But in the long run, high levels of immigration might make the difference between a workable demographic situation in Canada and an impossible one.

At the same time, we must keep in mind two likely effects of the global economy. The first is that we won't be able to afford to have more unproductive people. Our immigration policies should therefore emphasize valuable skills and education. We must dispense with the policy of letting immigrants with money buy their way to the front of the queue, and instead we should let immigrants earn their way, through superior qualifications. We don't need more money — we need more brains.

The second effect to keep in mind is the increase in productivity that will be brought on by automation. At the end of the last chapter, I mused on the long-term effects of automation and computers replacing people in the workforce. It is just possible that by dumb luck we will find ourselves in a position where the smaller number of workers supporting the retired baby boomers will be productive enough to be able to pay what the boomers have been promised and still be able to afford decent lives for themselves. This is not a certainty, of course. It will be a real toss-up, and we don't have enough information even to make a vague guess at present.

But one thing I can tell you: I don't believe we have the luxury to assume that we will be rescued by a *deus ex machina*. If we don't plan — now — to deal with the problems of the too-big generation born between 1947 and 1967, we may well die poor. And we will deserve to.

SEVEN

The Detonation
of the Population Bomb

Unlike plagues of the dark ages or contemporary diseases we do not yet understand, the modern plague is soluble by means we have discovered and with resources we possess. What is lacking is not sufficient knowledge of the solution but universal consciousness of the gravity of the problem and education of the billions who are its victims.

– Dr. Martin Luther King, in his speech on receiving the
Margaret Sanger Award in Human Rights, 1966

What is this plague that Dr. King warned us of in such strong terms, and where did it come from? *We* are that plague. We humans are increasing at such a rate that we threaten to overrun the Earth and destroy much or possibly all of life on this planet. To put it bluntly, if we do not solve the problem of the population explosion, the human race may not have to worry about any other problems, for many of us will die, and if we're unlucky as well as foolish, we may all die.

Isn't this a rather extreme position? Although there is overcrowding in some parts of the world, isn't population growth slowing overall?

No, it's not. World population growth — the number of people born each day — is greater than at any time in history. The number of people born over the last ten to twelve years exceeds the world population of 1800, less than 200 years ago. More than a quarter of a million babies are born every single day.

So when people ask me what I consider the biggest challenge humanity faces, there's no question in my mind: it is a human population that is growing too quickly. We have no experience in this problem, for it has never arisen before, so it's hard for us to understand why it is a problem. In answer, look at Figure 6 below.

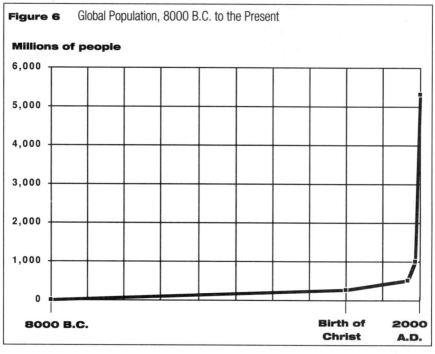

Figure 6   Global Population, 8000 B.C. to the Present

SOURCE: Paul R. and Anne H. Ehrlich, *The Population Explosion*
(New York: Simon & Schuster, 1990).

About 10,000 years ago, the entire human population amounted to something like half a million people — less than two days' worth of births today. At the time of the birth of Christ, there were probably no more than 5 million people on the planet — less than the population of Quebec today. By 1650 there were 500 million people, and by 1850 about 1 billion.[1] In 1990 there were more than 5.3 billion. By the end of this century, there will be 6 billion people, and by 2025 there may be 8 billion, with more than 10 billion expected by 2050.

Why don't we hear more about this? Very simply, because it's not part of our experience. Of the almost doubling of world population anticipated by 2050, about 97 percent will come from developing countries.[2] For instance, in 1950 there were only ten cities in the world with a population of more than 5 million. Of these ten, four were in developing countries: three in China, plus Buenos Aires in Argentina. By 2000 there will be forty-eight cities with a population of more than 5 million. Of these, thirty-seven will be in the less developed countries. The world's biggest city will be Mexico City, with a population for that metropolitan area alone that will almost equal the entire population of Canada.[3]

Just because we don't see this doesn't mean that it's not our problem. I said before that there *may* be 8 billion people by 2025 and more than 10 billion by 2050, because we're unsure what effects the Four Horsemen of the Apocalypse (Famine, War, Pestilence, and Death) will have. We don't know how fast population problems will emerge; but once they start to appear, they will explode upon us. To see why, consider a simple mathematical puzzle.

Suppose you have a lake with one water lily, and suppose the water lily population of the lake doubles every day so that there are two water lilies on the second day, four on the third, eight on the fourth, and so on. If the lake will be completely choked with water lilies at the end of thirty days, when will it be half full of water lilies? Answer: on the twenty-ninth day. In other words, virtually all the problems of over-crowding will occur during the last day! Before the last couple of days or so, there will not appear to be a problem. The same thing can be expected with human population growth. When the problems start to occur, they will come suddenly. Accordingly, if we don't start to act now, we may never have the chance, especially as population solutions literally take a lifetime to take full effect.

What kinds of problem are likely to crop up? Well, let's start with hunger. The harvests of 1985 and 1986 were bumper crops, the greatest in history. But if everybody in the world ate the way we do in Canada, there would have been enough food for less than one-half of the world's present population, never mind future growth.[4]

Earlier I said that we are experiencing a global revolution in food production that will depress prices. This is temporary and will last perhaps two or three decades (I confess I'm guessing). But this growth in food production has essentially been linear, which means steady, whereas human population growth is exponential, which means explosive.

Sooner or later, and probably near the end of the first quarter of the next century, we will outstrip the Earth's ability to feed us all, no matter how clever we are. This will lead to widespread famines of unimaginable proportions.

There are already concerns that our farming techniques are unsustainable because they cause precious topsoil to be either washed away or poisoned with salt from irrigation and the residues of fertilizers and pesticides used over decades. To take one example, grain production per acre in Illinois, in the heart of one of the richest grain belts in the world, fell by 2 percent in just five years, from 1979 to 1984, because of topsoil erosion.[5]

In underdeveloped countries, population pressures often cause truly foolish farming techniques to be used, such as the destruction of the rain forests in the Amazon and Java by hungry peasants in order to produce one or two years' crops. After that, these areas become barren and unproductive because of the poor quality of the soil, leaving the Earth with neither rain forest nor arable land.

Even more important than food is water. Although the surface of the Earth is almost seven-eighths water, the vast majority of this is salt water and therefore undrinkable. The globe's annual fresh water runoff — coming from the only sustainable source of fresh water: rain and snow — amounts to 40,000 cubic kilometres over land. Of this, less than 12,000 cubic kilometres is useful. Most of the rest is seasonal, not available when needed, and we have no conceivable way of storing such huge quantities. Of the 12,000 cubic kilometres that can be counted on to be available at the right time or that can be stored against future use, only about 7,000 cubic kilometres falls anywhere near where it is needed.

Because of the profligate way that we currently waste and pollute water, this 7,000 cubic kilometres of fresh, drinkable water will allow the global population to double only once more — which will occur sometime in the next fifty to sixty years if present trends continue.[6] Moreover, rainfall is a regional matter, not a global one. As a result, water shortages are showing up even now, and they will get steadily worse as population continues to grow.

120

Even if we cease using water wastefully for such things as golf courses in Palm Springs, or growing watermelons and rice in the California desert, and even if we ration it stringently and stop polluting it through industry — even with such measures, it's been estimated that we would be able to squeeze out enough water to last us, at most, until the end of the next century.[7] How much would you be willing to bet that the people involved will ever take such inconvenient measures before a crisis forces them to? And what do our grandchildren do after that?

Once we run out of water, we won't be able to sustain any increase in population. This means that any government that wants to accommodate an increase in its population will be able to do so only by taking — probably by force — the water supply of another jurisdiction. Other measures, such as desalinization, are so costly as to be impractical on any large scale.

Next, consider that population pressure has historically been a major cause of wars. Even such an apparently unique conflict as the Crusades can be traced in part to population pressures. In the Europe of that era, only the eldest son of a noble family inherited from his father. Accordingly, there was a need for the landless younger sons to find land of their own; and it was indeed mostly younger sons who went riding off to fight the infidel in the Holy Land. Their motives were at least as much mercenary as religious.

Because of population crowding and scarce resources, we can expect a rapidly rising drumbeat of regional conflicts, especially if the governments of the developed world continue to exploit and support weapons sales to potential hot spots and to countenance such sales by others. We have already seen how these weapons can be turned against us. What will it take for us to learn that while guns don't kill people, they sure as heck make it easier for people to kill people?

Next, consider plagues. The whole concept of a plague seems medieval, literally something out of the Dark Ages. Yet the more people there are, the more test animals there are for new diseases to mutate and develop. And if such people live in poverty, with substandard health care, poor water quality, and a near-starvation diet, they will have very little resistance to new diseases, making it that much easier for the diseases to find a host and flourish.

Lest we in the developed world decide that this doesn't affect us, remember that the AIDS virus is thought to have developed first in

Africa. It has become enough of a threat that it has changed our moral teachings in less than a generation. High schools now have condom vending machines in the washrooms of both sexes. Mothers confront their teenage children and insist that they take condoms when they go to the prom — something that would have brought gasps of shock and outrage twenty, or even ten, years ago. As a futurist, I know just how hard it is to get people to change their social behaviour. For AIDS to have provoked such a radical change so quickly, it must have frightened us deeply.

Nor are we in the developed world immune from the problems of population crowding. Major metropolitan areas throughout the OECD countries are experiencing gridlock on their highways, running out of places to dump their garbage, and suffering with infestations of homeless people who are sleeping on sidewalks and sticking their hands out for money. That these things are happening is no accident, nor are they aberrations resulting from a passing recession or bad planning by city hall. They are symptoms of problems to come — and if we had the wit and the will, we would recognize them as such.

All of this may seem unreal. Safe and secure as we are in our cozy Canadian homes, with our vast productive prairies and enormous untapped Arctic spaces, are we really threatened by overpopulation? Is it truly possible that our poorer citizens could face starvation or thirst on a massive scale within one to two generations? I seriously believe that it is.

So what are we to do about it?

OUR HOPE AND SALVATION

We probably cannot prevent the world's population from reaching 10 billion — that seems pretty certain, short of global war or natural catastrophe. It has been estimated that with this number of people, the gross world product — the sum of all nations' GNP — will increase by a factor of between five and ten times what it is today. Analysts doubt that the planet can sustain this,[8] so we have to slow and then stop the growth of humanity as quickly as we can.

Fortunately, there is good news. Population growth in the developing world has recently been slower than anyone anticipated — and in large part because of a much-vilified agent of change: television. TV programs aimed at educating women about contraception are being broadcast in many parts of the developing world. As recent studies show, when contraception is understood and available, women will reduce the size of their families, even in cultures that encourage large families. This, plus deliberate, carefully planned policies on the part of some Third World governments, has brought birth rates down, in some cases dramatically.

It's not enough, but it's a very hopeful sign. Excluding China, which has birth-control policies that we would find unbelievably draconian, 38 percent of married women in developing countries now practise some form of family planning. Although this compares poorly with the more than 70 percent in OECD countries, it's a great improvement over earlier periods. What this means is that in the developing world the average family size is falling from six children to four.[9]

However, the principal form of birth control is female sterilization, so by the time a woman decides to exercise birth control, she has already had as many children as she ever will. Thus, in order to lower the birth rate further, there must be a change in the desired size of families.

Some of this is being done by economics. One of the principal reasons for large families has been that children are a real asset as unpaid labourers in a farming society. However, in all countries the major growth, both in population and in economic activity, has been in the urban centres. In cities, the economic value of children is much lower and the cost of housing and feeding them much higher. Accordingly, couples are unable to afford as many children and do not wish to have as many. As a result, customs calling for large families are giving way to the reality of the need for fewer children.

All of these things are causing a slower rate of population growth than anticipated even ten years ago. Even so, the population is growing by 2.3 percent a year in developing countries, which implies a doubling every thirty-one years or so, or a tenfold increase every century.

Trying to change this growth rate gets into dangerous waters. Despite the severity of the problem and the potential for disaster, the most we can do is offer our help where it is wanted. If we in the developed countries try, either individually or through international organizations such as the United Nations or the World Bank, to force population restraint on other countries, we will rightly be accused of renewed colonialist ambitions. As the *Economist* has observed, "Many third-world leaders are wary of first-world efforts to persuade them to curb fertility. They suspect that the affluent north is mainly terrified by the prospect of hordes of swarthy immigrants, and more concerned for the future of the elephant than for the lives of black and brown babies."[10]

Nevertheless, there is still much we can do. The first is to help provide birth control where it is wanted. The demand for contraception dramatically outstrips the supply. Estimates that I've seen guess (and that's all they really are, guesses) that somewhere between 120 million and 200 million women of childbearing age in developing countries would use contraception if they could only get it. Estimates of the annual cost of providing such contraception range from $3.4 billion[11] to $8 billion.[12] On a global scale, this is a pittance, and one that could be raised in an afternoon of phone calls between world leaders.

What would be the prize if we could find this funding? We would see a reduction of the birthrate in the developing world from the current 2.3 percent to 1.6 percent — which would reduce world population by an estimated 1.4 billion by 2025 and would dramatically reduce the level at which world population eventually stabilized.[13] That's excellent news — but still not good enough.

The second-best contraceptive

The best contraception is contraception itself, but the next best is prosperity, and here we can make a real contribution without the slightest trace of colonialism and without a penny in foreign aid.

One of the biggest barriers that developing countries have had to face in their efforts to lift their people out of poverty has been the trade barriers of the developed countries. We're scared stiff that the cheap labour pools of the Third World are going to put us out of work, and so we shut their goods out of our markets. By one estimate, developed-country protectionism costs Third World countries more than $55 billion a year in lost exports — which is approximately what we give these countries as aid.[14] Yet this is wasted effort. As we saw in Chapter 2, there's no way we're going to be able to hold onto low-skilled and no-skilled jobs in any case.

Large families are often the only way the poor have of making sure that some of their male children are going to survive and support them when they are old. The attitude of Shankar Lal, a peasant farmer from the village of Biharipur, India, is typical:

> Shankar Lal had five girls before two sons came. Waiting for the two boys to survive infancy, he and his wife had two more girls. Then they discovered birth-control pills.
>
> "If I didn't have the boys, who would take care of me when I'm old?" Ram Sri asked, echoing the worry of almost every woman in Biharipur. "Who will feed me when I'm old? Who will take care of my land? The government? Will they take care of me if I stop having children?"[15]

If we drop our trade barriers, the standard of living in developing countries will improve, workers will be better able to provide for their old age, and they won't need to have big families.

Ironically, if we do throw our markets open to the cheap products of the developing world, not only will it cost us nothing in the long run, but it will actually increase our standard of living. Buying cheaper goods from these countries will give us more money to spend on other things, and this will further stimulate our own economy.

HOW BIG IS OUR LIFEBOAT?

Even if we decided to ignore global population problems until they eventually clobbered us, they would still intrude on our lives in the immediate future. They will force themselves to our attention in two ways: through the environment (which I'll discuss in Chapter 10) and through migration.

To the impoverished, Canada and other developed countries look like paradise, a place where people have enough to eat, homes to live in, free medical care, and even telephones, televisions, and cars. Is it any wonder that people from the Third World seek to come here by any means possible, legal or otherwise?[16] And as population pressures grow in the Third World, the number of these migrants will continue to expand. Yet the developed world is already showing signs of fear and apprehension.

In Canada we are protected largely by geography: the United States to the south, oceans to east and west, and Arctic wasteland and ocean to the north. Even so, we have a refugee problem and will consistently fill up our quotas, no matter what level we set them at. Meanwhile, the ever-growing surge of refugees will continue. We must expect this and prepare a long-term strategy. As a wise woman of my acquaintance said on another matter, "We mustn't let our bleeding hearts run away with our bloody heads."

In the United States, the leakage across the Mexican border is legendary. To my mind, one of the principal reasons why the United States, historically isolationist and protectionist, finally embraced the North American Free Trade Agreement was the belief that if it did not, it would be overwhelmed by a steadily rising tide of illegal immigrants. The reasoning is simple: let the dollar go to Latin America in the form of trade, or Latin America will come to the dollar as illegal immigrants.

Europe, bounded on both south and east by billions of poorer people, is being inundated with economic refugees, and this is generating a violent backlash. The rise of openly racist political parties, policies, and leaders, such as the neo-Nazis of Germany and Le Pen of France, is largely due to the flood of immigrants and refugees. The cries of "France for the French" (or "Germany for the Germans," or whatever) comes in reaction to the flood of "huddled masses, yearning to breathe free." Indeed, these masses bring real problems. They burden the already strained social safety nets of the developed countries; they aid the spread of diseases; and they can bring political and militant views that may be incompatible with their new homes.

We cannot ignore the world's population problems, for the world won't let us. As one world study group recently stated, "Arresting global population growth should be second in importance only to avoiding nuclear war."[17] To this, population analysts Paul and Anne Ehrlich add, "Whatever your cause, it's a lost cause without population control."[18]

So there are two choices, and only two: plan intelligently for a difficult future, or stumble and probably fall into a future full of pain and misery. If you choose the first of the two, it's important that you act on it, and soon — say, by writing to your MP to express your concerns and ask for action.

But doing nothing will hasten a tide of humanity that may swamp us all.

THE THIRD FORCE

Technology

E I G H T

The Computer Revolution Finally Begins

> Movies of the 1990s will portray [computers] as inconspicuous devices
> – more like watches than clocks. . . . Moreover, their relation to the
> user will change from that of an isolated productivity tool to that of an
> active collaborator in the acquisition, use and creation of information,
> as well as a facilitator of human interaction. . . .The networked
> computer . . . raises issues of security and personal and business
> privacy. It also raises the question of the distribution of power. The
> chasms between rich and poor could widen, for example, if the latest
> computing paradigm creates still more opportunities for educated
> people and still fewer for the uneducated.
>
> –Lawrence G. Tessler, Vice-President of Advanced Products, Apple
> Computer Inc.

The computer field is changing with unbelievable speed, but rather than try to describe how computers may change, let me show you.

The sawmill

As a spruce log rumbles up the gangway at a British Columbia sawmill, the computer screen lights up with the word SPRUCE. The mill operator glances at the trunk and touches the screen in the box marked "Correct," and the trunk moves off onto the conveyor meant

129

for spruce trees, picking up speed as it goes. The next trunk rumbles up and barely slows as the word MAPLE appears in the screen. The operator agrees, touching the "Correct" box on the screen, and the log moves off into the proper line.

The next trunk moves into place, but this time the line slows. The screen again shows the word SPRUCE but is followed by a question mark. The operator looks at the trunk and touches the box marked "Wrong." The line stops, and a menu appears in a new box on the screen listing the varieties of trees handled by this sawmill. The operator runs down the list until he finds "Pine," then touches that. The word PINE replaces SPRUCE on the screen, and the trunk moves onto a different conveyor, starting to pick up speed again.

This goes on through the day, with the operator having to make fewer and fewer corrections. By the end of a two-week training period, the computer is running logs through the sawmill at speeds humans could not match, and its ability to identify logs correctly at high speed is significantly better than that of the human operators who taught it.

The sawmill is now operating at a faster rate than ever before and with fewer errors. The total amount of time required to install and modify the software for the mill has been less than a month from the signing of the contract with the software company.

The commodity trader

The copper futures trader looks at the price-quote screen, watching the prices of contracts fluctuate randomly in the absence of any news. Just then, his desktop computer beeps, and a message appears on the screen: "Additional activity in orange juice futures triggers buy signal for copper. Copper prices now likely to rise by between 13 and 17 cents over the next three hours. Suggest we cover short positions and buy additional contracts." The trader wonders what orange juice futures have to do with copper, then shrugs and types in his orders to cover his short position. He decides against buying additional contracts — then later regrets his decision as copper prices rise by 18 cents that afternoon.

"It's bloody frustrating," he tells a friend over drinks that evening. "Half the time I have no idea why this damn computer is suggesting I buy or sell. It's like voodoo. But it's right more often than I am, so I feel pretty silly if I don't do what it suggests and end up losing money." As he sips his drink, he adds, "Do you know that over the past six months that bloody box has been able to forecast the price of copper three days in advance to within an average of 8 percent? I've never seen anything like it."

His friend wonders if they've had enough to drink yet, then casually says, "Any chance of getting a peek at this mechanical marvel?"

The first trader stares at him. "Not on your nelly! I spent two years teaching it everything I know. Now it's teaching me — and there's no way I'm going to share the wealth."

Lawyer

The lawyer rolls the wheelchair into his office, moves behind the desk, positioning himself so that he is speaking into a microphone stationed in front of his desktop computer. He says, "Jeeves wake up." The computer screen lights up. The lawyer pauses while the computer boots up and starts his word-processing program. When it's ready, he says, "Take a letter. R. L. Mackey, Briggs and Co. Fetch address. Standard opening."

He then dictates the body of the letter at speeds close to eighty words per minute, making corrections in the computer's choices of homonyms, pausing once to check the spelling of a name from his on-line phone index, and spelling out a word that the machine does not recognize. When the letter is finished, he says, "Standard closing. Print. Save document in file Briggs. Close document. Open file Briggs, open document 'Corporate structure.'"

A complex chart of holding companies and subsidiaries appears on the screen. The lawyer studies it a moment, then says, "Add same-sized box below 'Standard Holdings Ltd.' Label in new box reads 'Standard Holdings (U.S.A.) Inc.' Draw vertical line between two boxes. Line label between two boxes reads '100 percent.' Annotation to right of lower box reads 'Michigan private corporation.' Print chart. Save document. Close document. Open names file. Fetch address for R. L. Mackey, Briggs. Print envelope."

When this is done, he says, "E-mail to John, send copy to Margaret. Begin. John, I'm sending Bob Mackey a revised corporate chart, along with our suggestions on tax structure. Please follow up with him Thursday. Best regards, Mark. End E-mail. Jeeves, send. Jeeves, go to sleep."

The computer shuts itself off, and the lawyer maneuvers his wheelchair out of the room.

Grade 2 student

The seven-year-old boy sits down in front of the computer and says, "Charlie, wake up!" The computer makes a yawning sound, then says, "Oh, hi, Davey. What's up?"

"I wanna work on my story."

The computer replies, "You want to work on 'The Green Rabbit Space Invaders?'"

"Right."

The computer is silent for a moment, then the story appears on the screen. Davey looks at it, then moves the mouse, clicks where he wants the cursor to be positioned, and starts punching keys. After a few words, the computer says, "What's this word?" A word that Davey has just typed is highlighted in yellow.

"Dinosaur," Davey replies indignantly.

"That's not how we spell dinosaur. Try again."

Davey sticks his tongue out of the side of his mouth, backspaces over the word, then types "dinosoar."

Charlie replies, "Nope. Want a hint?"

Davey shrugs and says, "Oh, all right. But just a hint."

"The 'oar' sound in 'dinosaur' comes from two vowels working together. You've got the 'a' right, but the other vowel is wrong. Is that enough of a hint?"

Davey nods vigorously. "Oh, right, now I remember." He backspaces over the word again, and this time types it correctly.

"Bingo!" Charlie says enthusiastically. "You got it right with one hint!"

"Tell me my spelling score this week, Charlie."

The computer keeps a running tally of each student's spelling proficiency, and Davey can refer to his at any time to check his progress. The computer also supplies progress reports on this and other subjects for Davey's teacher, Mrs. Brown, and calls for her attention if Davey seems to be struggling.

Mrs. Brown worked closely with Davey on the first draft of his story, but now that he seems comfortably settled in English composition, the computer is doing most of the monitoring. This leaves Mrs.

Brown more time for students who still need her personal attention. Nor does she have to spend a lot of time on what she calls "administrivia." The computer handles most of that for her. She's much happier, because she's doing what she loves to do — teaching — and doesn't have all her time eaten up in paperwork.

The students are prospering because they are all working at their own speed. The more able students get enriched material to challenge them. The troubled students get additional material and explanations to support them, including explanations in their home language if English is their second language, plus their teacher's individual attention as needed. Nobody gets labelled as a "brown-nose" or "dummy," because nobody except Mrs. Brown and the principal know where anyone else is in the curriculum.

Best of all, the parents can call Charlie by phone in the evenings to find out how their children are doing (in a language other than English, if necessary), to pick up recorded personalized messages from Mrs. Brown about their child's progress, and to make sure that any homework assigned has been brought home. Parents feel more involved, and their kids benefit from their interest.

Airplane mechanic

A mechanic for Air Canada is performing routine maintenance on one of the airline's passenger planes. He is holding a computer that is slightly smaller than a piece of paper and has a screen but no keyboard. Its rubberized back is slightly sticky, so when he puts it down on the wing it doesn't slide off. He says, "Aircraft registration number NCC-1701-D. Routine maintenance. Port-side wing. Aileron assembly. Begin."

A diagram appears on the screen of the palm-top computer, showing the mechanic how to disassemble the aileron assembly for inspection. A voice from the computer says, "Inspect ventral hydraulic system for wear. This assembly is two years, three months, and four days old."

The mechanic removes the parts indicated on the screen, checking for wear. He finds a sleeve coupling with groove marks, and decides it needs replacing. He touches the screen diagram of the assembly to have it display the number of the offending part, then says, "Requisition replacement for this part, number 136-0075-24P. Deliver here immediately."

The computer screen highlights the offending part in red and replies, "Confirm order to replace part number 136-0075-24P, ventral hydraulic sleeve coupling. Correct?"

"That's right," says the mechanic.

The computer replies, "Part on order and should arrive within ten minutes." The mechanic nods and continues inspecting the remaining parts of the hydraulic assembly, asking the computer to show the parts in different stages of disassembly as he follows the inspection process.

The spare part will be brought directly to him, having been ordered through a short-range radio broadcast to central stores by the computer. The airplane's maintenance log will record the replacement and will note that these parts have been wearing in this manner more frequently than is considered normal. As well as calling this fact to the attention of the airline's chief maintenance engineer, it will E-mail a copy of the note to Boeing, the airplane's manufacturer.

The companion

The elderly lady sits in the chair, absently stroking the form on her lap. "Well, Kenny, my daughter didn't call again today," she says.

The cat lifts its head and says, "She did call on her way into work this morning, and it's only six-thirty, Doris. Be fair."

"I know, Kenny. But I get so lonely, and the only people around here to talk to are old. They're no fun."

"What about Hank Jennings, that new guy who just moved in down the walkway? He's from Alberta, and a widower."

The woman looks down at her companion. "Who? Where did you hear all this?"

"It's a new entry in the community bulletin board. I'd suggest you hustle on down and meet him before all the other women get to him."

"Well, it couldn't hurt. Would you please call him?"

The "cat" sits still for a moment, then says, "His line's busy. I've left the phone on 'ring again' for when it's free. By the way Doris, are you feeling okay? You sound kind of blue."

Doris sighs. "Oh, I don't know, Kenny. I just don't seem to have any energy any more. All I seem to be good for is —" and she stops abruptly.

Kenny stands up on her lap and looks into her face, then puts a paw on the vein at her neck. "Doris? Are you okay? Doris! Your pulse has gone irregular." Getting no answer, the computer, clothed in a cat puppet doll, calls the central nursing station of the lifecare centre where Doris lives: "Medical emergency. Doris Beakins, Suite 416. Code blue. Possible heart attack. Pulse irregular, eyes dilated, galvanic skin response indicates possible shock. Subject is breathing, but shallowly and irregularly."

The nursing station acknowledges the message and dispatches a paramedic, who arrives within three minutes of Doris's last comments. Meanwhile, Kenny calls Doris's daughter and informs her of the medical emergency. Doris survives and recovers, in large part because of the immediate call for help of her computer companion.

The salesman

The salesman is reading his morning paper when his phone speaks up: "Excuse me, sir, but there's a news headline I believe you'd find of interest. Toyota and Apple Computer have just announced that they will sell their Automated Driver's Assistant software to all professional car makers."

The salesman puts his paper down. He represents a company that designs custom cars for up-market clientele, and this is the first time Toyota and Apple have released their safety-enhancing software since it was introduced three years ago. "Show me the cost parameters, then give me a list of current prospects that have expressed interest in ADA."

A price list appears, taken from the press release just issued, followed by two names of prospective clients.

"Give me the makes and ages of of the cars they bought most recently from the lists in the Canadian Car Dealers' Association data bank."

There's a pause, then four cars are listed, two under each prospective client's name. It is apparent from the cars listed that one prospect is a family man, so the salesman decides to start with him.

"Retrieve my notes on John Cadderra."

A series of notes, made by the salesman from earlier contacts with Cadderra, appear on the screen, along with the dates of their conversations. The salesman studies them, then says, "Send Mr.

Cadderra an E-mail message that we can now offer him the car he was considering, but equipped with ADA. Tell him I will call his office at ten on Monday morning to speak with him about it. Take the technical information on ADA from the press release and add it to the letter. Note that Mr. Cadderra is an analytical personality type and prepare the letter accordingly. Notify me of his confirmation."

"Yes, sir."

The salesman sits back and ponders how much he can charge for the car and still make the sale. Up to this point, everything he has done has been completely within the law. Now, however, he decides to cross the line into unethical behaviour, thereby separating him from the large majority of his peers.

"Computer, call Source Alpha and confirm secure lines." Source Alpha is a technically legal operation from which people can make secure phone calls that can't be traced back to the original caller.

"Confirmed, sir."

"Tap into the 'Green' database in the Cayman Islands and get me all the information available on John Cadderra for the last thirty-six months." The Source Alpha computer randomly routes the call from Toronto to similar services in Geneva, thence to Lebanon, and finally to the Cayman Islands. It then gives the salesman's access code to a private but illegal database in the Cayman Islands and begins the search on John Cadderra. Shortly, the salesman has Cadderra's current salary level, bank balance, record of transactions, and automated bill payments. Looking over this information, he says, "Give me an average of Cadderra's monthly income and payments." Almost instantly, an income-and-expenditure account appears.

"Give me an estimate of the maximum amount a bank would lend Cadderra for a new car, based on a normal down-payment and monthly loan payments." The figure appears immediately.

"Save only this last figure in Cadderra's file, label it as my estimate of possible monthly car cost. Now get me his medical profile." A different series of data appears.

"Give me his blood type and an estimate of his regular hormone cycle." A graph appears on the screen with "Blood group A-positive" written across the top.

"Identify the scents and pheromones that would be most likely to make him receptive to a sale. Program them for the

Virtual Showroom when we make the appointment to view the car design."

"Yes, sir. Noted."

"Disconnect all phone lines."

The salesman sits back, satisfied that, with the help of the illicit information he has gathered, he will finally nail down Mr. Cadderra. He mentally starts counting his commission on the sale. What he doesn't realize is that his illegal information gathering was intercepted as it entered his phone and is now being unencrypted by the RCMP, based on a complaint by the Ethical Marketing and Sales Association, which has been concerned about this salesman's behaviour.

Unethical use of Source Alpha and the "Green" database in the Caymans has been producing a rising tide of newspaper articles, consumer anger, and complaints about invasions of privacy, to the point where Parliament has been talking about new, restrictive legislation that is not really necessary — if the association can help the RCMP enforce existing legislation. And the salesman is going to be the first arrest brought about by the two bodies working together.

How the computer will change our lives

These are but a few examples of how computers, coupled with instant, individual, completely portable communications, are going to change our lives. Indeed, the only thing of which I'm certain is that there are going to be more changes — and more radical changes — that I have envisioned.

Computers will act as our assistants and our intermediaries. They'll search out information for us, make dinner reservations on our behalf, act with our authority, order things with only short, simple instructions from us, buy information for us, assemble in-depth news on subjects that they know we will find of interest. They will learn our habits and patterns, and gradually improve their ability to anticipate our needs. They will adapt to us and in so doing will make our lives easier — if they are our computers.

But these same qualities will be used by others to watch us and anticipate our actions and movements. Commercial enterprises are even now seeking ways to make use of the mountains of information they already gather about us and our neighbours.

A small example: suppose you write checks for your groceries at the local supermarket chain. This means that the store has your name, address, phone number, and lots of other information about you on file. Suppose you buy a twenty-four-can case of Coca-Cola every week. As it passes over the checkout scanner it goes into the database, along with your name. Over time, the store builds up a profile of what you and your neighbours do and don't buy, and it tailors its stock to suit your desires — which is just good service.

But one day a bright laddie down at head office comes up with a new way to mine this mountain of data they have about you. The first result is that they send you a very nice letter. In this letter, they thank you for your patronage, and as their way of showing their appreciation, they give you a coupon for a dollar off your next purchase of twenty-four cans of their house brand of cola, which — for them — has a much higher profit margin. They know you buy a competing brand, and they are now starting to use that knowledge to increase their profits.

Are you pleased, upset, fearful, angry, or indifferent? I don't know either. But I do know that George Orwell's vision of one Big Brother watching our every move was completely wrong. It is thousands of Little Brothers that will watch our every move — and computers will be the lens that make their watching possible.

THE FUTURE OF THE COMPUTER

This is an appropriate time to describe two of the most common mistakes that futurists — and others who think about the future — make. The first is to assume that when something is technically possible, its use becomes inevitable. The second is that when something fails once, it will never become popular.

A prime example of the first mistake is to assume that CD-ROMs will completely replace books in the immediate future. The truth is that people like holding and reading physical books and will continue to buy them. Accordingly, this is not the last book you will ever buy. The same is true of newspapers: people enjoy rustling and browsing through a newspaper in a way that is not possible with a video screen.

Examples of the second kind of mistake are picture phones and computer-assisted medical diagnostic systems. Both were widely ballyhooed in earlier years, and both died a quick death. However, in both cases, the technology was not truly ready to deliver a cheap, reliable, usable product. Once that's possible, people may reconsider — as happened with the fax machine. The early fax machines were clumsy, slow, and unreliable, and people hated using them. Today, anybody who is in business must have a fax machine, just as they must have a telephone.

Both of these mistakes carry a very important message: technology cannot impose itself on people; people have to be willing to accept it. Which means there must always be a positive answer to the question: "What does this do for me?"

I'm spending a lot of time on computers in this section, not because they are more important than some other technologies but because they are about to go through what futurists call a phase change. This means that tomorrow is going to be quite different from today — and that's important in preparing for the future.

We've become used to the idea that computers continually become cheaper and faster. But humanity has never experienced changes in tools or techniques as rapid as those occurring now with computers. In the past, computers have doubled in speed and halved in price about every two and a half years, which means that over a ten-year period a $5,000 top-of-the-line desktop computer drops to a price-equivalent of less than $20. But this seriously underestimates the present rate of change. The product cycle is now under eighteen months, perhaps even under a year. Moreover, there are new developments that will accelerate the trend, such as massively parallel processing, RISC chip processors, and more.

This means that we are going to be caught off guard by how cheap basic computers become and how fast they get. This is a minor change, though, compared with the qualitative changes we are about to experience. As the quotation at the beginning of this chapter indicated, computers are going to change from big, clumsy, special-purpose boxes to small, unobtrusive devices that speed, assist, enable, and guide, often without our even noticing.

Indeed, it seems likely that the average computer of the future will be completely invisible, used to monitor and manage a function, machine, or process. You may already have three or four computers in your car, for instance, managing your fuel injection system or your traction control system, or what not. Yet unless somebody told you they were there, you'd never know — or have any reason or need to know.

Just as transistors changed from being rare and precious things that were used sparingly and became cheap, small components that were used with abandon, we are now entering the era of computer profligacy. Microprocessors are becoming cheap enough for machinery designers to be able, for example, to add two or three to keep your washing machine from banging around in the spin cycle if you have an unbalanced load of clothes, or to defrost your frost-free refrigerator only when it needs it, or to adjust the lighting level of your lamps as the sun goes down. In other cases, computers may be used to compensate for shortcomings in design in machines that will then not be able to function unassisted. Certain kinds of airplane are already designed like this — they would tumble out of control without computers to stabilize them from second to second.

What are some other implications of the dawning of this computer revolution? I can think of at least seven and am quite sure there are many more:

Voice programming

It is already possible to program or activate computers by talking to them. Moreover, as computers become more adept at this, they'll begin to anticipate what we mean when our speech is less than precise. For instance, "Over and out," "Sign off," "'Bye," and "End program" may all be interpreted to mean the same thing — if that's the way we want it.

The interpretation of speech is available today. Apple Computer already sells a line of computers that accept spoken commands. Various suppliers, such as Kolvox Communications of Toronto, sell voice-recognition systems that can be installed in PC-compatible computers.

Voice-recognition systems come in two types: speaker-independent (which work with anybody who speaks English but have very restricted vocabularies of perhaps 1,500 words) and speaker-dependent systems (which have to be trained to recognize the voices and speaking patterns of a small number of individuals but which have very large vocabularies of 80,000 words or more). With the speaker-dependent products, you can dictate memos, letters, notes, and other documents at speeds of 80 words a minute or more.

This is not the future, it's the present. What will change is that the cost will fall, and therefore the use of voice-activation will become much more popular. There is some debate over how popular it will be. Some people in the computer industry do not believe it will be important or used widely. I suspect that these are the people whose companies are lagging in the development of such systems. Personally, I believe that speech recognition will revolutionize the use of computers by making them easy to use and hence accessible to people who do not have, or do not want, keyboard skills.

When I sat down to write the stories given above, I found myself using speech recognition in almost every case, even though my only intention was to show how computers might develop. Speech is more convenient than writing or typing and will, I believe, become more popular as a means of communicating with computers. Moreover, the use of speech recognition is already making its way into applications that are not seen as being computer related (for example, programming a VCR by telling it what you want recorded and when); and businesses are increasingly using speech recognition to handle many of their routine calls from customers, as phone companies are now doing for collect or credit card calls.

Language translation

A likely offshoot of speech recognition is language translation. For instance, programs are beginning to appear for desktop computers that can translate English text into Japanese text, and vice versa. I suspect that in due course there will be computers capable of performing simultaneous translation that can be tucked in your ear like a hearing aid or used like tape-player headphones. They will allow you to understand the speech of virtually any known language, though subtleties, double entendres, and nonverbal communication will likely remain as much a mystery as they are now, with the translating done by humans.

Major-General Lewis MacKenzie, the Canadian who became famous as part of the peacekeeping force in Bosnia-Herzegovina, has the same speaker's agent as I do, and he once told me that the military routinely uses computers to translate text from one language to another. If speech recognition is added to this facility, together with substantial increases in speed, we may never need to learn another language — except for personal enrichment or cultural and literary reasons. The Koran (or Qu'ran), for example, cannot properly be understood in any language other than Arabic.

Computer locators

Computers will be able to keep track of us when we move from place to place — if we want them to. Suppose you're moving around an office building and someone is trying to contact you. That person can simply dial your phone number, and the computer will decide which phone is closest to you and will cause it to ring. This would be possible by having you wear an ID badge that broadcasts your location to a series of sensors.

Such a tracking system could be used for other purposes too. For instance, if three or more people were in a room together, the computer might assume that they were in conference and would not pass on any phone calls unless they indicated otherwise. Likewise, if you closed your door, your phone calls would automatically be intercepted by voice mail rather than intruding on your privacy, much as a secretary guards the boss's privacy today.[1]

Seeing will no longer be believing

The quality of computer-generated graphics has already reached the level of still photographs — a fact that has interesting, even frightening, implications. One of the computer service bureaus I use showed me a series of photographs from a wedding with an unusual "before and after" story. The bride's sister's marriage broke up shortly after the wedding and the former brother-in-law was front and centre in all the family photos. The service bureau was able to doctor the photographs to remove the brother-in-law completely, even though there were walls, windows, and bushes in the background that would have made it impossible simply to cut out the figure from the picture.

The implications of this are that soon it will be possible to create a fake "photograph" showing anybody doing anything one wants, and the fake will be indistinguishable from a real photo. The blackmail and faked news reporting possibilities in this alone are enormous.

The same capabilities are coming to video, though the problems of video are much tougher than for still photos. It's possible now to lift the moving image of an individual from one background and place it in another. This has already been done in a series of commercials for Coca-Cola, which showed deceased performers such as Humphrey Bogart and Louis Armstrong in a modern setting.

As computers become more powerful and cheaper, the ability to do this type of thing will become much more widely available — and more open to abuse. Something innocent said while mugging for the video camera on vacation, say, might appear damning if the person seemed to be speaking in the House of Commons.

The next step, the creation of full-action videos from scratch (without any existing images to start with), is much more difficult. It amounts to the creation of a cartoon that looks totally realistic. We don't know how to do this yet. Apparently simple things, such as matching the movement of facial muscles to speech, are enormously difficult, especially given the subtleties of nonverbal communication.[2] But it is virtually certain that we will know how to do this sometime early in the next century, if not sooner.

This could spell real problems for professional television and film actors. Studios could produce entire films without actors, using computer-generated actors and synthesized speech. These synthetic actors would never argue with a director over "artistic differences," would never be prima donnas, and, most important, would never collect royalties. Movie studios could create sequels to classic films, such as *Return to Casablanca* apparently reuniting Humphrey Bogart and Ingrid Bergman. Moreover, these synthetic films could be customized to fit specific target niches and individual tastes. Hence, a hero in a particular show could be white-skinned for homes owned by white people, and black-skinned for homes owned by black people.

More dangerous still, you could watch apparently live action from, say, Israel, and see an image that was completely synthetic, while believing that you were watching news of something actually happening. The propaganda potential is enormous — and worrisome. From now on, seeing may no longer be believing.

Virtual reality

Virtual reality is the creation of a synthetic, computer-generated world in which you can act as a participant, not just as an observer. Because of its sexy nature (sometimes literally), it has had a lot of press. The problems discussed above concerning the creation of synthetic images also apply to virtual reality. Nevertheless, good but not perfectly realistic computer graphics are often acceptable if the viewer — excuse me, "participant" — doesn't insist on "fool-the-eye" imagery. Consider the popularity of computer games among children (and many adults too), then imagine how much more popular they would be if the players could act out their roles in the game instead of just pushing buttons.

Then there are the less savoury potentials of virtual reality. There are already companies preparing to sell "virtual sex" activities. Pick your partner or partners, possibly based on images of living people; pick the activity, with nothing impossible or prohibited (how can you police pornography laws when the images disappear as the power goes off?). And remember that the mind does not differentiate between reality and something that simulates reality if it is done well enough. If you have concerns about the relatively static pornography of the present day, you ain't seen nothing yet. And perhaps ten years or so into the future, we may see the most degenerate application of virtual reality of them all: soap operas in which you can participate in the plot as one of the characters.

Yet not all virtual reality applications will be trivial, violent, or degenerate. Surgeons may be able to use virtual reality, coupled with microminiature operating tools, in such a way that they will apparently navigate through the body and be able to operate within it, without actually cutting it open — a significant improvement on current keyhole surgery techniques. Or, if that seems too whizzy and science fictional, then surgeons may well operate by remote control from sites hundreds or thousands of kilometres away by using a virtual-reality image of the patient they are operating on.

Teachers may be able to take their students on field trips to, say, the Amazon rain forest without ever leaving their classrooms. They could then have the computer identify the flora and fauna, and provide facts and information as a basis for discussion on the implications of clear-cutting, as well as allowing discussion with experts and other study groups in distant locations.

It might be possible to attend business conferences by virtual reality, so that the participants would all appear to be in the same room and could pick up the subtleties of body language and the feeling of "rubbing shoulders," even though they were far distant from one another. Moreover, they wouldn't need to dress up — a bathrobe could be transformed into a Savile Row suit or a Halston original. I suspect that the most startling applications and the ones that ultimately will be the most popular have not even been thought of yet.

"Do what I mean" programming

"Do what I mean" (DWIM) programming is starting to emerge. Until recently, one of the major drawbacks of computers has been that they take instructions in a completely literal way, and then only when we give the instructions in a special code that the computer can recognize (also called a programming language). This has restricted the number of people who can use computers to those willing to spend time and effort learning these programming languages and perfecting their use.

The desktop computer revolution has changed this to some degree by offering pre-programmed application software (which might be called "meta-programming languages") that have allowed people to do things without having to write all the program code required to accomplish it. Hence, you can use a spreadsheet and create an intricate financial model without knowing how to program in C++, Pascal, or assembly language. But this still restricts the use of computers to those who are prepared to learn the commands required for these application packages.

As DWIM programming develops and becomes more widespread, it will allow people to describe to computers what they want to accomplish, and the computers themselves will then write the programs. This will take the operation and supervision of computers out of the hands of a relative elite and will put it in the reach of a much broader segment of the population. Note, however, that people doing this kind of meta-programming will still have to be able to think clearly in order to give an accurate description of what they want.

Intelligent-seeming computers

Computers that seem to be intelligent will become common. How intelligent? I don't know. I do know that there are already situations in which computers can do things that seem to require intelligence and/or judgment. The sawmill story given above and the one about the commodities trader are both true and have already happened, though not exactly in the manner I've described.

145

Computer-assisted database searches, expert systems, and other artificial intelligence techniques will emerge and will help doctors diagnose ailments more accurately and more rapidly. This is particularly important considering that the amount of knowledge a doctor needs has expanded so greatly that it has long since outstripped the ability of any flesh-and-blood human to keep up unassisted. It is also likely that nurses and paramedics will use computers in sophisticated medical care, so that they will be able to deal with most routine problems as "paradoctors" and only refer cases to physician-specialists when they get out of their depth. As well, people may be able to diagnose themselves with computer assistance, possibly using a program on their home computer.

Another possibility might be a provincial health system that started with telephone screening. For instance, an individual patient with a problem that was not an emergency could phone, describe the condition to a paramedic with a computer (or even directly to a computer at the other end of the phone), and then be instructed to get a test kit from the local pharmacy. The patient would return the results to the pharmacy and get the proper referral by phone. This system, while completely by-passing the general practitioner, would give medical attention on demand, twenty-four hours a day, and would be a highly cost-effective use of medical resources — if people were willing to accept medical service over the phone.

Similar systems are likely to emerge for business consulting, law, human resources, materials sciences, engineering — indeed, most professions in which the availability of information is expanding rapidly. But the power available to those who can afford these systems versus those who cannot will widen the gap between the rich and the poor.

Genetic programming and neural network software (and perhaps hardware) are creating computer systems that are almost creepy in their ability to arrive at human-seeming judgments. The range of applications for these and other techniques is enormous. Self-driving automobiles are one example;[3] the computer companion in the story about Doris is another; and, of course, this type of "intelligent" computer may lead to the classic science-fiction robots who walk, talk, and act in a human manner.

One individual working in this field, who is a neuroanatomist by training and does not want to be named, states quite categorically that within ten years we will have computer programs capable of solving problems that are beyond the abilities of human beings — for instance, developing cures for certain difficult kinds of cancer. Others, such as Professor Eugene Fiume of the University of Toronto, disagree, saying that these developments are much farther off and may never happen.

I don't know who is right. All I know is that it takes only one person to make a breakthrough that previously seemed impossible. I also know that the pace of development in computers is accelerating, and probably faster than those working in the field realize.

So hold on tight. The computer revolution is only just beginning.

THE MERGING OF COMPUTERS AND COMMUNICATIONS

One French word for "computer" is "informatique," which is actually a much better description of what this kind of device does: it processes information. The biggest challenge of the information age is turning data into information, information into knowledge, knowledge into understanding, and understanding into useful action.

But information is expanding far faster than our ability to absorb it, and the rate of flow is increasing. It used to be that the limitation in the flow of information was the amount you could stuff down a phone line. As it happens, information flow is very much like plumbing: the width of the pipe and the rate at which water is being pumped determine how much water can flow through the pipe. Today, the flow of information is picking up as both the (figurative) diameter of the electronic pipe (the "bandwidth") and the force with which information is being pumped through it ("throughput" or "transmission rate") are picking up. So what used to be a trickle will quickly become a raging torrent.

First, let's look at bigger-sized pipes. Telephone wire is called a "twisted pair" because it is literally a pair of wires (actually, it's three wires, but the third is the ground and doesn't carry any information). A real alternative to the twisted pair that is already largely in place is coaxial cable, also called "co-ax." This is the kind of cable in most frequent use for cable-TV systems, and it can carry significantly more information than a twisted pair. Cable television companies, led in Canada by Rogers Cablesystems, are starting to think about what else they could deliver to the home that you would be willing to pay for. This may lead to "smart" TV, which might give you access to a lot more choices, not only in programming but in accessing information from commercial and public-access databases. Hence, if you are travelling to Orlando, Florida, and want to know what tomorrow's weather is going to be, you can wait for the WeatherNetwork's half-hourly resort forecast, or you might be able to access the U.S. weather service through your cable television and get tomorrow's Orlando forecast immediately.

Optical fibre and photonics

A "wider pipe" in terms of capacity, even though it is physically smaller than co-ax, is fibre-optic cable. The only limitation on the amount of information that can be transmitted through an optical-fibre cable is how quickly either the brightness or the frequency (i.e., colour) of the light can be made to vary. This limit will fall as we develop the technology to vary brightness or colour at ever faster speeds. And this means that the amount of information sent along a single strand of optical fibre, which may be thinner than your existing telephone twisted pair, will expand enormously. More, we won't have to change either the cable or the signal amplifiers along the route in order to increase the amount of information the cable can carry. This all means that optical-fibre cable has the potential to reduce the cost of communications dramatically.

In addition, there is a new field opening up: optical processing, also called photonics. Currently, we process and transmit information mostly through electronics. However, electronic transmission of information needs to be amplified and retransmitted frequently, or else the signal gets so weak that the information carried gets lost in background static. Worse, repeating the information signal over and over again electronically requires that each signal be reprocessed separately, which requires expensive equipment. All of this imposes costly limitations on electronic data transmission.

In comparison, optically transmitted information requires only a fraction of the expensive equipment needed for electronic transmission. More, to change the carrying capacity of an optical-fibre network only requires changing the equipment used to send and receive it, and perhaps the equipment at the major nodes of a network. It's not necessary to change either the fibre itself or the amplifiers along the way. All of this makes optical networks significantly less expensive than electronic nets.

The difference in the cost of optical fibre using pure optical processing with electronic devices only at the ends of the networks, and the same optical fibre using electronic processing all along the route is enormous and translates into greater carrying capacity. At present, a single strand of optical fibre using electronic switching can process hundreds or even thousands of simultaneous telephone calls. However, the same optical fibre, using optical processing, has been estimated to be able to carry all the telephone conversations of both the United States and Canada during the heaviest hour on the heaviest day of usage of the year — all on a single strand of optical fibre.[4] Imagine replacing all the millions of tonnes of copper cable used for telephony in North America with a single strand of glass! Or consider how much more information we could carry if our existing network of optical-fibre cables used optical processing instead of the current electronics.

This is good news for those who want cheaper communications, but it will cause monumental disruptions for telephone and other communications companies. A carrying capacity of this magnitude and at this level of cost could make communications so cheap that the phone companies would not be able to make enough money to survive in their present form. Of course, it won't happen that way, because the volume of information sent will rise as quickly as prices fall. However, it implies a completely new way of thinking about the pricing structure of the transmission of information — and major adaptations by those who do the transmitting. Accordingly, if I were a telephone company — or a cable company or television broadcaster, for that matter — I would be truly concerned about my long-term future.[5]

As for those who will benefit, over the last twenty-five years, computer processing capacity has risen more than a millionfold, while communications capacity has risen by about a thousandfold.[6] This means that while our ability to process information has expanded enormously, the cost of communicating it has become an expensive bottleneck. As an article in *Forbes Magazine* has explained, a technological wringer is "a new invention that radically reduces the price of a key factor of production and precipitates an industrial revolution. . . . During the next decade or so, industry will go through a new technological wringer . . . called the all-optical network."[7]

So although it doesn't seem as if we are lacking for information or communications, the flood we are currently experiencing is only a small trickle compared with what can and probably will be available to us.

For instance, the Canadian cable-television industry is currently worried about the rise of the "deathstar," a satellite-to-home broadcast system that completely side-steps cable systems. Such systems could offer more than 500 television channels to home viewers, compared with the 100-odd that are now possible using coaxial cable. This is causing people to worry about the survival of Canadian culture when there will be 500 channels available, comprised almost entirely of foreign (i.e., American) programming. In my view, this overlooks the real issue. As I said earlier, communications people and others should be thinking not about the effects of a mere 500 channels, but about what will happen when 50,000 or 50 million channels are available to each individual television set.

Of course, no one will bother to market a delivery system that offers 50 million channels, because this amounts to "video on demand," giving you exactly what you want, when and where you want it. And it will include the entire spectrum of information available to humanity, not just reruns of "The Flintstones." You'll be able to watch any desired episode of "The Flintstones," but you'll also be able to view the Mona Lisa, catch last night's performance of the Royal Winnipeg Ballet, listen to a concert from the National Arts Centre in Ottawa, access books from the U.S. Library of Congress, give a live speech to a group of 350 people in 350 different locations, publish your own book or poetry or painting — or do anything else you can imagine that is based on giving or receiving information.

The reason no one will bother with the expense of creating a 50-million-channel system is that there are better ways of delivering "video on demand." Which brings me to the second way of increasing the amount of information flow.

Data compression

So far, I've talked about pumping information through a notionally (though not physically) bigger cable with greater capacity. However, we can also increase information flow through a skinny channel — like a twisted pair — by changing the way we pump it. One technique for this is called data compression.

If, for instance, you are transmitting a television image that has a blue sky, the traditional way is to describe, line by line, the exact colour of every dot (called a "pixel") on the television screen. Hence, you wind up repeating the same colour of blue many, many times as you describe the total image. By contrast, data compression allows you to compress the amount of information transmitted simply by describing how many dots in the image are blue and where they are, and then letting the computer at the other end reconstruct the image based on your description. This is one form of data compression, and it is becoming more common and much faster as computer hardware and software improve.

Another form of compression is to transmit the entire picture once and then transmit only the parts of it that change from frame to frame. So if a car is driving up in front of a house, only those pixels that change from instant to instant would be described, and the receiving computer would keep the original image just as it was except for the pixels that had changed. Since only a very small portion of most images actually change, a lot less information would have to be transmitted to give a complete picture.

The combination of these and similar techniques, coupled with the improvements of hardware and software, mean that it will soon be possible to transmit a live colour picture over a twisted pair, which means that we could transmit a television program over a telephone instead of having to use massive amounts of radio frequency or the capacity of co-ax cable, as is currently required. This opens many possibilities. Telephone companies will be able to deliver movies, sporting events, news, sitcoms, or anything else, by phone. Video stores or production studios could take this on if the telephone companies weren't interested or were prohibited from doing so. What would this do to the economics of the broadcasting industry?

If video phones suddenly became cheap, requiring only a rudimentary video camera, a reasonably fast computer, and the proper software, I suspect they would also become popular. So teleconferencing would be affordable and easy, which could dramatically affect where we live, how we work, and with whom. Certainly this is the view of the Ontario Telepresence Project.

Cooperative work between Ottawa and Toronto can be used as an example to show how computer-supported collaborative work will fundamentally change the way business is conducted. The two groups hold regular meetings to exchange views and ideas and they now conduct the vast majority of these meetings and discussions through video conferencing. "Telepresence technology has greatly enhanced the collaboration," reports [Dr. Morris] Goldberg [of the University of Ottawa]. "Now people are very reluctant to go to Toronto for a two or three hour meeting." These same technologies have also made it possible for Goldberg to stay involved and informed on various aspects of the project. "As you know," he says, "I live in Europe. So I meet regularly through videoconferencing with Bill Buxton (Toronto Scientific Director) and with my group once a week. The meetings last from 15 minutes to an hour and there is no other way we could do this. It's just not possible. And these are technical meetings," Goldberg continues. "If I want to show a sheet of paper, I simply show the sheet. I don't have to go through the hassle of pre-shipping anything. It is much more natural."[8]

Genies and broadcatching

Clearly, the amount of information dumped on us in a given day is going to increase, but if we're already having problems with the amount of information we get, how will we cope with many times more?

In 1988 Apple Computer produced a stunning short video, based on what it then saw as the direction computing was taking. The video was about the computer of the future, which Apple called the Knowledge Navigator. Using speech recognition, DWIM programming, rapid and cheap access to distant databases, and video conferencing, it showed how someone could concentrate on doing creative work, leaving the grunt work to the computer. When the researcher in the video wanted to find a reference to a particular scientific article, he simply described it in general terms to the computer, and the computer found it for him. When he wanted updated information on the effects of clear cutting in the Amazon rain forest, the computer fetched more recent data for him.

This modern-day electronic genie is becoming more than a mere possibility. Apple calls such genies "personal digital assistants" (PDAs). Others call them "agents." Regardless of what they are called, computer assistants will fetch and carry, sift and filter, and watch the data flow for items that are of interest to us. Moreover, using neural network programs, rule-based systems, and other self-correcting, self-teaching software, computers will be able to select, for example, sets of news articles that we are likely to be interested in. This could eventually lead to personally assembled news delivery that showed only the articles we were interested in, skipping all the rest. Or it could filter through the 50 million channels to find the programs or events it knows we might want to see.

This leads to another new concept. We are all familiar with the idea of broadcasting — communicating with a large and scattered audience. As media channels of all kinds have proliferated, broadcasting is being replaced by "narrowcasting." With narrowcasting, you reach only those who have a specific interest in your message. Specialized magazines for motorcycle fans and cable-TV shows on fly fishing are perfect examples. Companies that sell to these markets advertise in these particular branches of the media rather than wasting their message on thousands of people who have no interest in their products.

"Broadcatching" is the ultimate form of narrowcasting: it appeals to a market of one. Moreover, broadcatching is initiated by the individual. If you can imagine someone sitting next to a raging torrent of information, broadcatching occurs when that person puts a smart fishing net into the torrent, and the net snags only those fish it knows the person wants, dodging all the rest. To appeal to such an individual, advertisers will have to know what will tempt a person's net to cause it to snag the advertiser's message out of the stream. Otherwise, the message will never be delivered.

This is one of the often-overlooked implications of computers: just as they will give companies and governments the ability to weasel their way into our private affairs, they will also give us the ability to craft intelligent moats and drawbridges to keep others from intruding on our privacy.

For instance, increasingly sophisticated phone systems — or, failing that, home computers set up to act as answering machines — will become gatekeepers against unwanted calls, such as those from telemarketers. Already, we are able to learn the phone number of a caller before we answer the phone. Suppose that our computer takes the caller's number, checks it to determine whether it comes from a personal phone or a corporate one, and then, if it is from a corporate phone whose number is not listed on our permitted list, refuses the call. This would put virtually all telemarketers out of business. Farther down the road, the computer might actually answer the phone and talk to the caller, shielding us from inconvenient calls, much as a good secretary would.

The "singularity"

A while back, a reporter from Société Radio-Canada, who was interviewing me about my views on the future, asked me a very interesting question: What will happen in the future that will catch us by surprise? After thinking for a minute, I answered that computers were going to surprise us because of the phase change I've described in this chapter. For the first time, we will have tools and nonhuman assistants that can talk back to us and with whom we can discuss matters. Certainly, these "intelligences" will be fashioned in our own image, but they will go beyond being mere echoes of our thoughts; they will add thoughts of their own.

Then, too, there is a future event that is discussed as being inevitable by some in this field and is dismissed as a fairy tale by others: the emergence of intelligent, self-aware computers. In the computer field this event is being called the "singularity." If and when it happens, humanity will be faced with new ethical as well as practical challenges: When do we recognize a nonhuman intelligence as a person? How do we tell whether an entity is "really" intelligent — or does that question mean anything? Does it matter that we created these intelligences or were at least responsible for their creation? Should they have "human rights," or is that something that will be forever reserved for homo sapiens?

It's going to be a different — and much smarter — world in which we live. Even if we don't like the idea.

NINE

Creations from Technology's Laboratory

Any sufficiently advanced technology is indistinguishable from magic.

– Arthur C. Clarke, *The Lost Worlds of 2001*

There are three great revolutions going on in technology. Two of them are very visible — information technologies (computers and communications) and biotechnology — whereas the third, materials technology, is almost completely invisible. Yet it's hard to decide which of the three will have the greatest long-term importance, especially as they are becoming ever more interdependent.

In addition, there's a revolution that has not yet started, one that may overshadow even these revolutions in importance. This is nanotechnology, which is the manufacture of objects by using very small machines — say, about the size of a virus. Most surprising of all, there is also the revolution that is widely expected and is not happening: the exploration and exploitation of space.

I discussed computers and information technologies in the previous chapter, and we'll deal with biotechnology as it pertains to humans in the Fifth Force: "Longer Lives," so for now, let's look at the other revolutions.

THE MATERIALS REVOLUTION[1]

In a sense, this is a misnomer. What we are experiencing is more like a very rapid materials *evolution*. However, the difference between a revolution and a rapid evolution is extremely subtle. We have been experiencing the materials evolution for millennia — the Stone Age, the Bronze Age, the Iron Age, and so on. Today, though, because of interdisciplinary cross-fertilization brought about by superior communications, because of the greater understanding of molecular chemistry and physics, and because of the far more powerful analytical tools available, materials scientists have been making enormous breakthroughs, though their discoveries have largely been ignored by the general public.

In Japan, breakthroughs in materials science are regular Sunday supplement stuff and occasionally make front-page headlines. Here, for some strange reason, you can hardly find anything on materials science. As a result, if there is an occupation with a bright future that is crying out for people, it is materials science (high school and college students, take note!).

There are so many things happening in materials, and in such diverse areas, that I'm just going to ramble through them in no particular order.

Composites

Composites are materials whose properties, when mixed appropriately, produce a compound that overcomes the weaknesses of each. Let me give you a common example. Plastic is relatively soft but tough; glass is hard but brittle; so when you put strands of glass in a plastic compound, you get a material that is both tough and hard: fibreglass.

The same principle is now being applied to many other materials. When graphite, a form of carbon, is spun into strands and then embedded in tough but heavy plastics, you can create lightweight but very stiff and strong materials. Graphite composites are being used for a variety of things, from airplane fuselages and parts to tennis and squash racquets. Indeed, it has revolutionized most racquet sports over the last ten years. With stiffer, lighter racquets, players can hit the ball harder, make shots that would otherwise be flubbed, and generally have more fun.

Other composites are being used in building, especially composites using wood. Wood is a natural material with incredible gifts: strong, reasonably durable, yet lightweight because it is not a homogeneous solid, but honeycombed, like a bone. The major problem with wood is, ironically, that it is in short supply and is becoming expensive. The reason why Canada, which has millions of hectares of forests, is running short of wood is that the environmental movements don't want lumber companies to cut down trees. Moreover, forest-product companies now recognize that social and political realities require that they plant at least one tree for each one they cut down. But they have a hard time justifying an investment that can take sixty years or more to mature.

As a result, there's a real need to find new substitutes for wood — and some of the best substitutes include wood itself. One of these is Parallam,[2] which stands for "parallel laminate." Plywood is a form of parallel laminate composed of thin sheets of not terribly good wood glued together, with the grains running in different directions to make a much stiffer, stronger composite. Parallam uses sheets of waste wood, often suspending the wood fibres in glue, in a kind of wood-and-glue equivalent of fibreglass: the sheets are then laminated together with other sheets of wood-and-glue material. Like plywood, they form a whole that is substantially stronger than the sum of its parts. Another wood composite is plastic wood. Here the wood fibres are suspended in plastic polymers; they lend strength and lightness, while the plastic gives toughness and durability, preserving the wood from rot and termites.

One of the oldest-known composites is concrete, though it is now undergoing radical change. Concrete has traditionally been formed of rock, a filler such as sand, and cement. Today, other materials, including plastics, are being added to give it additional or improved properties. As a result, we are approaching the production of superconcretes that will have greater strength and durability, and better resistance to such things as salt and weathering. Many of these new concrete composites will have to be manufactured indoors in carefully controlled environments and then hauled to construction sites for assembly. But in return for this inconvenience, they will allow buildings to be constructed with thinner walls, thereby increasing the "payload," or usable floor space, for the same building footprint.

Ceramic composites offer great promise for a variety of applications. Ceramics can be extremely hard, harder than metals. They can be made into very sharp edges, which make excellent cutting tools; and they can be made to withstand great heat, while being lighter than metals of comparable strength. But they are brittle and shatter easily. If they are made into composites, though, perhaps with graphite strands, they may become the new miracle material used to replace metals where weight or hardness are a factor. Even on their own, ceramics have great potential. They can be used as a coating on the leading edge of a metal surface of an airplane wing or a jet turbine, providing great strength and durability; and they have a big role in the computer and electronics industries, where they are now being used to create the semiconductors that largely dominate these industries.

Indeed, ceramics may be the key — or one of the keys — to the Holy Grail of materials science: superconductors.

Superconductors

The superconductor is one of those really sexy technological developments, like virtual reality, that gets investors excited because of its long-term potential. Meanwhile, its immediate future seems somewhat less exotic, especially when you consider that no one is making any money in the field yet.

Since 1911, it has been known that at low enough temperatures, certain materials offer no resistance when an electric current is run through them. Now, since electrical resistance is the result of the atoms and molecules in the wire bouncing around and impeding the flow of electrons, and since heat is essentially the motion of atoms and molecules, if you remove all the heat from an electrical conductor, the motion of atoms and molecules drops as well. Hence, at certain temperatures in certain substances, there is effectively no molecular motion, so there is no resistance.

The importance of this is that resistance slows down electrical processes and uses up electrical energy. So if there is no resistance, it may theoretically be possible to do things that are impossible in normal conductors, such as running a current around a circuit forever without losing any of its power. In theory at least, you could take the idle electrical generating capacity of Manitoba Hydro during the slack periods of the day — say 1 to 5 A.M. — and pump electricity into a superconductor, storing it with no power loss until you needed it during the peak periods. This would be a far more efficient means of storing power than with conventional batteries, and it would reduce the cost of electric power dramatically.

Superconducting wires will be able to transmit several times more power than a comparably sized conventional wire; this would be of great value to power utilities laying cables, or to computer manufacturers trying to shrink the size of all components in their products. Superconductors can also do things with magnetic fields that can't be done with ordinary materials, because superconductors repel both magnetic poles — north and south — and use no electrical power in doing so. In theory, therefore, you could build a magnetic levitating train that would float above a superconductor at zero cost. Although it would cost money to propel forward, the price would be much less than for a conventional train because the only friction would be from wind resistance.

Superconductors significantly speed up the transmission of electrical signals, a quality that could be particularly useful in computer circuits. They are also much better detectors of weak magnetic (and hence electrical) signals. As a result, they will be used in such applications as filtering out extraneous noise from cellular telephone signals, which would allow cellular systems to pack more phones onto existing frequencies. Superconductors will also mean that certain kinds of electronic equipment can be much smaller, more portable, and less expensive. For instance, in one already extant military application, an electronic component that measures less than 25 square centimetres is being used, where conventional electronics would require a 21-metre-long coaxial cable to produce comparable performance.[3]

An even more significant use of this property would be as a noninvasive means of detecting what's going on inside a human body, say, in the heart or brain, both of which produce very weak electrical signals. A superconductor-based monitor would be able to interpret these signals better than current electronics can do. This would allow the manufacture of much more sensitive devices, such as magnetic resonance imaging (MRI) scanners, and at substantially lower prices, which would make them more widely available.

So what's the problem? Well, first there's the temperature. When superconductance was first discovered, it occurred only at extremely low temperatures, within a few degrees of so-called absolute zero,[4] or $-273°C$. Needless to say, it is very expensive to get things this cold and to keep them that way. However, it turns out that not all materials need to be so cold in order to become superconductors. Current research is focusing on so-called high-temperature superconductors (say, above $-196°C$). This may seem like a trivial improvement, but in fact it is quite significant because $-196°C$ is the temperature at which nitrogen becomes a liquid and therefore can be used to cool such a material. Better yet, liquid nitrogen is cheap, costing only pennies a litre to produce.

This doesn't overcome all the problems by any means, because the ceramics that have superconducting properties at these temperatures are hard to manufacture in quantity, they tend to have lots of imperfections, and they're brittle, being more like chalk than metal, which is not what you want in a stretch of wire. Still, the research in this field is getting lots of money and attention because the prizes are so big. Moreover, it's still early days in superconductor development, for it was only in 1987 that the first vaguely practical high-temperature superconductor was fabricated by a group at the University of Houston.

As a typical new technology takes roughly thirty years to get to the stage of significant commercial application, a lot more research and development will be required before the enormous payoffs investors drool over start to roll in. Nevertheless, this is definitely a field to watch, for it has the potential to stand the entire electronics industry on its head. After all, the transistor was seven years old before it was used outside Bell Labs, and then its appearance was in a humble hearing aid. Not until an unknown Japanese inventor, Masaru Ibuka, built the first transistor radio did people start to see the potential of this new invention. And the company he built around that first product is one that most of us have heard of: Sony Corp.

Electroaccreted limestone

This is not so much a new material as a new means of creating limestone structures. The idea is that instead of building a structure, you let the structure build itself. To do so, you take a wire mesh — chicken wire will do — bend it into the form you want, place it in water that has limestone dissolved in it, such as sea water, run a small electric current through the wire, and wait anywhere from one to three months. Depending on how quickly you do this (slower is better), you can create load-bearing structures that are cheap and exactly the size and shape you want, yet are as strong as much more expensive materials such as concrete. Dr. Jorge Zapp, a Colombian materials engineer, has built self-supporting curved roofs that are 3 metres square and are able to bear loads in excess of 200 kilograms per square centimetre.[5]

The reason I find this particularly interesting is that the process has been suggested as a possible way of helping the Atlantic provinces' cod fishery. Using electroaccreted limestone fabrication, we could create a long pipeline down into deep ocean. We could then siphon cold, nutrient-rich water from the ocean depths and dump it into the inshore fishery areas. This would provide a much richer cultivating ground for all ocean life, including cod, and would substantially boost the rate at which the cod would regenerate. Because of the low cost of electroaccreted limestone fabrication, and the minimal costs of running a siphon, the entire project would be extremely inexpensive. Yet the returns to the inshore fisheries could be enormous, particularly if the water was dumped into fish and seafood farms.[6]

Moreover, as ocean water is an excellent source of dissolved limestone (calcium carbonate), the Atlantic provinces and British Columbia could create an industry in making electroaccreted limestone components for buildings at very competitive prices — if the concrete industry monopoly ever allowed it to get off the ground. But will the governments of Canada look at these ideas? Probably not. That would require something very much like imagination.

Biomimetic materials

Every day, all over the world, incredibly delicate yet strong structures are made that are many times more durable than the highest of hi-tech ceramics. More, these materials are manufactured in sloppy and poorly controlled conditions that few engineers could tolerate, let alone manage. Unfortunately, these structures are not made by humans. They are made by clams, oysters, abalone, nautiluses, even chickens. They are natural shells, spines, claws, coral reefs, egg shells, and the like, and we are only now becoming sophisticated enough to realize how incredibly good these materials are.

We are trying hard to duplicate them. By examining how they are made and from what, materials scientists are hoping to come up with new human-made substances that have some, if not all, of the properties of these natural marvels. For instance, whereas human-made materials tend to erode, crack, or develop stress points where there are discontinuities in the material and then see such cracks spread, shells that develop cracks tend to remain whole. Why? Well, it turns out that an abalone, for instance, controls how the aragonite crystals in its shell develop — a feat far beyond our abilities. It creates groups of hexagonal crystal bricks that fit snugly together, each one a mirror image of the next, thus creating a locking structure that has each crystal brick touching the next, with no space in between.[7] There are therefore no naturally occurring discontinuities, so cracks caused by being hit with a rock, for instance, don't spread.

As scientists start to understand how such structures are built, they will be able to start mimicking them, creating stronger, cheaper, more delicate and lighter materials. But that's only part of the story. Potentially greater rewards await us if scientists from different disciplines can work together to understand and duplicate the processes that allow these deceptively primitive animals to do things we can only dream of. If we can replicate some of the crystalline proteins these animals use to create and cement their structures, we may be able to mimic their development. A group of researchers at Northwestern University in the United States is working on the protein that makes up dentin, which forms the inner bulk of teeth.[8] Might it be possible to grow replacement teeth from their tough, original materials rather than using metal or ceramic fillings? We don't know — but it's an investigation that seems worth pursuing.

Biomaterials

Even as we humans seek to learn from nature, we are also looking at ways of assisting nature in human bodies. Hip replacements and heart valves are not news, but the potential for advances in materials that can be used as prosthetics and to repair breaks, tears, and faults is.

If I can oversimplify, there are two principal kinds of biomaterials: those accepted by the body, and those that might be subject to rejection. Titanium and steel and a wide range of inorganic materials are accepted by the body and hence are suitable for such uses as bone replacements. The second group involves many applications: parts that might be used in organ replacement; blood vessel replacements; implanted drug-release systems; biochemical sensors; devices to assist in tooth repair and replacement; hearing aids and/or replacements for part of the ear; eye repair and replacement devices; artificial arms and legs; and artificial or artificially grown skin for grafts and plastic surgery.

The challenges of this field are great — and so are the potential rewards, both human and financial. For the inorganic prostheses, the challenge may be to make materials that can last anywhere from twenty to eighty years for adults. (Children, of course, would need replacements that keep pace with their growth.) A young woman who needs a thigh bone replacement will not want it to wear out and have to be replaced later in life. Moreover, the best scenario for these materials would be if they could be accepted by the body, so that existing bones would bond with bone replacements.

One intriguing possibility is to use diamonds for joint replacement. Diamonds have some wonderful properties: they are the strongest, most rigid, and most transparent material known; they conduct heat four times better than copper; they are as slippery as Teflon; yet they are extremely stable. Their only drawback has been their cost. Now, however, industrial processes are emerging that would allow materials scientists to create thin film-coatings of diamond at relatively low cost.[9] This does not solve all the problems associated with diamonds — for instance, they don't bond well with other materials — but since they have such great potential, some kind of answer will likely be found.

For organic materials, the challenge will be either to side-step the body's immune system, which might otherwise cause the materials to be rejected, or to fool the immune system into believing that the material comes from the body. Neither course is simple. For instance, pig heart valves are very similar to human heart valves and might be used to repair hearts damaged through heart attacks. First, though, they would have to be put through a process to eliminate all the materials that might prompt the immune system to attack them, and they would have to be treated to give them added strength so that they would last.

Nevertheless, the potential rewards from the development of biomaterials could be enormous, bringing many people significant improvement in the quality of life, and even the length of life.

Carbon — the dark horse of materials science

Carbon is one of the most common elements on earth, and, along with nitrogen, hydrogen, and oxygen is one of the principal building blocks of living organisms. Now there is a new family of carbon compounds that has strange and wonderful properties. They have been named "fullerenes," after futurist Buckminster Fuller. The attraction of fullerenes is that they form spherical or cylindrical shapes that are incredibly strong, and they may eventually lead to structures that are almost unimaginably strong. The principal reason for this strength is that we are gradually learning how to make materials that are free of defects by assembling them a molecule at a time. I'll come back to this a little later. In tests, fullerene has been shot at metal walls at speeds of 32,000 kilometres per hour. The metal molecules shatter, but the fullerene either bounces off or pierces the wall.[10]

One fullerene compound likely to be available in the immediate future is Rhondite, a material in which the fullerene forms around an iron atom and is then formed into helical (i.e., spiralling) strands. The result can be likened to a diamond-studded steel that is cheap to make (about 50 cents per kilogram) yet will be of significantly greater strength than the steel we are currently producing.[11]

As for the long term, the sky — literally — may be the limit. Although we don't yet know how to do so, the day may come when we can spin defect-free fullerene strands that would be, by today's standards, almost unimaginably strong. Such a filament would be almost unbreakable and incredibly light for its strength. This might lead to the heretofore impossible "space elevator" that science fiction stories have hypothesized.[12]

The idea of the space elevator is to put a satellite in stationary Earth orbit, then to run cable both up and down from the satellite in such a way as to keep the centre of mass unchanged. If we ran elevators up and down the cable when it reached the ground, this would allow us to put payloads into space so cheaply that it might reduce the cost of leaving the Earth's gravity well by a hundredfold.[13]

"Smart" materials

The profligate use of computers that I anticipate, coupled with new materials and existing materials, such as optical fibres, will enable us to create "smart" materials that will be self-diagnostic or even dynamically adaptable to changing conditions. For instance, it may be possible in future to build office towers in Florida that sense hurricane winds and lean into them so that they are more resistant to wind damage. Airplanes may have sensors and optical-fibre networks built into them to sense microscopic cracks and to call for maintenance before the damage becomes expensive — or life-threatening.

Similarly, bridges and support structures will be built with optical systems that measure load and structural distortions, such as stretching or twisting, so that problems can be remedied before they become dangerous. One bridge in Calgary that incorporates some of these ideas is currently being built as a pilot project. Had the houses and bridges in Los Angeles been built with such sensors, the engineers overseeing the rebuilding after the earthquake of early 1994 would have been able to tell which ones were safe and which needed to be repaired, torn down, or abandoned. As it was, many people lost their homes unnecessarily purely because they couldn't be sure if the houses were safe or not, and bridges were pulled down for the same reason.

Although smart materials are only just beginning to be used, they show great promise — and the best applications have probably not even been thought of yet.

NANOTECHNOLOGY

This is a revolution that has hardly started, and we may not see even preliminary results for ten or twenty years. However, if the promise of this field holds true, it may completely change how we make things and what kinds of things we make.

Nanotechnology involves the use of very small machines — perhaps getting down to the size of a virus. These machines would have two properties that would make them dramatically different from the manufacturing technologies we use today. First, they could be used to manufacture things on a molecule-by-molecule (or even atom-by-atom) basis, allowing us to produce materials with unprecedented strength, durability, and purity. We could thus create new materials as needed, with the specific properties required for each particular task.

Second, nanomachines could replicate or reproduce themselves. Obviously, one machine the size of a virus would not be able to do

165

very much of value. However, if these machines did the work they were designed to do and made more copies of themselves as well, they would then be able to produce significant and valuable results.

So you need a drug tailored to the unique genetic pattern of a specific individual? Nanotechnology would allow it to be created, as well as producing a tiny device to deliver it by navigating through the bloodstream to the precise site where the drug was needed. Or it could allow us to build machines that could travel through the body, killing cancerous cells and repairing damaged ones. Or how about a machine that rebuilds the mechanism of your inner ear, reversing the deafness that often comes with aging? Or a new eye with perfect vision? Or a new kidney, built from scratch but matching your genetic pattern exactly?

Or what about an organic computer, grown rather than built? Today's computer scientists talk about "massively parallel processing" with perhaps a thousand microprocessors. What kind of computing power will we have when massively parallel processing means trillions of processors capable of enormously greater speeds because of their atomic scale?

How about a virus-sized machine that could be dumped into sea water to sort the molecules by type, putting the salts and impurities on one side of a membrane and pure water molecules on the other? Or one that would take water and separate it into hydrogen and oxygen? Or one that would produce petroleum feedstock from scrub plants grown on wasteland? Then again, imagine a man-made assembler that you can dump into a vat, along with the requisite raw materials, leave for a time, and then have a new, completed automobile roll out, fully equipped down to the stereo system and corporate logo. If this sounds absurd, remember that this is more or less how living organisms are created.

Once we are able to make machines that can manipulate atoms and molecules directly, we will be able to undertake tasks that are beyond our imagination today. But nanotechnology is not something to watch from day to day or even from month to month. We are, I think, at least ten years from any significant preliminary developments and probably fifty years from the kinds of application I've described above. There are formidable technical problems to overcome before we get there, even though the scientific principles are all known today. But if the promise does become a reality, nanotechnology may be a technological revolution beside which all previous ones pale into insignificance.

THE EXPLOITATION OF NEAR-EARTH SPACE

Freeman Dyson, director of the Space Studies Institute, had this to say about the Apollo moon-landing program:

> Everybody agrees that the Apollo program was a brilliant success technically, yet a failure historically. . . . The order of priorities in Apollo was accurately reflected by the first item to be unloaded after each landing on the Moon's surface, the television camera. . . . The missions beyond Apollo 18 were cancelled and the project brought to a halt, because the purpose of providing public entertainment had been achieved, and further repetitions of the same takeoff-and-landing spectacle would not have added much to the quality of the show. . . . [Hence, the] opportunity to do cost-effective exploring of the Moon was missed.[14]

Recent talk of a joint Russian-American effort to reach Mars strikes me as more of the same: 99 percent grandstanding, 1 percent real value.

In researching material for this book, I spoke with many people who are involved in the space program in one way or another, and asked the same question: "Can you give me any good commercial reason for going into space, other than for weather and communications satellites?" Despite a lot of interesting discussions, the answer was almost always the same: "No." Perhaps I just spoke to the wrong people.

The funny part about the entire space effort so far is that, badly managed though it has been, it has paid for itself many times over in spin-off technologies. Just a few of the things that have arisen out of, or been accelerated by, the space program have been:

• the development of the microprocessor and microminiaturized electronics, and hence the computer revolution as it is now;

• image-enhancing software (originally developed to convert images, sent by weak radio signals from satellites orbiting other planets, into clear pictures), now used with such medical equipment as computerized-axial-tomography (CAT) scans and magnetic-resonance-imaging (MRI) systems;

167

• the Doppler ultrasound stethoscope, which is used for medical diagnostics, especially for the examination of soft-tissue injuries, as well as for determining the health of unborn fetuses in the womb;

• the telemetry of medical data in hospital intensive-care units;

• improved weather forecasting, because of weather satellites, which has saved thousands of lives, as well as billions of dollars in property that would otherwise have been lost in hurricanes;

• countless improvements in metallurgy, ceramics, and composite materials that have been of enormous benefit in a host of industries and applications;[15]

• and, of course, the billions of dollars of communications traffic that goes by satellite every year.

Since these benefits are spread over many industries, they are not counted among the benefits of the space program, which is therefore regarded as a waste of money. Despite this, I believe humanity needs to open up the exploitation of space. There are several reasons for doing so. One that has immediate appeal is that if we placed our factories in orbit rather than on the ground, we could stop polluting this planet. We could mine the moon and the asteroids for raw materials, rather than tearing up the ground below us.

But there are two other important reasons for going into space. One is to open a frontier for humanity, to provide an escape valve for those who are dissatisfied or adventurous. The other is to provide long-term insurance for the survival of the human race. Here I should make it clear that I'm talking about survival of the race in the event of a global catastrophe, not survival of individuals. In other words, I'm not advocating that we try to solve the world's population problem by shipping excess people off to space colonies. That is simply not possible; as well as being infeasible logistically, it would be far too expensive.

Why are even the enthusiasts flagging in their ideas of why we should go into space? First, because the cost of getting into orbit using existing launch vehicles to escape the Earth's gravity is so high as to make large-scale development unrealistic. And second, because most of the developments to date, such as the space shuttle, have been grandstanding stunts rather than building blocks aimed at making space travel practical.

Ironically, even with current technology it might be possible to build a reusable rocket that could put payloads into orbit at roughly the cost per kilo of shipping things from Canada to Australia by air.[16] However, since NASA has wasted so much money on its white elephant space shuttle program, it would be less than pleased to see someone else succeed with a more practical program.

In the long term, there is at least one compelling reason for exploiting near-Earth space that should lead us to continue our efforts: nonpolluting sources of energy. In Chapter 7, I described how the gross world product could be expected to increase by between five and ten times as a result of global population growth over the next century. Because there is a direct correlation between economic growth and energy consumption, this means that there will be a similar growth in energy production, which implies that we'll need new sources of clean energy if we don't want to choke ourselves on pollution.

At present, there are three primary sources of relatively clean energy available in commercially useful quantities: nuclear power, hydroelectric power, and combined-cycle gas turbines burning natural gas. Each has its own problems. Those associated with nuclear power — most especially the public relations problems — are well known. Hydroelectric power has several problems that are now being given more prominence: destruction of wildlife habitats, native land claims, shorter life spans than originally expected because of silting, and so on. Combined-cycle gas turbines produce relatively clean, relatively cheap electric power, but they burn hydrocarbons, and there are several reasons why the long-term future of energy does not include burning hydrocarbons.

For many years, solar power has been spoken of as a good, clean alternative form of energy, and it will gain greater currency as the technology of converting sunlight to electricity gradually improves. But solar power still has a significant drawback: the sun doesn't shine on us all the time. Worse, it's usually not sunny enough in the places where you want the power — like Toronto, Montreal, or Vancouver.

However, it's always sunny in space; there are no clouds, and the sunshine doesn't get filtered through the atmosphere. Accordingly, enthusiasts have advocated building solar power satellites (SPS). These would collect solar energy in space and convert it to microwaves, which would then be beamed to a receiving antenna on Earth. Power losses would be on the order of about 25 percent of the power generated. The only problem is that putting up an SPS would be a big project, roughly on a par with building a major hydroelectric dam, mostly because of the costs of lofting the material into orbit. Accordingly, SPS advocates have talked about mining asteroids or the moon as a way of cutting the gravity costs associated with the project, but this would put the time schedule well into the future.

There is, however, a way of exploiting space for power right now that would be relatively cheap and would produce significant benefits, as well as providing a stepping stone to SPS projects later. Moreover, it's one that offers significant opportunities for Canada to develop a new export market for a high value-added product and to take the lead in a new technology.

Suppose that instead of generating the power in space and beaming it to Earth, we generated the power on Earth and beamed it to space and then back down to Earth again. We could do this if a relatively lightweight, inexpensive satellite that was really just a glorified mirror for microwaves was placed in geosynchronous (i.e., stationary) orbit around the Earth (see Figure 7). This would allow us to generate power wherever we could do so in a clean, efficient manner, and then supply it wherever it was needed. There would inevitably be some power losses because of the more than 70,000 kilometres the microwaves would have to travel up to the satellite and back, but these losses would be about the same as those involved in transmitting power from James Bay to New York City by land line.[17]

We might, for example, tap the hydroelectric potential of Newfoundland or build nuclear power stations in remote towns that wanted to increase local employment. It wouldn't matter where we located them — the cost of transmission would be almost the same, regardless of ground location.

Where would we sell the power? Well, how about selling it to Mexico City, which has a major pollution problem, or to any of the Latin American countries? Certainly, they need the power and would probably prefer to get it in a nonpolluting way. Or if that's too far-fetched, we could sell it across time zones in order to get the most efficient use of utility plant and equipment. Hence, Newfoundland might sell its off-peak capacity to British Columbia or Europe. This would allow Newfoundland to generate employment, pay for the development of its natural resources through export sales, and allow its customers to get by with lower native generating capacity.

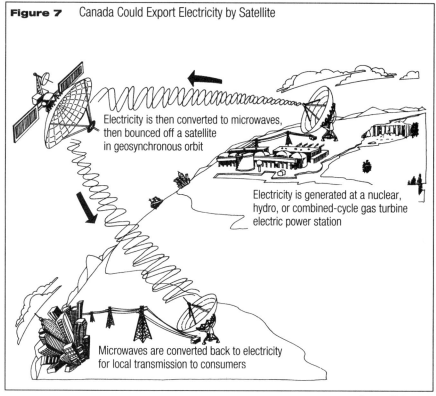

Figure 7   Canada Could Export Electricity by Satellite

Electricity is then converted to microwaves, then bounced off a satellite in geosynchronous orbit

Electricity is generated at a nuclear, hydro, or combined-cycle gas turbine electric power station

Microwaves are converted back to electricity for local transmission to consumers

Source: IF Research

In total, then, it would be a win-win proposition. We would get export sales for electric power, employment in remote locations, and there would be less global pollution. I've tried to interest two of Canada's provincial power utilities in this idea, but I've come up against two major problems: it wasn't their idea (so they didn't like it), and it's too different. There are no rewards for boldness in a bureaucracy.

And that, in a nutshell, is why you probably won't ever have a chance to vacation on the moon. Forget your childhood dreams: NASA and pusillanimous paper pushers have buried them in red tape and gold-plated incompetence for at least a generation.

THE FOURTH FORCE

Environmentalism
and the Ecology

T E N

The End of Infinity

For millions of years we looked at the ocean and said, "This is infinite. It will accept our garbage and waste forever." We looked at the sky and said, "This is infinite: it will hold an infinite amount of smoke." We *like* the idea of infinity. A problem with infinity in it is easily solved. How long can you pollute a planet infinitely large? Easy: forever. Stop thinking.

Then one day there are so many of us the planet no longer seems infinitely large.

– Spider Robinson, "Melancholy Elephants," 1984

In 1962 Rachel Carson published a book that changed the world: *Silent Spring*. There had been people before her who had warned of the dangers of desecrating the Earth, but it was Carson who brought it into the consciousness of the American public, and thence into the councils of the developed world.

I was a teenager when *Silent Spring* began to get attention, but I can still remember the furor it caused. Television specials showed some of the effects Carson had written about, such as birds dying from eating insects sprayed with pesticides and fish dying from industrial waste dumped into rivers. Learned "talking heads" denounced her as an alarmist, a fool, a communist, an anarchist. There were few defenders.

Indeed, the biggest problem that those concerned with the environment have had is the indifference or outright hostility of

175

consumers and corporations, who don't want to hear a message that tells them: "You can't go on doing what you've been doing. You're going to have to shape up, clean up your act, or you will kill us all." Since it's easier and seems cheaper to keep on polluting, and since it's hard to use resources intelligently, the first inclination has always been just to ignore the problem and hope it will go away.

But Carson's message has not gone away, because what she said was true. The message that we cannot go on desecrating the Earth is as controversial today as it was in 1962. Now, however, there are new dangers arising from the environmentalists as well. I believe that the environmental movement is degenerating into a series of media events, that the truth itself is suffering, and that we are putting ourselves in needless danger as a result.

ENVIRONMENTALISM AS MEDIA CIRCUS

Some of those arguing the environmental case are doing themselves — and the Earth — a disservice, for they contend that nothing is too extreme and no price is too high to defend the Earth from polluters. At the far extremities of the movement are the eco-terrorists, who are willing to cause the death of other humans to make their point.

I remember one cartoon that seemed to epitomize these extremists. It showed a man presenting a petition to another, saying something like, "We're petitioning to have humanity wiped out as the only true solution to environmental problems." I smiled, but then stopped and thought: there probably are people who believe this.

The environmental movement, partly to make the issues understandable to a general public that has a hazardously short attention span, portrays ecological issues in simplistic good/bad, black/white terms. Therein lies the danger, because the details are important, and they are too often lost in the shouting. Let me give you an example.

A story in which environmentalists win and the ecology loses

In the simplistic world of environmentalist public relations, manmade materials such as plastic are bad and natural materials such as wood and paper are good, even when the evidence proves otherwise. Take, for example, the environmentally inspired pressure campaign of 1990 that forced McDonald's restaurants to jettison the polystyrene foam clamshells they had been using to keep their hamburgers warm and to replace them with coated paper. The knee-jerk reaction was that polystyrene was bad, but paper was good. The reality is more complicated.

If you look at the complete cycle costs and problems of paper versus polystyrene, it is polystyrene that actually does less damage to the environment. Paper uses more energy and creates more pollution when it is manufactured. And coated paper is neither recyclable nor biodegradable. This is not to say that polystyrene foam is completely innocuous; it's not. In particular, it creates a problem in landfills because it takes up a lot of volume relative to its weight. But it can be broken down into base plastic and recycled, and in 1989 and 1990 McDonald's was revving up a major recycling effort to do just that — until the environmentalists pressured them to switch to coated paper. So far as I know, McDonald's is making no effort to recycle the coated paper it currently uses to keep its burgers warm. Despite this, the Environmental Defence Fund has called this "an environmental touchdown."[1]

I'm not trying to advocate either paper or polystyrene foam as a perfect material. What I am saying is that a bad choice was made from good motives. The environmentalists won — but the environment lost.

The dangers of environmentalism as media circus

There are several dangers with the direction the environmental movement seems to be taking. First, it's become part of the scenery, such an everyday thing that it creates headlines only when something extreme goes on. This means that the only way to draw attention to an environmental cause is to do something extreme. In turn, this creates the impression that environmentalists are, or should be, extremists.

Related to this is the fact that there are too many environmental causes and no priorities. Since the environmental movement is not organized in any way, anybody can adopt any cause and embark on a crusade for it. There's nothing legally or morally wrong about this, but it creates a babble of voices, all urging people of the importance of doing different things, and this creates confusion. Is it more important to save the whales or the Temagami old growth forest? Is dealing with solid waste more important than drift-net fishing? Have we licked air pollution only to have to worry about global warming? Is it enough that I put plastic bottles in the blue box for recycling, or do I need to take transit to work more often as well?

What's really important here?

The self-proclaimed experts don't seem to be able to agree on priorities. Add to this the self-serving "green products" of companies trying to cash in on legitimate concerns about the state of the world, and it's easier for people to shrug off the whole issue than change their life-styles.

Unless environmentalists can organize their movement and give a sense of priority, they are going to be faced with increasing reluctance on the part of consumers and voters to do more. This is especially true during difficult economic periods, when people are more interested in food-on-the-table issues than they are about saving the dolphins. Which brings me to my next point. The sexier issues get more attention even if they're less important.

During the NAFTA negotiations, President Carlos Salinas of Mexico made several speeches about how Mexico was banning drift-net fishing to avoid killing dolphins. But when was the last time you heard a politician get up and give a speech about saving the aquifers, stopping groundwater pollution, or making better use of existing water resources? There are going to be far more problems resulting from the misuse of water than from killing dolphins. But dolphins are cute and cuddly and don't require making difficult political choices, so they get attention and aquifers don't. This is no way to make tough decisions.

Environmentalism — today's secular religion

In a very real sense, environmentalism has become today's religion in the developed world. Every politician, everyone in the media, and most people in public life regularly put their hands over their hearts and pledge allegiance to environmental causes. That's not a bad thing, because if we are to survive as a race and as a planet, we cannot ignore the wastes we produce. But it has reached the stage where anyone who challenges the established dogma of environmentalism is accused of heresy. As a result, scarce resources and energy often get committed to causes that are not vital, or to ones where the outcomes are uncertain or where the proposed actions are just plain wrong.

Take, for instance, the debate — or, rather, lack of debate — over global warming. Everyone who talks about global warming assumes that it is happening, that humanity is the cause of it, and that we must act immediately to counteract it. But it ain't necessarily so:

> A recent Gallup poll conducted for the Institute of Science, Technology and Media found that of those scientists actively involved in global climate research, 53 percent do not believe that global warming has occurred and 30 percent don't know, leaving only 17 percent who believe that global warming has begun.[2]

Indeed, Professor R. E. Munn of the University of Toronto's Institute for Environmental Studies suggests that the warming trend frequently cited in the popular press has not happened. "There's no statistical demonstration that the climate has warmed up," he says. "There's some evidence, but it's within the range of probability."[3] He quickly adds, though, that this doesn't mean that it's okay for humanity to continue to dump greenhouse gases into the atmosphere.

Or consider Canada's homegrown guru on the environment, geneticist David Suzuki:

> The uncertainty in predicting the long-term effects of this excess of greenhouse gases merely reflects our state of scientific ignorance. If we know so little about what affects weather and climate that it's hard to predict weather accurately from day to day, how can we anticipate climate change from year to year? . . .The fact is that we don't know what will happen. By tweaking parameters and factors in complex computer models of the upper atmosphere, we can get predictions ranging from an impending Ice Age to catastrophic heating.[4]

So, given our lack of understanding and the lack of a clear climatic trend, what is Dr. Suzuki's solution? "We have to decrease greenhouse gas output because the atmospheric changes, whatever they are, will have massive consequences so they must be minimized."[5]

Now, I have a problem with much — though not all — of what Dr. Suzuki and other commentators have to say on this matter. Of course, it doesn't surprise me when they call for action right now on an issue that has a lot of public appeal, even when they acknowledge they don't know what's going on — but that doesn't mean I have to agree with them.

So is global warming real? What's going on out there?

The truth is that we don't know what's happening with the Earth's climate. It is true that the average temperature measured by specific reporting stations, principally in the Northern Hemisphere, has been rising fairly steadily since about 1970. But in 1991 two Danish scientists, Eigil Friis-Christensen and Knud Lassen of the Danish Meteorological Institute, may have blown a hole in the global warming boat by suggesting that it was the sun, not greenhouse gases, that was responsible for the recent warming trend:

> Furthermore, a strikingly good agreement between [the eighty- to ninety-year solar activity cycle and Earth's surface temperature] is revealed. There is a close association between these two curves in the up-going trends from 1900 to 1940 and since 1970, as well as in the important decrease from 1945 to 1970. . . . We therefore find that this agreement supports (although it does not prove) the suggestion of a direct solar activity influence on global temperature. . . .
>
> We . . . compared the [eighty- to ninety-year] smoothed sunspot cycle lengths and a 22-year running mean of the extent of sea ice around Iceland. The comparison clearly shows that each maximum in the long-term solar activity around 1770, 1850, and 1940 has been accompanied by a corresponding minimum in the 22-year running mean value of the extent of the sea ice around Iceland.[6]

In plain English, this means that the sun goes through an eighty- to ninety-year cycle of activity. During certain parts of this cycle, the sun warms up, and seems to cause Earth's average temperature to rise. Accordingly, the evidence assembled by these two climatologists seems to indicate that this century's increase in global temperature could be entirely natural. Moreover, they also concluded that if humanity is responsible for an increase in global temperature, there is no sign of it as yet.

What a novel idea: the sun, the ultimate source of all our energy, the principal reason why Earth has a climate at all and isn't just a frozen ball of dirt, might be the major reason why the climate changes. Who'd have thunk it?

Well, again, the truth is that we don't know. We do know that the sun is a variable star, which heats up and cools down from time to time. We know that it has been emitting fewer neutrinos, a by-product of solar fusion, than we would expect, which might indicate that it is entering a cooling phase. We know that Earth has gone through many warming and cooling trends throughout its geologic history, without any help at all from humanity. And, yes, we also know that humanity has been producing more of the gases that cause heat from the sun to be trapped within the atmosphere.

There seems to be an emerging consensus among climatologists that if humanity continues along its present path in producing greenhouse gases, there might be a measurable increase in global temperature of between 1.5° and 4.5°C over the next fifty years.[7] But in the first place, we don't know what the temperature would be without human interference — it could be warmer or cooler than today. Secondly, we don't know what effects this would have, because even the best estimates are merely educated guesses.

Maurice Strong, the current chairman of Ontario Hydro and former secretary-general of the Earth Summit in Rio de Janeiro, is cited as saying that it could cost as much as $600 billion a year to lower carbon-dioxide emissions.[8] So where I part company with many environmentalists is that I can't see spending hundreds of billions of dollars to restrict the emission of greenhouse gases when we have no idea whether it will keep Earth from overheating — or even whether overheating is a problem. It might be, for instance, that a warmer climate would do beneficial things, like causing the Sahara to blossom into fertile land again, and would give us a better climate. This type of thing has happened before. But we simply don't know, and taking action out of ignorance could be very expensive — and even outright destructive if we subsequently proved to be mistaken.

Like most religions, environmentalism has unreasoned dogma

I guess the attitude that causes me the greatest concern is that many environmentalists seem to have rigid dogmas, preferring to stick to their beliefs rather than consider solutions that run counter to those beliefs. Take nuclear power, for instance. Anyone who thinks about it for more than five minutes will realize that over the next two decades we are going to be faced with a steadily rising need for more energy, and that the vast majority of this energy will have to come from our current conventional sources: fossil fuels, hydroelectric power, and nuclear energy.

Nuclear energy has many desirable qualities: it doesn't create greenhouse gases, it doesn't pollute the atmosphere, yet it produces significant amounts of energy and can be located almost anywhere that's convenient. It has two public drawbacks: hysteria over the possibility that a nuclear power plant will go "boom," and concerns over disposing of the spent nuclear waste in a safe manner. (It may also have an economic drawback because the decommissioning of nuclear plants may turn out to be much more expensive than originally thought. However, this has received much less attention than the other two issues.)

Preventing a nuclear plant from exploding is more a matter of proper design than anything else. Chernobyl demonstrated this by illustrating the problems of bad design — and Three Mile Island confirmed the value of good design because it didn't explode.

Since North America has gone out of the nuclear power business (largely because of environmental public relations), I suggest that it will be very interesting to watch Japan's continued development of nuclear power. The Japanese' great attention to detail and willingness to take a good basic design and continually refine it may mean that twenty years from now we may be buying power stations (or power) from them, rather than selling designs to them.

However, the question of disposing of spent nuclear fuel may already have been solved — and the environmentalists don't want to know about it. I was at a conference recently where a speaker noted that we could ship spent nuclear fuel to a designated site on the moon and stockpile it there. As the moon has no ecosphere, it would do no harm, and it would be far removed from human populations yet could be retrieved at a later date if we needed it. Before money was invested in assessing the practicality of this idea, one of the researchers had called Greenpeace to find out how environmentalists might react, and had received the reply: "That's a really good idea. We'll fight it every step of the way." Why? the researcher wanted to know. "Because it would encourage the use of nuclear power." The Greenpeace people didn't want to fix the problem. They just wanted nuclear power not to happen.

It may be that nuclear power is not the wisest choice for the future. But to reject possible solutions without good reason is an

182

infantile reaction — and one that guarantees that we will make foolish choices for the future.

THE EARTH'S ECOLOGY

The word ecology means "1: a branch of science concerned with the
interrelationship of organisms and their environments 2: the totality
or pattern of relations between organisms and their environments."[9]
I suspect that it may be the most complex subject humanity will ever
undertake to study. One aspect of the global ecology that is usually
ignored in environmental considerations is money and economics.
Environmentalists frequently give the impression that money is irrelevant, because you can't eat or breathe it, and that environmental
matters must be put first no matter what the cost.

To say that money — a human invention for representing time,
effort, and skill — is irrelevant is to ignore its relationship to the
ecology. If we could force developing countries, for example, to stop
producing greenhouse gases, many of their people would die from
lack of food or medicine. There is always a human cost to money; it
is never free.

Part of the problem is the illusion that corporations can be
forced to pay for environmental issues and that their money is free.
But corporations are legal fictions; it is people, in the form of
employees, shareholders, and consumers, who pay the costs borne
by these human creations.

Since we in the developed world are the ones with money, some
environmentalists are calling for a reduction in our standard of living,
even a redistribution of our wealth to the poorer countries of the
world, for the sake of the environment. In response, I think that it's
important to remember that people will not willingly choose to be
poor. Heck, most people won't even pay an extra buck to buy a
completely biodegradable dish detergent. It is therefore foolish for
anyone to call for the impoverishment of the developed world for
environmental reasons, because it won't happen.

Unfortunately, this reality is one reason why sincere, dedicated
environmentalists often resort to extreme, black-and-white rhetoric.
They believe that anything less has no chance of convincing the public of the need for action. Nor are their concerns misplaced.

We are a significant part of the problem

We in the developed countries use the vast majority of the currently developed resources, and produce the vast majority of pollution. Paul and Anne Ehrlich give an equation to describe the impact humanity has on the planet:

$$I = P \times A \times T$$

Where I = impact or effect; P = population; A = affluence, or per capita consumption; and T = technology, or the effect of technology in producing each unit of affluence.[10] What this means is that 27 million Canadians living in an affluent society and employing a significant amount of technology to maintain it will do more damage to the ecology than 270 million people living in mud huts and herding goats in Africa. The facts, as presented in the Economist, confirm this: "The average person in a developing country uses the equivalent of one or two barrels of oil a year of fuel (apart from what is scavenged directly from forests and fields); the average European or Japanese, the equivalent of between ten and 30 barrels a year; the average American, 40 barrels."[11]

Paul and Anne Ehrlich have estimated that one person in a developed country such as ours produces as much pollution as a hundred people in an underdeveloped country. I don't know if the number is correct, but if you just think about it, you'll see that we must create more pollution than people in poorer countries. We have more cars, putting exhaust into the atmosphere. We use more electricity to watch television, to run the dishwasher, to keep food cold in the refrigerator. We just plain use and consume more stuff, and that creates more pollution. Accordingly, even though the developed countries represent perhaps 20 percent of the global population, we probably produce more than 80 percent of global pollution. Which is why environmentalists are convinced that the only way to save the planet is to get us to cut back our standard of living.

However, while this formula provides great insight, it is not complete. First of all, as countries become more affluent, the technology they use becomes less wasteful and more efficient. Hence, beyond a certain point, technology actually reduces the pollution produced rather than increasing it (as noted in Chapter 2). In addition, this formula doesn't consider the future. It presents a static picture of the world as it is, instead of viewing the dynamic, rapidly changing world as it will be.

Bear in mind that almost all global population growth (about 97 percent) will be in the developing countries. That's the P in the equation given above. Next, as you will recall from the first section of this book, many poor countries are increasing their prosperity by developing their economies and industries. This means that their A affluence and T technology will increase, and at a much faster pace than in the developed countries. As a result, almost all of the increase in pollution and environmental harm will come from the developing countries, not from us rich fat cats.

The best way to minimize the ultimate amount of pollution is to help these countries restrain their population growth and manage their industries more efficiently. But that's not what's happening, and China is a good example. Over the past several years, China has had one of the fastest-growing economies in the world. Because it also has the largest deposits of coal in the world (most of it low-quality and highly polluting), it is building coal-fired electric generating stations at a rate equivalent to 1,000 megawatts a month to power its expansion.[12] At this rate, by the year 2020, China will account for about 20 percent of the world's carbon-dioxide output. Short of invading China and forcibly stopping it from polluting, our only hope is to offer it a more attractive alternative. This goes for the other developing countries as well.

We know the pollution produced by developing countries is going to expand rapidly as their population and levels of affluence increase. We must show them that they will get rich faster by being efficient than by building wasteful, polluting industries.

In 1991 a study was done for the World Resources Institute entitled "Energy for a Sustainable World," authored by Jose Goldemberg, Thomas B. Johannson, Amulya K. N. Reddy, and Robert H. Williams. In this study, the authors imagined what would happen if developing countries adopted the best technology likely to be commercially available by the year 2000. The authors concluded that these countries would be able to afford a standard of living comparable to Western Europe in the late 1970s while their energy demand would be only slightly higher than it was in 1993.[13]

185

Unfortunately, this is not the direction of the developed world's policies. Instead, the rich countries are using two methods: bribes and sermons. The sermons go something like: "You shouldn't be clear-cutting your rain forests. Don't you know how important they are to the welfare of the planet?" To which the answer comes back:

> If it is in the interest of the rich that we do not cut down our trees, then they must compensate us for the loss of income. Yet, instead, what has the North done? It launched a boycott of our timber, reasoning that if it does not buy, we will stop cutting our timber.
>
> In doing so, however, they ignore the hundreds of thousands of people whose lives depend on the timber industry. They ignore the loss of government revenue with which we subsidize and support our people, particularly the poor. In other words, they want to preserve Malaysia's forest at our expense but at no cost to them.[14]

So said the prime minister of Malaysia, an exemplar of many in the developing world who hold this view. And it's hard to fault them. If you had to choose between letting your people starve and your children die from lack of medical care, or harvesting trees that you own but that some self-righteous Western hypocrite tells you are important to the long-term welfare of the globe, which would you choose? They look at our standard of living and how we achieved it, and feel that they have the right to follow suit.

Which is where the bribes come in. Some OECD leaders, realizing that we have no moral position from which to preach to developing countries, offer them "foreign aid" to leave the rain forests uncut, or to leave coal deposits in the ground. Indeed, this seemed to be the leitmotif of the Rio Earth Summit of 1992: let the rich countries pay us if they don't want us to pollute this environment which they say is so fragile.

I don't think bribes will work in the long run. We can only lead by example, by improving our own record in the use of resources and eliminating our own waste and pollution. I believe that if we do this, we will be able to sell the technology to developing countries at a profit — for them, for us, and for the Earth.

So what suggestions do I have to offer?

A list of ecological priorities

First, anyone in business should accept that the environmental move-ment is not going to go away. It's been here for more than thirty years, and hoping that it will vanish is foolish. Environmentalism will continue to grow as a force in consumer relations and govern-ment, which means that smart management will try to keep their companies in the forefront of environmental concerns. Indeed, this can be a valuable competitive force: by staying ahead of regulations, then working with governments to shape them, you can put pres-sure on your competitors. But corporations should also take the time to think about what they're doing. In other words, if you're in busi-ness, you should research the facts (as opposed to opinions) as care-fully as the current state of science and knowledge allows, and take the course of action that is least wasteful. This step often costs very little and may pay enormous dividends.

If you're a consumer, you need to understand that consumers create more pollution and waste than corporations do, and that ulti-mately you will pay the costs incurred by both governments and corporations. So it's in your own best interest to ask yourself which alternatives are the least wasteful. Can you buy the same product without bubble packaging? Is there another use for the material you're about to throw away? If you add environmental concerns to the list of things you want when you shop for a new car or refriger-ator, can you find better choices?

But while becoming an informed and thoughtful consumer, beware of the crisis-of-the-day syndrome promoted by 30-second television coverage of environmental issues. As Professor Munn of the University of Toronto pointed out in a 1987 conference of cli-matologists, "The emergence of McLuhan's 'Global Village' has resulted in the phenomena of 'Trial by Television,' in which the opinions of millions of persons are shaped by inadequate and often incorrect reporting of environmental issues."[15]

Indeed, it's time we opened our eyes to some of the very real problems ahead of us. As best I can discern, based on the research and reading I've done in this field, the top seven ecological priorities are as follows:

1 Overpopulation

Human overpopulation is by far the most important ecological issue, for it is the source of all the other problems, as the *Scientific American* recently pointed out: "None of the preceding measures [to conserve energy or preserve the environment], nor all of them taken together, will be enough to save us from the folly of failing to stabilize world population. The growth of population aggravates every resource problem, every environmental problem, and most social and political problems."[16] Since I've dealt with this subject extensively in Chapter 7, I won't belabour the point here.

2 Transportation

Coupled with overpopulation is the global increase in the use of transportation, especially automobiles. The rate of increase in cars is significantly greater than the growth rate of population, and cars are probably the single most destructive technology we use.

However, improvements in the standard of living since the Industrial Revolution have been rooted in the heavy use of transportation. So environmental "solutions" that propose banning cars, for instance, won't work. People won't accept the decline in their standard of living that would go with such a measure. Which means that the only solution is to produce cars that cause less pollution and are more cost-effective. This makes California's experiment with so-called "zero pollution" cars[17] (due to start in 1997) all the more interesting and important.

3 Energy

Energy is central to most other ecological concerns. We use energy to do almost everything, but when we use it inefficiently it does enormous damage to our ecology.

Interestingly, the key to energy is not just the production of it. Equally important is storing it and having it available when and where we need it. This means we should be watching for improvements in battery and transmission technologies, and perhaps especially for the superconductor research discussed in the last chapter. In terms of generating power, renewable sources will be a small but growing factor in the near future. Windmills are now becoming efficient enough to compete with more conventional power sources for market share, and solar power cells, while not there yet, are approaching that level.

As I noted earlier, the problem with renewable resources is that the wind doesn't always blow, and the sun doesn't always shine. For this reason alone, wind and solar power are not likely to be a significant source of energy in the near future unless there are dramatic improvements in our ability to store and transmit power.

One of the best medium-term sources of energy may be burning hydrogen or using it in fuel cells. The "waste" produced when you burn hydrogen is water vapour, which does no harm at all.[18] But there are also problems to be overcome in using hydrogen. Although the gas itself is extremely light, it takes a lot of energy to produce and compress hydrogen gas, and you need heavy equipment to store it.

In the long run, it's possible that nuclear fusion will be our principal source of energy. In theory, fusion is extraordinarily cheap because it gives back more energy than it takes to produce. It creates no dangerous wastes, and a malfunction causes a fusion reaction to stop entirely, unlike nuclear fission generators. However, it is so difficult to start and sustain a fusion reaction that we are decades away from being able to do so on a commercial basis.[19]

Before we can successfully harness fusion, I believe we will get our power from solar satellites in space. In the meantime, however, most of our energy supplies will continue to come largely from traditional sources: fossil fuels, nuclear generation, and hydroelectric projects. Accordingly, it behooves us to learn how to use these sources with the greatest possible efficiency, producing the least possible harm.

4 Water

Since I have already discussed this at some length, let me just summarize my concerns. We are using too much water, we are using it wastefully, and we are destroying our water supplies through the casual pollution of aquifers. There will be hell to pay in the future unless we change our ways.

5 Waste and pollution

Our economies developed in a world where it didn't matter how much waste we produced, we simply dumped it. The world was so big and we were so few that it didn't matter. This is no longer the case, so we must change our behaviour.

I have a cartoon from the *Futurist* magazine that brilliantly illustrates current attitudes. It shows a factory whose chimneys are spouting smoke. There are two message balloons. One points to the factory and says "Our property." The other points to the smoke belching from the factory's chimney and says "Not our property."

Suppose that whoever created pollution was responsible for seeing that it was properly treated and dealt with, and bore the costs of doing so. For instance, every consumer product would bear two prices: the cost of buying the item, and the eventual cost of disposing of it, packaging and all. Suppose, further, that consumers had to pay both prices at the outset, instead of having the costs of disposal hidden in municipal taxes, as they are at present. I guarantee that if the cost of producing waste was obvious to all, competitive forces would reduce the amount of waste enormously. I dislike this idea if only because I have no faith that governments would implement it well.[20] But we do need some way of tying the cost of disposal to the person or company that produces the waste.

6 Wildlife conservation

We must stop killing off other forms of life. I'm not high on cuddling dolphins at the expense of more important issues, and I would choose the life of a lumberjack over that of a tree every time. But I do recognize one stark reality: humanity cannot survive on this planet without the other forms of life. Ours is a closed ecology, and we are only a very small part of it. Without the other parts, we would die.

Unfortunately, the spread of humanity has been like a plague for almost all other plants and animals — except possibly raccoons, rats, and mosquitoes. We destroy natural habitats. We pollute. We consume. We exterminate. And if we keep it up, we run the risk of exterminating ourselves.

7 Ignorance

Ignorance is perhaps the greatest danger of all. Scientists are our pathfinders, and for our own preservation we need to support their work. Moreover, money spent on scientific research, even in the most abstract areas, has been proven over and over again to produce long-term economic benefits. We are stumbling blind into areas that will affect our future and our survival — and scientists working in ecological issues are the ones working on finding flashlights.

Pollution equals waste equals lost profits

At the end of the day, even when I disagree with their reasoning, I wind up in essential agreement with commentator David Suzuki and climatologist Ted Munn. Whether global warming is a problem today or not, if humanity continues to dump carbon dioxide and other wastes into the Earth's ecology in steadily growing amounts, we will certainly create problems, both those we expect and others we haven't yet imagined.

One of the things Dr. Suzuki said in the article I cited earlier was that we can save billions of dollars while reducing greenhouse gases such as carbon dioxide, but that the benefits from the capital investment required to do so may come over a period of years. And one of the emerging principles in ecological management is called the "no regrets" policy, whereby things that we suspect should be done for long-term environmental reasons can be justified in other terms that make them worthwhile, regardless of whether our long-term fears turn out to be well founded or not.

In addition, I think we need to remember that, in the long run, reducing waste is in fact more profitable than polluting. In Chapter 4, I talked about how Toyota went to a lean-production system because it could not afford the wastage and high inventories of the North American car manufacturers. It was lean production that allowed the company to produce a higher-quality product at a lower price. How did Toyota do this? By dedication to a central organizing principle: that less waste was more profitable.

I believe that we are faced with a similar choice in environmental matters. We can have more efficient industries with higher profits by deciding that our central organizing principle is to get the most out of the resources we use, to reduce the resources we need, and to waste as little as possible — ideally, to waste nothing. *Business Week* noted this trend in 1991:

> In 1987, Du Pont changed its tack. Management had the company's existing quality teams add waste reduction to their agendas. Dramatic gains

followed: One plastics plant, by making modest changes in production and shipping procedures, saved 15 million pounds of plastic a year that now goes into products, not landfills. . . . And quality management can "become a road map to pollution prevention, which puts you ahead of regulations," says George D. Carpenter, director of environment, energy, and safety systems at Procter & Gamble Co.[21]

Or consider a national example given by a former foreign minister of Japan:

The composition of the energy supply is a major determinant of air pollution levels. Japan was able to reduce its dependence on oil to 55.6 percent — down from 77.6 percent. The country also managed to raise its use of natural gas to 9.8 percent from 1.6 percent and of nuclear power to 10.9 percent, up from 0.6 percent, during the period 1973–88. This shift away from petroleum has done much to help cut down on the amount of carbon dioxide spewed into the atmosphere.[22]

Gustave Speth of the World Resources Institute has commented that "if the efficiency in energy use current in Japan today could be matched in the US and around the world, total economic output could be doubled globally, and virtually doubled in the US, without increasing energy use."[23]

What would it do for your company's profits if you could produce the same output with half as much energy as you currently use — and with less resources? Conversely, what would it do to your market position if your competitors did these things and you didn't?

This is not a simple course of action, nor can it be done easily or quickly. But if we dedicate ourselves to it, it should be rewarding, not only in money but in satisfaction. We will all, quite literally, breathe easier.

THE FIFTH FORCE

Longer Lives

ELEVEN

How Much Is Enough?

The number of adults over 65 is expected to double by the year 2030, and the fastest-growing segment of the elderly is those over 85, nearly half of whom have Alzheimer's.

– *Economist,* "At the Races," April 14, 1992

Do you want to go on living? Silly question; of course you do. How long do you want to live? As long as you can, I imagine. But is it possible to live too long? Ah, that's a more subtle and difficult question, one that I'll come back to later in this chapter — and one that many of us may come back to later in our lives.

The life span of humans in the developed countries has exploded, doubling over the last two centuries. As mentioned in Chapter 6, since the beginning of this century our life expectancy has increased from about forty-five years to about seventy-six — which means that it has gone up by almost four months for every year since 1901. That's an incredible increase.

How did this happen? Most people would chalk it up to modern medicine, but that's only part of the story. A good case can be made that what we think of as medicine had relatively little to do with our present longevity. According to the Economist, "there is, surprisingly, little or no evidence that modern doctors, pills or surgery have improved people's overall state of health. The increase in Americans' average life span from 63 years in 1940 to 76 today has

195

been ascribed more to increased wealth, better sanitation, nutrition and housing, and the wide-spread introduction of the refrigerator than to modern medicine."[1]

Perhaps the single exception is the discovery of antibiotics in the late 1930s. Before the use of antibiotics, people routinely died of the many diseases that have plagued humanity throughout history: typhoid, dysentery, whooping cough, smallpox, cholera, and so on. Tuberculosis, which used to be called "consumption," was one of the biggest killers: more than 99.9 percent of the people who contracted it died.

Unfortunately, we have improperly used and overused antibiotics, for drug-resistant strains of some of these dreaded diseases have been emerging. Tuberculosis, for instance, is now reappearing in North America and Europe, and the new strains are resistant to the traditional antibiotics. As well, new epidemics have appeared, such as AIDS, which kills by destroying the body's ability to resist other diseases, thereby making a person easy prey to the first malady that happens along. Moreover, it's a virtual certainty that new diseases, as well as new drug-resistant strains of old diseases, will continue to emerge.

Despite this, the odds seem very high that life expectancy will continue to increase, perhaps at the rate of four months per year; perhaps even faster. We are on the verge of developments that are every bit as revolutionary as the discovery of antibiotics or the invention of refrigeration or the widespread use of good hygiene. But our longer lives will bring major new problems as well. So although longer life may be a blessing, it will be a mixed blessing unless we plan how it is to happen.

THE NEW TECHNOLOGIES OF LONGEVITY

Ironically, physicians will be largely left out of the picture in the new technologies of longevity: individualized nutrition, biomedical engineering, and genetic engineering. These fields are populated not primarily by physicians but by engineers and geneticists. Indeed, coupled with the advances in computers described earlier in the book, physicians may see their roles on centre stage changed and even partly usurped by other professionals. Let's consider these one at a time.

Individualized nutrition

Many of the developments in this area may well come about as a result of research into human genetics, but I've elected to treat the subject separately because not all developments in this area are due to genetic research. Strange as it may sound, we are becoming aware that what we eat and drink may have profound effects on our health. I say this is strange not because it is a hard concept to grasp, but because it is so obvious — and consequently it seems strange that more effort has not been devoted to it.

It seems to me that this new awareness about nutrition and food preparation may represent a major new industry waiting to be born, and the only question in my mind is whether the research and subsequent marketing will be done by the food companies or by someone else, such as the pharmaceutical manufacturers. Perhaps there will be an alliance between the two. You see, the food companies do relatively little research of this kind, so are not geared for it. But the pharmaceutical companies, which do mountains of research, do not have the manufacturing and distribution facilities to deal with the retail end of things. It is, as I say, an industry waiting to be born.

I'm personally quite aware of the importance that what we eat and drink can be vital to our health, because it is vital to my own. My mother tells me that one of my great-uncles died of a mysterious wasting disease. No matter what he ate, he continued to lose weight and eventually died of this inexplicable malady. Today, looking back on his tragic end, I would bet that he died of malnutrition because of vitamin deficiencies, calcium deficiency, blood iron anemia, and so on. You see, I suspect he was a celiac, and I make this guess because I'm a celiac and I know that celiac disease is genetically linked. But celiac disease was not discovered until after World War II, so my great-uncle's doctor and family had no possible way of knowing what was wrong with him.

A celiac cannot eat wheat, barley, rye, or oats, for they prevent him from absorbing the nutrition of the food he consumes. If he eats these grains, over an extended period of time (upwards of ten years or more) he will develop nutritional deficiencies, which can eventually cause death. As my great-uncle lived and worked on a farm, it is certain that his loving family urged him to eat lots of bread and other foods containing these grains — and it killed him. Today we know that all celiacs have to do is avoid eating wheat, barley, rye, and oats, and they'll be fine.

Since being diagnosed as a celiac, I've become aware of the large number of people with food allergies and medical intolerances, some of which are much more severe than mine. In fact, there seems to be an explosion of such allergies. There are two possible explanations for this: either our environment is becoming much more dangerous (which may be mildly true but is unlikely to be the cause of lots of new allergies) or we are just now developing the means of identifying them and becoming aware of their importance. I tend to favour the latter explanation, though both are probably contributing factors.

Nor does it stop with food. Recent studies have suggested that drinking highly chlorinated water can produce a subtle but pronounced shift in the way the bloodstream deals with cholesterol. These studies indicate that prolonged exposure to highly chlorinated water may shift the bloodstream away from transporting high-density lipoproteins ("good" cholesterol) to transporting low-density lipoproteins ("bad" cholesterol). Further, chlorine may actually destroy polyunsaturated fatty acids, which are essential to health.[2]

Moreover, some of the results of genetic research seem to indicate that certain foods will cause problems, such as triggering cancer, in specific individuals. As time goes on, we may reach the level of sophistication where each of us has a tailor-made diet to keep us healthy. And I suspect that as we learn more about both food and drink and about our individual genetic patterns, we may be able to lengthen our lives significantly — provided we stick to our diets.

Biomedical engineering

"Biomedical engineering," says Dr. Hans Kunov, a professor of this discipline at the University of Toronto, "is often confused with genetic engineering, but the two fields are very different."[3] Biomedical engineering works to produce man-made or engineered devices that deal, directly or indirectly, with the individual. In other words, they include devices such as hearing aids, eyeglasses, pacemakers, artificial hearts, and prosthetic arms and legs, as well as information and imaging systems. Among those that have recently emerged from biomedical engineering labs, or are about to do so, are the following:

Medical imaging technologies

These include computerized-axial-tomography (CAT) scans, positron-emission-tomography (PET) scans, and magnetic resonance imaging (MRI), all of which allow doctors to examine what's happening inside the body, especially within the body's soft tissues and organs. In future, as computer speed and capacity continue to improve, doctors may be able to watch real-time, full-colour, three-dimensional images of what's happening inside a patient, and surgeons will be able to use these images to guide them as they operate. This will be a significant improvement over the present situation, where surgeons have to rely on what they actually see with their eyes during an operation.

This imaging will also be able to supply the surgeon with additional information. For instance, the surgeon will be able to compare a patient's heart in its present condition with a similar image taken at an earlier date. As well, surgeons will be able to call up information from data banks (say, relating to the most recent developments in medicine and surgical techniques) and superimpose the information on the images of the patient's body.

Imaging will also allow for much more sophisticated "keyhole" surgery, where instead of slicing the patient open to reach an organ buried deep inside his body, the surgeon makes a small incision, then inserts a long rod with the appropriate surgical tools at the end, and guides it to the correct surgical site to perform the necessary procedures.

Robotic surgery

Robots in surgery sound both science-fictiony and kind of scary, but they are neither. Robotic devices could be something as simple as an artificial third hand that would enable a surgeon to hold or support something for extended periods without tiring, or they could be as sophisticated as robot micro-manipulators that perform surgery on very small tissue under the direction or immediate manipulation of the surgeon. In future, surgeons may don sensing gloves and have the micro-manipulators mimic their movements as they watch the results on an imaging device, such as those described above.

Robotic surgery might even include remote-controlled robots coupled with real-time, high-definition images that would allow a surgeon to perform surgery in one location while the patient was far away, perhaps even on the other side of the globe. A development such as this would allow medical skills to go mobile, so that doctors would be able to perform high-precision, specialized surgery in isolated communities in the Far North, in inner cities, and in war zones and disaster areas, simply by having mobile surgical equipment flown or driven to where it was needed. Another possibility is that, in emergency surgery, the ambulance dispatched to the patient's home might actually become an operating theatre for the surgeon, who would be based back at the hospital.

Expert diagnostic systems

I mentioned diagnosis in Chapter 8 when dealing with developments in computers. There will probably be resistance to computer-based diagnostic systems, since diagnosis is at the very heart of the role for which physicians have trained. Yet physicians are going to need help because information is exploding far faster than any flesh-and-blood practitioner can possibly cope with: "An average American doctor spends nine hours a week educating himself. And for most doctors, integrating data generated in each hospital on each patient and applying the knowledge gained from reading journals has become an art as much as a science. The information can often be conflicting and few doctors have any idea how to resolve such conflicts."[4]

Help might come in the form of reminders to the physician to check for certain indicators; it could be new information from recent publications on relevant issues; or it could be information from the patient's own record that correlates with other information (for example, an allergy that is triggered by a particular drug or anesthetic).

It's also possible that preliminary diagnoses and testing might be performed by nurses or paramedics in tandem with a computerized diagnostic system. These systems would likely be based on the knowledge and experience of the finest diagnosticians in their fields, thus making their knowledge available much more widely than would normally be possible. And these experts might well be paid a royalty for access to the information, much as rock stars are paid for the music they have recorded.

Then, too, if properly tailored versions of these systems were available to the general public, people might be able to initiate health care on themselves, perhaps buying prepackaged medical test kits from a local pharmacy, much as they do with present-day pregnancy tests. These systems would allow people to monitor the results of their treatment more frequently and on a more timely basis than a health-care practitioner could ever do, and they could answer questions that puzzled or worried the patient.

Of course, having diagnoses performed by people who are not physicians will undoubtedly be fought by physicians, on both medical and financial grounds. However, since physicians account for a significant percentage of the costs of the health-care system, I suspect that they would ultimately lose this battle.

Centralization and automation of health records
The centralization and automation of health records is bound to come, along with on-line access to them as needed. At present, the health-care system winds up duplicating patient information in many different places and often performing tests that have already been done (or need not be done) simply because not all the information is available from other locations. Moreover, practitioners — who are highly trained and highly paid specialists — are forced to spend a significant amount of time in clerical work that would be more suited to modestly paid workers — except that it has to be done correctly so that patients come to no harm. Automating the record keeping will remove much of this burden, particularly if the practitioners can dictate the results as they work, rather than having to take time out specifically to write up patient notes, fill in requisitions and prescriptions, and file the necessary forms for billing.

Early indications are that automated and centralized record keeping is very cost-effective indeed. Sweden, with a universal coverage system similar to our own, experienced a health-care crisis when the costs reached almost 12 percent of GNP. As part of its overhaul of the system, Sweden centralized its records. Since then, it has saved billions of dollars each year, though just how much relates to record keeping is not clear, since there were other reforms as well. But it is clear that the exercise was well worth the trouble.[5]

In a more controlled experiment in cost containment, the Regenstrief Institute at the University of Indiana performed a trial in which doctors used computers to order tests for hospital in-patients

201

and then received reminders about follow-up treatments. In 1993 the institute published the results of this test, and its figures suggest that there were savings of over $800 per patient, or about $3 million per year for the hospital.[6] Note that this was for only one step in speeding up information flows.

Of course, such databases of sensitive information are always open to potential abuse. If your computerized information record bècame available to insurance or pharmaceutical companies, or to potential employers, it could influence their judgments about how to treat you. Nevertheless, given the financial position of our health-care system, I believe that centralized, automated record keeping is almost inevitable.

Xenotransplantation

This two-dollar word means transplanting organs from one species of animal into another. However, in practice it means taking organs from animals that have an internal anatomy similar to our own and transplanting them into humans. Pigs and baboons may be the likeliest candidates (and you can read whatever you like into that).

It's well known that transplanting foreign tissue into the human body triggers a defensive reaction by the immune system, which will quickly reject it (probably killing the human patient in the process) unless powerful antirejection drugs are used.[7] Accordingly, researchers are looking at ways of either fooling the immune system into thinking that a pig's liver, for instance, belongs to the patient's body, or suppressing the immune reaction to prevent rejection. Both are being worked on, and there is a high probability that in future human hearts, livers, kidneys, and other vital but vulnerable organs will be replaced when needed by organs taken from animals.[8]

Mechanical assistance for those who need it

This might be prosthetic arms or legs for people who have lost a limb, or it could be some sort of mechanical assistance for the elderly which would allow them to cope with the challenges of living in their own homes in a state of reduced mobility and with lessened strength.

One of the greatest fears of the elderly is of falling and breaking a bone. They would be able to live in their own homes much longer if there were some device that could prevent them losing their balance and help them stay upright. Likewise, some means of monitoring their health and signalling for help in the event of an emergency would make them much more comfortable about living alone — as well as providing greater peace of mind for friends and relatives.

However, the real promise of biomedical technology will come if engineers ever succeed in crossing the human/machine boundary. "The human body is a robust machine," comments Dr. Kunov. "It is highly successful at preventing outside signals from interfering with the brain's control of the body. But, of course, that also means it's much more difficult for us to get in to correct problems directly. All we can do so far is tack on equipment to compensate."

As an illustration of what may eventually be possible, Dr. Kunov points to recent experiments in which researchers have grown retinal tissue from a human eye so that it attaches directly to nerve tissue. This would seem to imply that we might be able to feed impulses directly into the nervous system. For instance, we might be able to repair someone's hearing directly, rather than just increasing the volume of sound the ear receives, as present hearing aids do. This might be possible if we could create a retinal-tissue/nervous-tissue growth, implant it in the ear, then set up a small laser to stimulate the appropriate retinal tissue in response to particular sound frequencies.

The implications of this are remarkable: "If we can learn to speak the language of the neuron," says Dr. Kunov, "then we can deal directly with the body to effect repairs." But biomedical engineering faces obstacles that have nothing to do with neurons, for its products tend to be expensive. "More effective treatment will repay the capital investment required many times over," Kunov notes, "but unfortunately the health-care system doesn't get the financial credit for restoring a person to health and productivity. All that shows up in the ledger is higher health costs, even though society benefits from healthier people who require less subsequent medical treatment."

Genetic engineering

"We have learned more about the importance of gene defects in causing disease in the last ten years than in all previous human history." This statement comes from a man who knows: Dr. Ron Worton. He works at the Hospital for Sick Children in Toronto, and heads up Canada's contribution to the international Human Genome Project.[9] Nor is that all that Dr. Worton has to say:

"Developments in genetics are filtering through academia and into medical practice very slowly," he comments. "Most physicians have very little training in genetics, and so are resistant to having to learn an entirely new field to treat diseases they've seen all their careers. This is not terribly important today, because we don't have very many solutions to genetically linked diseases right now. But within five to ten years, it will be a very different situation. We could well see a crisis in the practice of medicine over new gene therapies being developed today."

The Human Genome Project — an international project coordinated by HUGO (Human Genome Organization), with principal offices in Bethesda, Maryland, for the Americas; London, England, for Europe; and Osaka, Japan, for the Pacific — is engaged in mapping out all the genes of the human species and trying to determine the function of the proteins encoded by the genes. This is not, as scientists say, a trivial exercise. There are an estimated 100,000 human genes, and each has 30,000 nucleotides whose sequence determines the function of the encoded protein. What this means is that the researchers working on the project are trying to map and understand a code that consists of 3 billion sequence elements (nucleotides).

Despite the size of the task, the researchers expect to complete it by 2010 — a mere sixteen years away. And what will be the prize? Well, it's becoming clear that many diseases and conditions that we have traditionally thought of as being due to external agents (such as germs) are in fact either caused by genetic defects or are triggered by genetic predispositions. Accordingly, if we are to find cures or treatments for cancer, heart disease, Alzheimer's disease, diabetes, and even obesity and baldness, we must start to use tools developed through genetic engineering.

In the near future, this may lead to success in dealing with diseases that result from single gene defects. For example, cystic fibrosis (CF) is caused by a defect in a specific protein, with the result that the lung membranes improperly regulate the passage of chlorine ions from epithelial cells. This means that insufficient amounts of water permeate the epithelial membranes (including that of the lungs) through osmosis. As a result, the mucus in the lungs gets very thick and sticky, interfering with the person's ability to breathe. Through genetic engineering, researchers have been able to use an adenovirus (one of the viruses that cause colds) to carry a gene with the corrected code to the epithelial cells in the lungs. Once there, it prompts the proper regulation of chloride ion transport. This starts the flow of water by osmosis and thus thins the mucus in the lungs. Without this rewritten and corrected gene, CF sufferers eventually die of suffocation. With it, they may be able to live normal, healthy lives.

Muscular dystrophy (MD), severe combined immunodeficiency disease ("the bubble boy" disease), and sickle-cell anemia are also caused by single gene defects, as are many other ailments — more than we ever suspected. New ones are constantly being found as the Human Genome Project plots its way through the code of life. But the big problem is how to introduce corrected genes into the body.

There are several difficulties to overcome. First, no one solution works for every problem because of the different mechanisms of different parts of the body. For instance, although viruses seem an ideal way to deliver tailored genes (because they are so good at invading the body's cells), they can have several side effects as well. One of these is the possibility that they will trigger other genetically linked diseases. One of the things we've learned from the Human Genome Project is that some diseases, such as certain kinds of cancer, result from a genetic predisposition. This means that someone who has this predisposition may get the cancer only if exposed to a specific set of environmental conditions. Accordingly, using a virus to perform gene therapy runs the risk of triggering some previously unsuspected concern from otherwise normal body cells. Hence, in curing one disease, we may cause another.

New drugs may be an alternative to viruses in gene therapy. For instance, it might be possible to take the corrected CF gene, surround it with a layer of lipid (fatlike molecules) that would protect the CF gene, and carry it to where it was needed. In this way, we would be able to correct the defect without exposing the patient to a virus. For some diseases, this might effect a cure, but in others it could require repeated treatment.

Another possibility might be to alter diseased cells genetically in order to attack them. This might be done by introducing tailored genes into cancerous cells, causing them to produce antigens. The appearance of antigens on the surface of such cells would stimulate the production of antibodies by the body's immune system, which would then attack and kill the cancerous cells. Or it might be possible to cause the cancerous cells — and only the cancerous cells — to absorb a specific poison, which the healthy cells would reject. The many possibilities for the treatment of single gene defects means that we can expect a rising stream of cures and treatments for previously intractable diseases.

Treating diseases caused by multiple gene defects will be more difficult. Instead of being caused by an error in a single gene, some diseases result from errors in several different genes, or from an incorrect interplay between genes. These diseases — which might include several types of cancer, diabetes, asthma, epilepsy, heart disease, Alzheimer's disease, schizophrenia, even obesity — will be much more difficult to track down and will be correspondingly difficult to treat and cure. We are, as yet, in the very early stages of research in this area.

Slowing the aging process

There are other implications in genetic engineering that are even more startling. Many of the effects of aging, for instance, may be the result of accumulated genetic defects. One hypothesis, developed by Dr. Silvia Bacchetti and her colleagues at McMaster University in Hamilton, Ontario, suggests that we may be able to slow or stop the process of aging — although at a cost.[10]

The vast majority of the body's cells, called "somatic" cells, regularly reproduce and replace themselves, and in the process they duplicate the chromosomes contained in each cell. Now, the chromosomes in all body cells end in what are known as "telomeres" (literally meaning "ending part," or "ending boundary"). Every time a somatic cell divides to replicate itself, it loses some of the telomeres. It has been suggested that when the chromosome gets too short, it may act as a signal to the cell not to divide — and the cell dies without being replaced. When enough somatic cells die, this may trigger many of the things we associate with aging: organs fail, tissues shrink, and the body generally does not function the way it should.

According to the hypothesis developed at McMaster, if we could prevent chromosomes from losing telomeres, we might be able to slow or stop the aging process. As it happens, the body's germ-line cells — those used to produce sperm and ova, and to pass on our genetic code to our children — do not suffer this loss of telomeres. It now seems as if this difference between somatic cells and germ-line cells may be due to an enzyme called "telomerase," which is inactive in somatic cells but is active in germ-line cells. The implication is that if telomerase could be activated in somatic cells, there might be no shortening of the telomeres, and the somatic cells would continue to reproduce — thus lengthening our lives.

However, there is a risk inherent in such treatment. As it happens, one of the unusual things about cancer cells is that they seem to have stable telomeres. By preventing somatic cells from losing telomeres, we might run the risk of tipping them over into acquiring some of the properties of cancerous cells. Clearly, this is all at a very early stage of research. But for the first time in human history, it is conceivable that we may be able to slow or stop the aging process.

Eliminating genetic defects before birth

Another area of rapid development is our ability to eliminate disease in children before they are born. It's much easier to develop tests to detect genetic defects than it is to find ways of fixing them. We can already test a zygote (fertilized egg) to determine whether it has certain kinds of genetic defects, and if it does, we can prevent it from coming to term (i.e., abort it). As we expand the range of genetically linked diseases that we can test for, we'll be able bring a steadily healthier human race into existence, and significantly extend human longevity by doing so.

By far the cheapest and medically easiest approach to doing this is to wait for a woman to get pregnant in the usual way, and then test the fetus for genetic defects. This kind of genetic screening is being done right now (using amniocentesis) for such conditions as Down Syndrome. It's also sometimes used to determine the fetus's sex.[11] Checking for other, more subtle genetic outcomes, then, would merely be an extension of existing practice. Of course, the ethical questions surrounding abortion for such purposes will remain controversial. In addition, the abortion of fetuses known to have genetic defects will raise new questions about the morality of testing for genetic purity.

There are, however, alternatives to abortion. Most of them involve in vitro fertilization, which means fertilizing an egg outside the mother's body, then implanting it back into the womb. In vitro fertilization is already possible, though it is both difficult and expensive.

Perhaps the least difficult ethically (though the most complex and expensive medically) would be to take a fertilized ovum, determine which genetic imperfections were present, and rewrite those genes before implanting the ovum in the womb. It's not possible to correct such defects in a zygote today, but it might well become possible early in the next century. However, if such techniques are developed, they will be horribly difficult and expensive, and accordingly will probably never be used.

A simpler and cheaper possibility would be to take several ova, fertilize them, then select the one with the fewest detectable defects, implant it using in vitro techniques, and bring it to term. This would still be difficult and expensive, but it will probably be done sometime in the next century, especially with parents known to be carriers of genetic defects. However, this approach retains the ethical problem of disposing of fertilized ova, which some people consider to be human beings.

As we become able to detect more and more genetic defects and genetic predispositions to disease, we open a range of thorny new questions that have no neat answers. For instance, it would be very helpful to know that you have a genetic predisposition to colonic cancer, because you could then be checked regularly in order to catch malignant polyps before the cancer established itself. But suppose your genes indicate that you're likely to get Alzheimer's disease in your sixties, thus losing your ability to function as an independent human being. Would you want to know that while you were in your thirties?

Advances in genetic engineering will produce many formidable moral, ethical, practical, and even economic problems. But we may also be able to eradicate genetically based diseases, thus greatly extending human longevity. And the combined effects of the biotech revolution mean that we can confidently predict that life expectancy in the developed countries will continue to expand. The Economist, in a special survey on medicine, has forecast that the average life span may stretch into the eighties by 2010, and to a hundred by 2050.

But is this automatically a good thing?

HOW DESIRABLE IS LONGER LIFE?

A hundred years ago, when life expectancy was forty years, the average Canadian was twenty-one years old. This meant that by the time you became an adult at the age of fifteen or sixteen, you had perhaps five to ten years before your parents died and left you in charge.

Today, by the time you reach the status of adulthood (say, at the age of twenty-one), you will have to wait, on average, twenty-five to thirty years before your parents die and you inherit. Indeed, there's an excellent chance that you may spend more years worrying about your aged parents than you do about your children before they are full-grown. This has profound implications on the shape and nature of society, on the economy, on work, and on our relations with one another.

The implications for work, the economy, and personal finances

First, consider the costs of living longer. Earlier, I noted that it costs at least seven times as much in health services for someone aged sixty-five than it costs for someone of fifteen. This is not unexpected, but throughout recorded history, before the modern era, only one person in ten lived to age sixty-five, whereas in North America today nearly 80 percent do. Therefore, as life expectancy continues to expand, the total medical needs of society will rise much faster than the size of the population.

As mentioned before, a substantially higher percentage of retired adults vote than young adults, and they tend to vote as a block. This means that increasingly those over sixty-five (who will constitute a steadily rising percentage of the total population) will skew the political system in favour of the aged, thereby robbing the young of their share of society's resources. Children and young parents will likely be the victims of an aging society, even though the aged have no desire to victimize them.

This will hurt on a personal level as well. If you retire at age sixty-five and have saved up enough money to support you until you are seventy-five but then find yourself living to well over eighty, you may be trapped in poverty. On the other hand, if you plan for a longer retirement, it will affect your standard of living when you're young. Suppose you are forty-five when you start saving for your retirement (though you really should start earlier). If you can achieve a 6 percent rate of return both before and after retirement, and if you want to have a pre-tax income of $40,000 a year when you retire, then you're going to have to save quite a lot during your working years. As Table 5 shows, you would have to save $4,469 more each year (which would mean that much less to spend) if you expected to live twenty years in retirement rather than ten.

TABLE 5 Savings Required Each Year from Age 45 to Retire with an Annual income of $40,000 at age 65

Number of years of expected retirement	Total amount you will need to save by age 65	Amount you will need to save each year before retiring
10	$294,403	$8,003
15	388,490	10,561
20	458,797	12,472
25	513,334	13,900

Likewise, if life expectancy continues to expand, companies that have planned their pension funds with the expectation that they will pay a pension for only ten years will find their pension liabilities shooting up. As noted earlier, the stage therefore seems set for an increase in the retirement age, perhaps to seventy years old or more. But do you really want to wait that long to retire? On the other hand, if older workers stay in the workforce, they will take up jobs and make life that much more difficult for the generations that follow them.

This all seems like a prescription for certain strife between generations — unless we plan for what we know is coming and work out some rules today. Moreover, we're going to witness prejudice and discrimination on the basis of age, in both directions. Already, older workers are looked on with suspicion, even though research shows this is unwarranted. While it's true that older people tend to work more slowly than younger people, they have fewer on-the-job accidents, and they tend to make fewer errors and better decisions, especially in situations where judgment and experience are important.[12]

In fact, the whole direction of society, business, and work is making it possible for people to remain productive for longer.

Muscles and physical stamina are no longer as important as they were, since more of our work is done at a desk or a work station. Rather than commuting to work, people may be able, or even encouraged, to work at home. And, of course, people are staying healthy and active longer than ever before.

Another factor is that people who are nearing or past retirement age represent a vast treasure store of knowledge, contacts, and experience. If their talents and abilities could be tapped on a continuing basis, in a manner that did not destroy the prospects of the young, it would be of enormous benefit to Canada and Canadians. Or, to put it another way, will our society be able to afford a large and increasing number of people who produce nothing?

Please note that I am not accusing the elderly of freeloading. No, my question is more abstract: How many consumers can be supported by each worker? From the discussion in Chapter 6, it is clear that this number is going to rise dramatically as the baby boom ages. What effect will this have on our economy? Will rising productivity cover the relative shortfall in workers? I don't know — but I suggest that we should be thinking about it.

Social implications

At the other end of the scale are young people, who are routinely and widely discriminated against today but accept it without question. To see this, suppose that wherever you went you found that, because of your skin colour, you had to pay more to get into the movies, had to pay a premium to buy food, and could only use certain counters at the bank. Suppose there were clubs that you were not allowed to join, special benefits you were not eligible to receive, and vacation trips that were only for people of the right race. Would that constitute discrimination?

Now substitute the word "age" for "skin colour" and "race" and you'll have an accurate picture of how discrimination is currently at work in our society. I suspect that much of our indulgence for this kind of discrimination is due to the fact that we expect to join the ranks of the elderly one day. Accordingly, we are prepared to extend special courtesies, partly out of respect, and partly out of an understanding that "there with the grace of God, will go I."

For many people, their worst nightmares might be summed up in an account taken from the *Toronto Star*.

> She's 82, and lives alone with her cat. She's legally blind and cannot walk. She has no relatives willing to look after her, no neighbours who stop by regularly. Most of her friends have died. She cannot watch television or read a magazine. Asked how she spends her days, she replies, "I cry a lot."
>
> . . . One day, the homemaker forgets to put the woman's supper in its regular spot in the refrigerator. The woman spends hours feeling around the inside of the fridge but cannot find the food.
>
> So she settles for what she can find — a few crackers and part of a chocolate bar.[13]

In earlier generations, family ties were strong because one generation depended on another. Today, we go through long periods of our lives — decades, in fact — when we are independent of our parents. As a result, our family ties are weakened, and consequently the prospect of being a lonely old man or lonely old woman is much greater than ever before.

Nor is this the only change and challenge. My mother's mother grew up in a world where people travelled by horse and buggy, yet she lived to marvel that a man had walked on the moon. My father's father had never flown in a plane until he got too old to live on his own and moved across the continent to live with my parents. He found it an odd and somewhat frightening experience. The shock of change and the pace of change are turning the elderly into strangers in a strange land.

We will experience similar or even more discomfiting things as we age. For our own self-interest, then, we need to re-evaluate how we treat each other and what it means to be old, for there is no age that defines greater or lesser humanity.

THE SIXTH FORCE

The Decline of the Nation-State

TWELVE

The Fate of Canada

In Canada we have one of the richest nations on earth, a country so uniquely blessed with space and opportunity that the world's poor are beating at the door to get in, and it is tearing itself apart. . . . If one of the top developed nations on earth can't make a federal, multi-ethnic state work, who else can?

– Author Michael Ignatieff, English-born son of a Canadian diplomat

How are the following events related? Yugoslavia breaks into tiny pieces, and the pieces go to war with each other. Canada, Mexico, and the United States sign a North American Free Trade Agreement, which will inevitably draw them closer together. The former Soviet Union breaks up into groups of countries, big and small. Quebec separatists seem stronger and more dedicated than ever to the idea of pulling Quebec out of the Canadian confederation. Scottish and Welsh nationalists want to take Scotland and Wales out of the United Kingdom. And the old established nations of Europe are working together to form the European Community, which will have many of the trappings of a central government for most of Europe.

It took me a long while to find a pattern. On one hand, it seemed that countries were flying apart, but on the other hand, the conglomerations of nations, especially the European union, seemed to indicate that something different was going on, that countries should become bigger, not smaller. It didn't make sense — until I realized that both were indications of the same force at work: the declining importance of the nation-state.

The concept of the nation-state was conceived in 1576 by the French lawyer-politician Jean Boudin (1530–96) in his Six livres de la république. It came to life with the implementation of the American constitution and the outbreak of the French Revolution, both of which occurred in 1789. Before then, there were kingdoms, city-states, and principalities, but no aggregates of citizens under the direction of a single government.

We have a hard time seeing this because we think of nations as the natural political structure in which people are organized. Yet historically there is nothing natural, automatic, or God-given about the existence of nation-states, and it may be that we are experiencing the beginning of the end of this artifice. Certainly it seems to me that we are witnessing its decline, though not its demise. Peter Drucker noted this change when he wrote: "Beginning perhaps in the 1970s, the nation-state has begun to come apart. It has already been out-flanked in crucial areas where 'sovereignty' has lost all meaning."[1] Similarly, Daniel Bell, Henry Ford Professor of Social Sciences at Harvard University, stated: "The nation-state is becoming too small for the big things, and too big for the small things."[2]

But why is this happening? And why is it happening now?

WHY THE NATION-STATE IS IN DECLINE

Originally, nation-states had two primary reasons for existence: national security and the managing of international trade. National security includes not only defence from external attack but also internal security, which means such things as the policing of public safety, and a citizen's assurance of being treated with justice and equity. Over the years, especially since the two world wars, governments have taken over many other areas of life. For now, though, let's stick with the two principal functions of the nation-state and look at the factors that are eating away at them.

The end of the Cold War

The years since the end of World War II have turned out to be a time of relative tranquillity. While the Soviet Union and the United States

216

were locked in confrontation, the other nations of the world (with many localized exceptions) remained essentially at peace. But it was a period of great polarity: communism versus capitalism; the dictatorship of the proletariat versus democracy; bad versus good; us against them. In a world faced with the prospect of a war that might truly end all wars and perhaps most human life as well, nations huddled together in one camp or the other, sheltering under either the red skirts of the communist camp or the red-white-and-blue skirts of America and its allies. Each country's need for national security pushed it into a defensive posture mandated by a major external threat.

With the collapse of the "evil empire" and the apparent end of the Cold War, the confrontation — and the stability — of the past has disappeared. As the appearance of a massive external threat has declined, so has the perceived importance of that component of national security. Ironically, today's world is less stable than the world of the Cold War. Today's threats are viewed as requiring a good global police force rather than major military alliances. As a result, the countries allied with the two former adversaries feel less need to band together, pooling their resources and strengths to be secure against a massive external foe.

Personally, I'm not convinced that the world is now safe for democracy. First, there is no certainty that Russia will remain stable and friendly. It is experiencing enormous economic strain, brought on by the collapse of the hopelessly uncompetitive economy that was built up under communist rule. Accordingly, it's possible that the Russians could follow a charismatic dictator in an effort to return to the "good old days" of imperialism and military adventurism. They might say to one another, "At least under the communists we had bread to eat and places to sleep." So although it may not be probable, I believe it is possible that the confrontation between the United States and Russia could return in a somewhat changed guise. Therefore, it's important to watch the shape and nature of Russia's leadership.

Next, there is a growing danger either that there will be a regional nuclear war or that terrorist attacks on cities in the developed world will use nuclear, chemical, or biological weapons. The technologies for manufacturing these weapons are spreading around the globe like an evil virus. In some cases, the capabilities are being developed by countries that are unstable or are headed by odious leaders with enormous egos and dreams of conquest.

We must therefore keep a watchful eye on the development of weapons of mass destruction by countries like North Korea, as well as on the determination with which the community of nations opposes such renegades. It is quite conceivable that if North Korea and others were allowed to do so, they might wind up both developing and selling these weapons to other renegades, such as Iraq or the Irish Republican Army.

Next is the perception that what the world needs now is a good "globocop" and that this role should be handled by the United Nations. I'm not sure this assumption is justified. In the first place, there are no clear rules indicating when the United Nations should intervene. Accordingly, intervention seems to come when a problem either catches the attention and whim of the Western media (as in Somalia) or when it is near and dear to the hearts of the white, rich countries of the West (as in Bosnia). Meanwhile, conflicts that are not captured on television or are far from the white-skinned voters of the affluent West (as in Sri Lanka, Liberia, and Ethiopia) are largely ignored, regardless of the number of people who are killed or the needs of the populace. This is producing a perception that the United Nations, and especially the Security Council, is a tool of the rich for the rich — never a good image for a police force.

Furthermore, the United Nations has no military and therefore has to rely on the generosity of those of its members, such as Canada, that have shown a persistent humanitarian willingness to serve. But in an age where the military is being de-emphasized for financial and economic reasons, peacekeepers are going to be progressively harder to find.

Finally, the United Nations is a bureaucracy built on the bureaucracies of its member governments. Its operations are politicized as well as being bungling, sluggish, inefficient, and at times incredibly stupid. As a result, its peacekeepers are often ordered to do impossible things, are not given enough troops or equipment to do the job, are exposed to needless danger, and are then hung out to dry by the memo-writing, bottom-covering, cookie-pushing diplomats in New York. It is a tribute to the military units of all peacekeeping nations that they do as well as they do.

218

Nevertheless, it is clear that, despite these things, the average citizen believes that there's far less need for a powerful national government to guarantee safety from external threats today than there was during the Cold War.

Economic might is replacing military might

At the end of World War II, Japan was forbidden by its American masters to have a military. At the time, it looked as if Japan was being hobbled, forced into a position of dependency on the military might of the United States. In retrospect, we can see that Japan turned this apparent weakness to its advantage, for it meant that the Americans took over the protection of Japan from external enemies — and paid for the privilege of doing so — leaving Japan free to devote its resources to building its economic strength.

Since Japan's economy had been so decimated by the war, this seemed at first to be an unimportant wrinkle in its rebuilding program. But in the 1970s and 1980s it became clear that the United States was competing at a disadvantage because it had devoted such a big chunk of its GNP to defence. Far too many of America's brightest brains and too much of its R & D spending went into building better tanks, rockets, and bombs. In contrast, virtually all of Japan's brightest engineers and all of its R & D monies went into producing superior cars, televisions, VCRs, and other consumer goods. During the Cold War the Americans couldn't do much about this. Now that the Cold War is deemed to be over, the United States, along with every other developed country, is trying to rethink and reduce its military spending in order to free up resources for economic competition.

This trend seems likely to continue. Even regional disagreements, such as the historic enmity between Argentina and Brazil, or between France, England, and Germany, are being submerged by the recognition that military competition is being replaced by economic competition. Here's what Richard Rosecrance, associate director of the University of California at Los Angeles's Center for International Relations has to say about this:

> From a "balance of power" [i.e., military] standpoint, it is very difficult to understand what is now happening in Europe. The integrating and enlarging Europe is becoming an ever stronger force. On typical historical precedents, one might expect the fringe countries to form an alliance against this strong central group.

219

> Instead, the fringe nations including Eastern Europe, nations of the former Soviet Union, Turkey, Morocco and others are trying their best to win an association if not direct admission to the councils of the European Community.
>
> The result is that one of the main features of the post-1989 world is that typical balance of power effects are absent. Instead, a central coalition, centering on the European Community, but drawing in the U.S. and Japan as well, is in process of formation. For economic reasons, this group is highly interdependent. Violating all historical precedents, nations of the former USSR, rather than seeking to balance *against* this strong central coalition, are rather trying to join it. It seems impossible in these circumstances to imagine, say, that China and India would form an opposing bloc to balance against the central group. They, too, in time, will be drawn into association with it.[3]

This development further reduces the importance of a strong national government and at the same time focuses attention on the rules of trade.

Defining the rules of trade

There is a recognition that trade is too important to leave to the whims of narrowly focused, jingoistic domestic politics. Governments have tacitly acknowledged that if they were to adopt the protectionist trade policies urged on them by special interest groups, this would lead to a repeat of the disastrous trade wars of the 1930s. Accordingly, national governments around the world have given up ever greater amounts of sovereignty to international trade organizations and treaties, often in defiance of domestic pressure groups.

This isn't invariably the case. France almost wrecked the Uruguay Round of the General Agreement on Tariffs and Trade (GATT) in its efforts to appease its fat and greedy farmers. Canada seems to have traded away the interests of millions of consumers in order to retain a supply management scheme that favours a few thousand egg, dairy, and poultry producers, most of whom are in politically sensitive Quebec. And the United States government apparently agreed to persecute Canadian durum wheat exporters (knowing that its position was indefensible under the rules of the GATT treaties) in order to buy the support of certain members of Congress for the NAFTA treaty. Nevertheless, in the main, national governments have recognized that world trade must work to an agreed-upon set of rules that supersede and at times violate national sovereignty.

Global competitiveness: the great leveller

Earlier in this book I talked about the emergence of a global economy and the need to be competitive internationally. Governments are now recognizing that they have an important part to play in aiding the competitiveness of the companies within their borders. If, for example, a country raises its tax rates too high, it encourages its brightest citizens and its major corporate employers to leave. If its environmental or employment regulations are too tough and too far in advance of the country's major economic competitors, it will scare away the companies that form its economic base.

This means that the countries that are going to remain competitive will find that their tax rates and their laws and regulations gradually approach the same level of cost and effect as those of their competitors, whether they like it or not. And, of course, this means that much of the creation of social policy is being taken out of the hands of national governments. Because of this, such things as protection for workers and environmental standards seem destined to seek a global common denominator.

In rough terms, there is no immediate relief from this reality, as the alternatives are even less palatable. To persist in policies inconsistent with our existing and emerging competitors would cause Canada's industrial infrastructure to evaporate over time. This would make it impossible for us to help those Canadians who need it, because we would be too poor to do so. The alternative is for the developed countries to force our standards on the underdeveloped and developing nations of the world. We could, in theory, keep our minimum wage high by forcing developing countries to adopt the same high level of minimum wage. This would nullify the advantage of their low-wage labour and would allow us to preserve our high standard of living. Indeed, this is precisely what some developed countries, led by the United States, are trying to do.

This initiative will fail, however, for the developing countries see very clearly that it is an attempt by the rich countries to keep them poor. They know that they must start with low wages before they can afford high wages if they are to gain market share internationally and build up their infrastructure at home. There is no way — short of massive bribery by the developed nations (which would be self-defeating)

221

or military conquest — that the developing nations will willingly accept a plan that keeps them in poverty. As a result, in the far distant future we can expect to see a world that has more or less uniform incomes, work standards, environmental rules, fiscal policies, and, in general terms, government policies. The trick will be getting to that world, and this will be both painful and difficult.

Countries will be able to choose local policies that are different from those of their competitors, as long as the costs work out much the same. For instance, Canada could keep its government-run health-care system with higher taxes, while the United States kept its privately organized (or disorganized) system with lower taxes, because both countries would wind up with much the same price for the different results they had chosen.

But the overall image remains: in the long run, each nation's government policies will be dictated by a kind of democracy among nations, with the most popular policies being enforced by competitive pressures. And this, of course, further reduces each nation's freedom to act and hence diminishes the importance of national governments.

The global capital markets

In the spring of 1994, Canadian interest rates shot up almost two full percentage points without any economic need or justification, and at a time when the economy was just starting to pick up some momentum. More, this happened under the watchful eyes of a new, supposedly more sensitive governor of the Bank of Canada and under a new Liberal government that had been highly critical of the Tories for forcing interest rates up during a time of recession. But although it was against government policy, the Government of Canada had no option but to force up the level of interest rates. The alternative would have been to see the Canadian dollar come under increasing attack by foreign-currency traders, which would have forced up the level of inflation and done even greater damage to the economy.

Time and again it has been demonstrated that there is no national government — indeed, there is no group of national governments — that can stand against the international financial markets. In Chapter 3, I described what happened to New Zealand when the bond markets stopped buying its government's bonds. All governments are now ultimately accountable to the bond and currency markets. If they lose the confidence of the cynical, opportunistic, fickle, and crassly commercial traders who buy and sell bonds and currencies, then governments can fall, and nations and peoples can be blighted financially.

These traders are beyond governing, for all they need are telephones and access to information, and they can get these anywhere in the world. If Canada were, for instance, foolish enough to try to regulate the actions of these individuals in order to gain a measure of control over the capital markets, the traders would simply pack up shop, move to another country, and the game would continue beyond our reach.

However, bond and currency traders have an exploitable weakness as well: they will buy anything if they think it will make them money. They have no allegiance but profit. And what they think will make them money is predictable, so far as government bonds and currencies are concerned. What they want is a country where the currency is hard (in other words, where inflation is low or nonexistent), where the productivity of the people is high and steadily rising, where government policy regulation is predictable and welcoming to foreign investors, and where governments have their financial affairs in order and thus borrow a little but not a lot. Such countries have the greatest leeway in forming national policy.

Accordingly, true Canadian nationalists should be picketing Ottawa and the provincial capitals for fiscal and financial self-discipline, for it is only by such probity that our governments can rule in Canada without having their policy hands trumped by the international financial markets. Governments that do not get their financial and economic affairs in order are surrendering their financial sovereignty to the international markets, much as drug addicts surrender their independence to their pushers.

Environmental concerns

Pollution doesn't recognize national boundaries — and, increasingly, neither do environmentalists. This is perfectly illustrated by the efforts of environmentalists in Europe to influence the forestry policies of the Government of British Columbia. I think it's pretty safe to say that environmental concerns will continue to span borders and thus will continue to interfere with a government's untrammelled ability to formulate its own policies.

In the past, when the topic of sovereignty came up, people from other countries often backed away, saying that while it was a shame that the Brazilians were clear-cutting the Amazon, it was their business, and there was nothing we could do about it. Now, people are starting to say to hell with sovereignty — let's save the trees, let's save the seals, let's save the Earth before it's too late.

But the consequences go far beyond trees or seals or pollution, as we will see.

Information technology and the media

Richard Nixon was brought down by an act that was, relatively speaking, a peccadillo in the sometimes tawdry history of American politics. However, the images of him trying to twist and squirm his way off the hook ("I am not a crook") were enough to defeat him. He himself had said earlier in his career that political power was based on blue smoke and mirrors. The television cameras dispelled the blue smoke and showed the mirrors for what they were, and Nixon was revealed as a petty man in a powerful post.

When Mikhail Gorbachev was imprisoned in his dacha and a junta announced that it had taken control of the Soviet Union, the junta was unable to make its coup stick because it didn't control the flow of information. Fax machines, telephones, photocopiers, and television revealed the junta's lies and the depth of the opposition to its actions, and did more to defeat it than guns or troops.

When the Chinese government sought to crush dissidents in Tiananmen Square, it brought in tanks and troops. The dissidents brought in Western television correspondents with their cameras, then defended the correspondents with their own lives. They knew what Mao Tse-tung might have learned had he lived: today, power grows out of the barrel of a television camera.

The Americans learned the same lesson in Vietnam, where they won most of their military battles but lost the public relations war. Accordingly, in their subsequent invasions of Grenada and Iraq, they made sure that they controlled where the barrel of the camera was pointed.

All these are examples of how the media and information technology are leaching away the power of national governments. Governments now stand trial in the court of international opinion as portrayed in the media, and leaders ignore this fact at their peril. Hence, atrocities committed in Bosnia and displayed on television may cause foreign bombs to rain down on the perpetrators, even though the killing in Bosnia amounts to a civil war. In another day and age, foreign governments would have kept out of the fray. Today, sovereignty is less of a consideration than the news on CNN.

Local and regional governments and bureaucracies

The additional powers that governments have assumed during this century — prompted particularly by the Great Depression of the 1930s plus the two world wars — have brought a proliferation in the machinery of government. The bureaucracies of the developed countries have now reached the stage where they actually constrain the abilities of the government. Changing the bureaucracy is often perceived to be the biggest obstacle to changing policy, as is so pointedly portrayed in the British television series "Yes, Minister." Civil servants, in many cases, believe that it is up to them to provide the stability that the here-today-gone-tomorrow politicians cannot; and the public now believes that the bureaucracies are there to serve themselves, not the public. Indeed, there are many real-life examples that support the underlying truth of the British television comedy.

Moreover, political power has been divided and subdivided, and then subdivided again, with bureaucracies flourishing at each level, so that changing policy often involves more than one level of government and more than one set of bureaucrats. Where I live, in downtown Toronto, I am subject to the Government of Canada, the Government of Ontario, the Metro Toronto regional government, the City of Toronto, the Metro Toronto School Board, and the City of Toronto School Board. In all, this makes six levels of government to which I pay taxes, and it means six layers of bureaucrats who exist, presumably, to serve my needs.[4]

As with the larger, global forces at work, the net result is a gradual seeping away of power from the nation-state of Canada. This is part of what Daniel Bell meant when he said that nation-states are too big for the small things. Regional and local governments have taken charge of the small things, the day-to-day issues that are of most immediate importance to the individual and are within the individual's ability to influence. For example, a national "war against drugs" has less effect on drug use than the policies of cities and police; and a "war against poverty" is best implemented at the local level and based on the needs of the region.

I suggest that most people can reach their city councillors, and thus influence local politics, far more easily than they can affect policies that come out of Ottawa. This has been clearly illustrated by the frustration many Ontario voters feel with the members of the Liberal caucus in Ottawa. Ontario Liberals form the largest group within the Liberal caucus, yet they seem powerless to sway government policy on their constituents' behalf.

It has been a long time since I heard anyone say, "Boy I really feel that the federal government is representing my interests. I'm glad it's there." I believe that most Canadians — and likewise most Americans, English, French, and so on — feel distant from the events that happen in their national capitals. And because people are feeling powerless to influence their national governments, they no longer identify with them.

Politicians

The modern nation-state has seen the emergence of a class of politicians — usually trained in law — who view politics as a career and act accordingly. The priorities of such politicians are to look good for the cameras, to make sure that they always have a good 30-second sound bite ready for the reporters, and to take those actions that will please the party leaders and party faithful. Serving the needs of the people who elected them as their representatives is often regarded as a necessary evil, falling under the heading of "constituency work."

Moreover, politicians seem to feel that they need to do something — after all, that's why they were elected — even when the best course of action may be to do nothing. Their actions often have nothing to do with the best interests of the nation. As the *Economist* put it, "The degree to which most modern politicians are out of touch with the reality of most people's working lives is almost frightening. . . . The career politician's natural ambition also causes him to operate on a timescale and to respond to incentives that probably have nothing to do with his country's actual well-being. National problems are mainly long-term; politicians are trained to think short. . . . Rejoicing in constant change themselves, they thoughtlessly impose the often enormous costs of change on others."[5]

If people feel that government is irrelevant or that their elected officials are insensitive to their needs or interests, they will ignore governments and politics, and turn their attention and allegiances elsewhere.

Allegiance to groups and group rights

The powerlessness that individuals feel regarding their national governments, and their frustration with governments generally, is causing people to pledge allegiance to special interest groups. They feel that by joining with others who have similar interests, they will have a better chance of influencing events and gaining the outcomes that they want. This is producing a trend towards group rights as opposed to individual rights. A perfect example is the passage of an amendment to the Canadian constitution on February 1, 1993, which entrenched the rights of certain English- and French-language communities in New Brunswick.

But while it might be a worthy thing to protect the rights of minorities, this trend is causing chunks of governmental authority to be taken away from governments and given to groups. The end result is a splintering of the national character and identity, and a lessening of the nation as a whole. At its extreme, it results in groups fighting and killing one another for the biggest share of the pie, as the conflict between the Bosnian Serbs, Croats, and Muslims shows.

It happens in more peaceful ways too, as when women's rights groups fight with right-to-life groups, only to be criticized by Real Women, whose arguments are in turn attacked by lesbian women.[6] Or when status Indians seek to eject non-status Indians from reservation lands in order to maintain the purity of their bloodlines and their land claims. (This is ethnic cleansing by another name, but don't get caught saying so.)

Theodore Roosevelt noted this trend in the United States, and his worries were echoed by the noted American historian, Arthur Schlesinger: "'The one absolute certain way of bringing this nation to ruin, of preventing all possibility of its continuing to be a nation at all,' said Theodore Roosevelt, 'would be to permit it to become a tangle of squabbling nationalities, an intricate knot of German-Americans,

Irish-Americans, Scandinavian-Americans, or Italian-Americans, each preserving its separate nationality.' Three-quarters of a century later, we must only add a few more nationalities to T.R.'s brew. This only strengthens his point."[7]

But, of course, no one has any interest in the thoughts of either a dead white male or a live one, especially as both are obviously American imperialists. I'll have more to say on this in Chapter 13.

WHY DOES THE DECLINE OF THE NATION-STATE MATTER?

The successor to nationalism may not be internationalism, despite the example of the European Community. It may, instead, be tribalism, in which petty and narrow interests replace enlightened self-interest, and the needs of the whole are brushed aside in a fight to secure the rights and privileges of the few. A world without coherent large groupings of people who are dedicated to mutual support and defence is a dangerous world — one in which terrorists will have freer rein to wreak havoc and in which more groups will feel isolated, disenfranchised, and persecuted, thus producing more terrorists. Much of the blame for this comes from the basic motivation for forming a separate state — the desire for uniformity, the belief that ethnic, religious, or linguistic sameness should be the binding force in a nation. The word "balkanize" means "to break up into smaller and often hostile units." One need only look at the current state of the Balkan peninsula to realize the dangers this can bring.

In matters of trade, there's only one rule: might makes right. The large trading blocs and the multinational trade agreements have come about only because no one country can dominate the world and dictate the terms of trade. If the United States, for instance, could dictate the terms of trade, it would. You only have to see the way it regularly tries to bully its trading partners to know that if they were left to the tender mercies of U.S. pressure groups and lobbyists, American legislators would quickly seek to exploit other countries to suit the preferences of their voters. But the United States realizes two things. First, Americans are better off trading with prosperous countries that have prosperous markets into which they can sell American goods, which means that the U. S. must allow its partners to sell as well as buy. Second, it is not strong enough to defy everyone else. It is for these reasons that there are free trade agreements. They do not arise out of bonhomie and goodwill; they spring from reluctant self-interest.

Nevertheless, it is as well to remember that trade is a game in which the rule is that might makes right. Consequently, countries that can maintain their prestige and status will have a distinct advantage and will be in a stronger position to bargain. No one would argue, for example, that Belgium or Liechtenstein would have more clout on their own than they would by working through the European Community.

The logical extension of current free trade trends is a global trading community with no restrictions and with a single currency, free movement of labour to wherever the jobs are, and labour laws and environmental regulations that are more or less comparable from jurisdiction to jurisdiction. When, in the distant future, these things happen and a true globocop emerges, your nationality will make about as much difference as your postal code. But we are a long way from this. Accordingly, nation-states, weakened though they are, will have to serve us for a while longer. We are not yet citizens of the world.

In the meantime, wherever there is a minority that is geographically concentrated and believes it has a current or historical grievance, the declining power of the nation-state will tempt wannabe nationalists to break away and form their own nation-states.[8] Which brings us to Quebec.

Will Quebec separate?

Born as I was in a foreign country and having become a Canadian citizen of my own free will, I have no emotional baggage to drag with me from Canada's past. None of my forebears fought on the Plains of Abraham. It's clear to me that injustices were perpetrated on French Canadians in the past, just as it's clear to me that the present culture of francophone Quebec is far more vibrant than the culture of anglophone Canada. Accepting Quebec as a "distinct society" is no more than an acknowledgment of current reality.

It is also clear that Pierre Trudeau and Brian Mulroney, in the egoistical pursuit of personal glory, each committed acts of enormous hubris when they attempted to repatriate the Canadian constitution. Regardless of the merits or defects of the Meech Lake Accord and the Charlottetown Accord, the rejection of these agreements was seen by francophone Quebeckers as a slap in the face and a rejection of Quebec's legitimate claims for recognition within the Canadian confederation. I greatly fear that Trudeau and Mulroney, along with Clyde Wells of Newfoundland, Gary Filmon and Elijah Harper of Manitoba, and the others who acted out of narrow, parochial interests in blocking one or both of these accords, may come to be remembered as the people who triggered the avalanche that destroyed Canada.

As for the Quebec separatists, I can see how the declining influence of the Canadian nation-state makes the prospect of an independent Quebec seem more tempting and more likely than ever before. But I believe they have minimized or overlooked several significant dangers, both for Quebec, and for the rest of Canada (ROC).

The first of these is in matters of trade. I dealt with these in Chapter 3 when I called Quebec separatists destructive fools, so I won't repeat those thoughts here. Next, the same forces that are bringing about the decline of the Canadian nation-state would work just as strongly upon an independent Quebec. Indeed, they might have a greater effect. There are several reasons for this.

First, I believe that a separate Quebec would go through a long period of very painful and expensive adjustment, which would produce a much lower standard of living for the average Quebecker. Far from being the amicable divorce that Lucien Bouchard and Jacques Parizeau say they want with the rest of Canada, I suspect that the ROC would recoil at Quebec's rejection and would become hostile to Quebeckers. This might well result in higher trade barriers than at present and a decline in trade that would hurt both sides, notably Ontario and New Brunswick in the ROC.

In addition, the uncertainty of the situation would likely scare away global investors, as described in Chapter 3. The economic and financial crises that would result would increase social friction and prompt lobby groups to push for special treatment in both Quebec and the ROC. Lean economic times are times when discontent rises easily to the surface. In a separation-inspired recession, all conflicts would be exacerbated.

Then there is the question of the rights of the aboriginal peoples and anglophones in Quebec. Would they all be willing to accept a Quebec state as their homeland and quietly surrender their Canadian nationality? I doubt it. And if the ROC, plus the Crees and Inuit living in Quebec, were hostile to a separate Quebec, what would happen with Ungava, the northern portion of present-day Quebec? Ungava did and may still belong to the Cree and Inuit, depending on the outcome of land-claim negotiations and various court cases. The land was a federal responsibility whose administration was handed to Quebec in 1912. However, this was not a gift, and many in both the ROC and among the Cree and Inuit would argue that Ungava could not go with Quebec. This would undoubtedly be hotly disputed by a Quebec national government, especially as Ungava is the site of Hydro-Québec's James Bay and Great White Whale hydroelectric projects, in which the provincial utility has invested tens of billions of dollars.

All told, there would be many reasons for conflict between the several parties, regardless of who was technically correct. I suspect that these conflicts would produce occasional violence. How extensive that violence would be, I do not know, but to my mind the greatest danger would be of starting the kind of vicious "martyr-begets-martyr" cycle that exists in Northern Ireland and Bosnia.

I suspect that Quebec separatists have vastly underestimated the costs and problems of separation, and may live to rue their folly. I also believe that even though Quebec separation is only a possibility and is not necessarily the most probable outcome, the rest of Canada is significantly underestimating the determination, skill, and clarity of purpose of Quebec separatists, as well as down-playing the potential costs of separation.

It is a dangerous situation, and the danger is compounded by the failure of all concerned to face the facts. It is cold comfort to know that what happens here, good or bad, will be a textbook case study of the decline of the nation-state. Perhaps, if divided we fall, other countries will learn from our mistakes.

Then again, perhaps not. After all, how much have we learned from Yugoslavia?

THE SEVENTH FORCE

The Shattering of Society
and the Isolation of the Individual

T H I R T E E N

Alone

Teenagers who attend religious services are considerably more likely than teens who never attend services to place a high value on such traits as honesty, forgiveness, concern for others, politeness and generosity. . . . The decline of organized religion in the last half of this century is nothing less than tragic, if equally effective new players that foster civility and address spirituality fail to appear. To date, their arrival is in question.

– Dr. Reginald Bibby, "Who Will Teach Our Children Shared Values?" 1994[1]

"It's a small world, isn't it?" No, actually, it's not. It's a huge world, and one that is getting bigger, at least insofar as the amount of influence individuals can have on the societies in which they live. Each of us represents an ever-diminishing part of an ever-growing whole of humanity, so that our voice among the millions or billions in the world gets lost very quickly and leaves us feeling powerless.

Meanwhile, television, telephones, satellites, and jet planes convince us that the entire world is just around the corner. We find ourselves believing that everyone is our neighbour and that the people in Asia or Bosnia are as important to us as the people in Montreal or those at the other end of the city, or even next door. This makes it even harder to understand why things never seem to go the way we think they should. Why don't our elected representatives seem to look out for our interests? Why doesn't the United Nations do

235

what's right? Can't they see what's so obvious to us here? Why are there so many angry people in Canada, in the United States, in Europe? Why is there so much arguing between so many groups? *What's going on?*

What's going on is that the world is getting bigger, and we are feeling dwarfed by its problems. So you would think that our natural reaction would be to huddle together among our friends, co-workers, and families for comfort and support.

But you would be wrong.

A while back, I had a neighbour who built a fence. First he got me to take down the ancient chain-link fence, on the understanding that we would replace it with a similar new one. Then he "changed his mind" and without consulting my wife or me, put up a solid wooden fence that was more than twice the height of the original one, and was exactly the kind of fence he knew we didn't want. I was angry, but more than this I was sad, because monster fences have become commonplace. They mean that I have ceased to live in a neighbourhood and now reside in a bedroom district.

There are people who live four doors away from me whom I have never met. They get up in the morning, walk down the stairs into their garages, get in their cars, and drive off to work. In the evening, they drive their cars into their garages, close the garage doors, and climb the stairs into their houses. Their backyards have high fences, too. I never see them.

Nor is my part of the city unique. People use their houses as places to sleep but don't want to have any messy entanglements with the people around them.

But the problems go way beyond this. What we are witnessing is nothing less than the shattering of society and the isolation of the individual.

THE DESTRUCTION OF COMMUNITIES

Futurists talk about the secondary and tertiary effects of developments as well as the primary effects. For instance, the primary impact of the automobile was to make transportation easier, faster, and cheaper. The secondary effect was to allow industries to grow more rapidly and the standard of living to rise dramatically. The tertiary effect was to destroy communities.

My maternal grandparents were born, lived, and were buried in the same small-town community. They knew and were known to just about everybody who lived there. My parents grew up hundreds of kilometres apart from each other, met and married by virtue of the automobile, and set up housekeeping hundreds of kilometres from either of their parents. Over time, they developed their own friends, but they were otherwise strangers to the towns where they settled. My wife and I grew up in communities on different continents, and we met and settled down in a place that was distant from both of our birthplaces.

One of the older members of my church once commented that when she was a girl, her family's whole social life — and therefore most of their entertainment — came from being members of the local church, with the suppers and parties that arose out of church membership. Today, television, movies, videos, and computer games have given us ways of getting our entertainment out of a box instead of from the company of the people around us. We no longer have as many reasons to seek out other people, to be in their company, be interested or involved in their lives, or have them involved in ours. Increasingly, we are living alone among millions of strangers, kept company primarily by our television sets.

THE DWINDLING FAMILY

Other changes have transformed the family. In our grandparents' day, the extended family was common, with members of three generations often living in the same house while maintaining a close relationship with nearby cousins, uncles, and aunts. This was not for some romantic or heart-warming reason; it was because most people tended to stay in the communities where they were born. Moreover, people relied on other members of their family in times of trouble and sickness, and the elderly needed the younger generations to help them survive when they were too old to continue working. Today, the relationships and support of the extended family have been largely replaced by institutions and governments, and by impersonal care givers.

As people became more mobile, the extended family gave way to the nuclear family, and this structure became the foundation of our society. When I was in high school, there might have been one kid in a class of thirty or more who came from what was called a "broken home." A few others came from families where both parents were forced to work, and so had to make do without a mother at home. These children were objects of pity, spoken of in whispers, and allowances were made if their behaviour was erratic or occasionally antisocial.

Today the nuclear family is crumbling. A large percentage — perhaps even a majority — of my children's classmates come from families that have gone through divorce or separation. Many now belong to single-parent families. Moreover, in families that have two parents, it's almost inevitable that both parents are working.

Nor is this unique to my neighbourhood. In today's society, only about 12 percent of families with children have the "traditional" pattern of one parent staying at home with the children while the other goes out to work.[2] Across Canada, about one-third of all marriages end in divorce, and more than 70 percent of pre-school children are cared for on a regular basis by someone other than their parents.[3] In the early 1960s, less than one-third of Canadian women worked outside the home. Today, nearly two-thirds of women with children under the age of six are in the workforce, and it's expected that by 1996 something like 80 percent of all women will be in the workforce.[4]

Yet we can now prove that coming from a "broken home" affects children and that it does so severely. Divorces tend to place women and children in poverty, and poverty is known to create emotional, academic, even physical problems for children. A study done by Professor Ross Finnie for Laval University shows that in an average Canadian divorce, a mother who gets custody of the children experiences a shocking 41 percent drop in income in the first year. Fully 60 percent of such mother-and-children families wind up living below the poverty level. By the end of three years after a marriage break-up, single mothers get by, on average, with less than half the family income they had before. In comparison, the standard of living of fathers who do not have custody of their children goes up by an average of 30 percent.[5]

But not all the harmful effects of divorce are related to poverty. According to research done by Sara McLanahan, a sociologist at Princeton University, children who grow up in single-parent families resulting from a divorce are more likely to drop out of school, marry in their teens, have children out of wedlock, and experience a breakdown in their own marriages.[6] Another study, performed by Martin Richards, a Cambridge University psychologist, concluded that the chance of a child going to university is cut in half if the parents are divorced.[7]

You can see the societal importance of the family just by looking around you. Those ethnic groups that have strong family ties tend to be doing well in Canada. In contrast, the groups that have a large number of single-parent families, with children frequently born out of wedlock, are not integrating well into Canadian society. Naturally enough, with all the poverty and stress they have to cope with, they are producing a disproportionate number of young people who get involved in crime and drugs.

Nor is it just the children of divorced parents who are in trouble; there has been a rising number of reports of violence in schools, as Michael Valpy of the *Globe and Mail* has pointed out:

> In the Gaspé coast town of Ste-Anne-des-Monts, student violence and defiance of teachers closed down the secondary school for the second consecutive day.
>
> In the Northern Ontario community of Atikokan, a 15-year-old held a teacher and another student at gun-point in a high-school classroom for two hours in a dispute over mustard spattered on clothes.
>
> In the Toronto suburb of Scarborough, a local school board approved a policy sanctioning permanent expulsion for students who use or threaten to use weapons in school or cause harm to teachers or other students "requiring medical intervention."
>
> That is a day in the life of Canadian children.
>
> [In Canada, we] are creating a lot of dysfunctional kids because adult Canadians to a distressing degree have been treating the family as an institution whose form and durability is a matter of personal convenience rather than as the enduring and protective cradle of child development. As a society, we are not making the necessary commitment, devoting the necessary time, employing the necessary energy to raising our children.[8]

A GENERATION OF NEGLECTED SAVAGES

How did things come to this? To explore this question, let me take a detour. What is the biggest problem with our educational system? I've pondered this question for several years now, and certainly there is no shortage of scapegoats. But I have come to the conclusion that the biggest problem of all is parents. We parents, as a group, hold more responsibility for the ills of the system and are doing less about it than any other group.

As I mentioned in Chapter 3, the children we are delivering to school and society are too frequently ill-mannered, over-stimulated, violent, undisciplined brats, addicted to television and video games, ill-disposed to learning, unreceptive to the efforts of their teachers, and incapable of taking a constructive place in our society.

A couple of summers ago, a young friend of mine named Kadey Schulz was working as a camp councillor and was put in charge of a group of seven-year-old boys and girls. When she found one of the boys punching one of the girls, she separated them and told the boy that kind of behaviour wasn't allowed. To which he replied, "Why don't you suck my dick, bitch."

If you were to tell this story to any teacher in any school in the country, I suggest that you would get a knowing nod in reply because they all meet children like this every year. And in too many of our high schools you will find teachers who are fearful of student violence. It's not that all our children are like this, or even most of them. But a sizable minority are, or are even worse.

As someone who tries to anticipate the future, I often look at what's happening in other parts of the world to see if there are trends that are similar to ours. I grew up in the New York City suburbs and have stayed in touch with Dr. Peter Lawton, one of my teachers who saved me as a student and changed my life. He's been teaching for over forty years and was selected as one of the top fifty teachers in the United States a few years ago. When I was visiting him recently, we talked about what's happening in American schools.

It's a grim picture. Violence has become a way of life, with kids bringing weapons to school. Indeed, some schools spend as much as two hours a day putting students through metal detectors. But could this happen here in civil, courteous Canada? As noted above, it has already begun. It's not widespread, but it is happening.

Next, I asked Dr. Lawton how students had changed over his years of teaching, and he identified three major differences. First, he said, today's students are observers, not participants. They're neither involved nor interested in their own education. It's almost as if they're being forced to watch a boring television show. Next, he said, they're lazy and have no work habits. They don't much care if they're caught without their homework done or if they fail a test at school. They don't seem to think it matters, as if it really doesn't have much to do with them. Finally, and perhaps worst of all, he said that they're intellectual cowards. They won't rise to a challenge because they're afraid that if they care, they might fail, and then they would be mocked by their peers.

Now, I suspect that while Canadian students may be somewhat more diligent than their American peers, a lot of what Dr. Lawton said applies to Canadians as well. The sum total of all these things is that children are becoming unteachable. It won't matter how well we reorganize the educational system or how well our teachers teach if the children choose not to learn. Worse, if we raise a generation of renegades who don't care what happens to anyone but themselves, we will be destroying ourselves, and our society will fall.

How has this happened to our children? Well, the first and easiest places to lay the blame are television and video games. Both tend to violence, encourage noninvolvement with other people, and are experienced in a detached fashion. And despite what some so-called experts say, I firmly believe that the glorification of violence, the denigration of thrift, work, and thoughtfulness, and the treatment of other people as pleasure objects to be used and discarded, all have a harmful and lasting effect on both adults and children.

But television and video games don't come out of a vacuum. Someone has to allow them into children's lives, and that someone is parents. I am absolutely flabbergasted when parents tell me that they can't get their kids to turn off the television, put down their video games, and do their homework. Maybe I'm foolish, but it seems to me the answer is simple: turn off or take away the television or video game, and let the kids cry if they must. Similarly, I am regularly dumbfounded by the things parents allow their children to do in public. If our children don't know the rules or choose not to obey them, it's not their fault. It's the parents who are to blame.

As parents, we have responsibilities and obligations to our children and to our society. Canadian society invests more than $100,000 per child in education, health, and support services, and is entitled to have us live up to our end of the bargain: to produce responsible citizens. It is our job to teach our children how to be human beings, not savages, and we need to do it by setting firm boundaries and by teaching through example rather than by occasional lip service.

Unfortunately, the stresses of the parents are being visited on the children. So many of us live in situations where both parents must work to keep their heads above water, or where there's only one parent to cope, that we don't have the time and energy we'd like to spend on our children. But there are also too many people who are just bad parents. They give their kids too much money, let them watch adult films and videos, allow them to go to bed late, get up groggy, and eat what they please. These parents fail to supervise their kids' homework, studiously avoid any involvement in PTA meetings, and generally raise their kids with the least possible effort. They teach neither morals nor ethics, and the rules of the household tend to be inconsistent, reflecting the mood of the parent rather than the needs of the children.

Today, it's particularly important that we teach our children moral values. Our school systems were never designed to teach behaviour and self-discipline, only to supplement the teachings that children received at home. As sociologist Reginald Bibby noted, "Canadian schools operate in a milieu that is highly conscious of cultural diversity, where people are extremely suspicious of anyone who wants to postulate values. 'Whose values?' is the predictable objection."[9] In a multicultural society, especially one in which sensitivity about not abusing other peoples' cultures is so high, public schools are forced into an impartial, value-free stance. All the moralizing they can manage is to say, "Don't assault other people, use condoms, and don't do drugs." Hardly the stuff of civilization.

So the ball winds up back in the parents' court — and more and more of us are dropping it. As a society, by neglecting our children, by passively accepting the disintegration of the family, and by ignoring the traditional rules of custom, behaviour, and morality, we are cutting our own throats. And instead of trying to fix the problems, we are spending our time trying to fix the blame.

PETTY LITTLE INTEREST GROUPS

In the last chapter I quoted Theodore Roosevelt's warning about the danger of the United States being broken up into ethnic groups. I view America as a leading indicator of what may happen here and therefore watch trends and events there to help me anticipate them here. This is particularly true concerning racial friction and pressure groups. In that light, Roosevelt's comments barely scratch the surface of my concerns for Canada and, indeed, for much of the democratic world.

Saul Bellow, the Canadian-born novelist and professor of literature at Boston University, who won the 1976 Nobel Prize for Literature, put it this way: "As a onetime anthropologist, I know a taboo when I see one. Open discussion of many major public questions has for some time now been taboo. We can't open our mouths without being denounced as racists, misogynists, supremacists, imperialists or fascists. As for the media, they stand ready to trash anyone so designated."[10]

Arthur Schlesinger, historian and author of the frightening book, The Disuniting of America: Reflections on a Multicultural Society, also commented on this trend:

> Oberlin [College] was for a century and half the model of a racially integrated college. . . . [Today] Asians live in Asia House, Jews in "J" House, Latinos in Spanish House, blacks in African-Heritage House, foreign students in Third World House. Even the Lesbian, Gay, and Bisexual Union has broken up into racial and gender factions. . . . And it is sad, though instructive, that the administrations especially disposed to encourage racial and ethnic enclaves . . . [are] the ones experiencing the most racial tension. Troy Duster, a Berkeley sociologist, finds a correlation between group separatism and racial hostility among students.[11]

Author Shelby Steele — who is not a white male — described how individuals try to skew the rules to get extra benefits:

> Ultimately, black power was not about equality or justice; it was as its name suggests, about power. By the 1970s, the marriage of race and power was once again firmly established. Equality was out: the "politics of difference" was in. From then on, everyone would rally around the single quality that makes them different from the white male and pursue power based on that quality. It is a very simple formula. All you have to do is identify that quality, whatever it may be, with victimization. . . . Grievance identities are thus "sovereignties" that compete with the sovereignties of the nation itself. . . . Those with grievance identities also demand *extra* entitlements far beyond what should come to us as citizens.[12]

Having noted this trend in the United States, I then started to watch for its appearance in Canada, and to my dismay I saw the same type of "politically correct" divisiveness gaining ground here. In December 1993 Allan Kaufman, a lecturer at the University of Ottawa's law school, learned that five of his fifty-four law students had been given six hours to write an open-book exam instead of the normal three hours allocated to the rest of his class. These five were members of visible minorities. Kaufman filed a protest with the University of Ottawa senate, calling the policy "reverse discrimination against white students" and adding that it suggested "that these visible minority students are inferior." He added, "It may be well-meaning, but it's doing a terrible harm to the [minority] students."[13] The faculty agreed to suspend the policy and to set up a committee to produce a new exam policy. But both Kaufman, who is a director of the National Capital Alliance on Race Relations, and the University of Ottawa became the targets of attack by minority groups, who accused them of racism.

Next, consider the May 1994 meeting of the Writers' Union of Canada, held in Vancouver, whose attendance was to be restricted to "writers of colour and First Nations writers" — in other words, anyone but whites. Pierre Berton, the noted Canadian author who was one of the founders of the Writers' Union, objected to the restrictions. "If people want to hold an exclusive meeting, that's fine. I can understand the reason for it," he said. "But the Union can't, with its members' money or its imprimatur, officially support any organization — any organization — which excludes people from any function because of the colour of their skin."[14]

Berton was heckled for his troubles, and his defenders were shouted down — a long way from Patrick Henry's democratic ideal.[15] Moreover, the proponents of the anybody-but-whites conference seemed to feel that the opinions of whites were automatically wrong and were maliciously intended. Makeda Silvera, the publisher of Sister Vision Press, said, "As far as I'm concerned, we should have the right, the space, and the taxpayers' money to meet as African writers — forget even the writers of colour. Okay?"[16] The inference was that even excluding whites was not divisive enough for some members of the union, who clearly believe that they are entitled to taxpayers' money for openly racist purposes.

History makes it clear that many groups have been abused and put at severe disadvantages. Nor do I doubt that racism and sexism still exist and need to be opposed. But when we seek to combat bigotry and discrimination with more bigotry and discrimination, we commit ourselves to failure from the start. Worse, if we allow ourselves to be divided into petty, snivelling little interest groups, whose sole purpose is to rip shreds of power from society as a whole, we will end up with a society that cannot function, and we will be both ungovernable and hateful.

TELEVISION: THE DESTROYER OF CULTURE

So much has been written about the evils of television that there's little chance I can add much that is new. Let me then comment on how television and its relations and descendants — videos, video games, proliferating cable TV, and virtual reality — are going to affect the future.

First, television is usurping the role that used to be filled by religion: providing a social conscience and a sense of community. It tends to sever the relationships that naturally grow between people and to replace them with entertainment. Moreover, this is mainly the type of entertainment that glorifies materialism and encourages the view that other people are pleasure objects and violence is an acceptable way of solving problems. There have been numerous studies showing how this affects the way children view themselves and behave towards others.

For example, Sandra Campbell, a Canadian educational consultant who has done extensive research on the effects of media on children, says that children's imaginations are being "colonized" by television, and the result is often an expectation that the world is a violent and frightening place. Moreover, it tends to rob them of initiative and creativity. "They are passive receivers of someone else's world," she comments.[17] In addition, a report of the U.S. National Institute of Mental Health has found that there is "overwhelming" evidence that violence on television leads to aggressive behaviour in children and teenagers.[18]

I would go further. Although I know of no studies on this point, I strongly believe that television has a profound, long-term effect on the behaviour of adults towards one another and that these effects are not beneficial.

Starting with news reporting, which is supposed to be serious viewing, television affects our attention span, so that we expect 30-second explanations to suffice for even the most complicated matters. It thus creates unrealistic expectations that complex and difficult problems can be solved quickly and easily. It tells us what we should consider important and excludes everything else from our consideration. Problems that do not appear on television do not exist. Those that do, attain instant prominence out of all proportion to their true relevance.

Thomas Jefferson once commented that someone who reads nothing but newspapers is little better off than someone who reads nothing at all. Television, with its slick production values and minimal content, is far worse. And, of course, television and film entertainment are even worse than the news programs. At a time when the cornerstone of our society, the family, is under attack, programs such as "Married . . . With Children" and "The Simpsons" send exactly the wrong message. Terminator 2 is not only a technical tour de force and a fascinating film, but it is an almost nonstop glorification of violence as the way to settle disputes. The result of all this will be that people will become less and less involved in one another's lives; they will be more alienated and distrustful; and they will develop a shallow outlook on life, giving little thought to the consequences of their actions.

Yet even if television were wholesome and thoughtful, I would be opposed to it for two reasons: first, because time spent with television is time that cannot be spent on more creative or thoughtful things. Second, television and films represent not only trivial culture but *American* trivial culture.

THE AMERICANIZATION OF GLOBAL CULTURE

Now, I have no problem with American culture — in America. Certainly, there is much to commend in the lofty ideals and examples set by the United States over the last two centuries and by its many talented artists, statesmen, and writers. But very little of this shows in the television programs and films that America exports in such profusion to the world. Instead, we mostly get the lowest common denominator — the simplistic Archie Bunker view of things, the culture of "Dallas" and "The Young and the Restless."

Moreover, even if the message were uplifting and edifying, it would still be American. What works for children in New York or Los Angeles or Duluth is mostly not appropriate for the rest of the world. Worse, it threatens the roots of other cultures, because the children of other countries spend more time learning about trivial American things than about their own societies. And the glossy production values of American programs are coupled with unbeatable cheapness. Because American producers recoup their costs in their home market, they can then sell American programs in foreign countries at a small fraction of the cost of a native production.

Nor are television and films the only agents of Americanization. There's always Coca-Cola, McDonalds, Levi's jeans, and the self-proclaimed "boy toy" performer, and while it's true that there are non-American media icons involved in the homogenization of global culture (such as the Rolling Stones, for example), the majority of such icons are American. The global economy carries the greatest commercial successes, not necessarily the finest exemplars of culture.

When children of other cultures spend more time with the icons and images of trivial America than in learning about their own roots, traditions, and history, it produces a loss of national identity and a sense of aimlessness. I suspect that this is another reason why so many people are starting to identify with their ancestry, their race, or some other foundation that helps them decide who they really are. For without roots, we feel anxiety and, in certain circumstances, a reactionary desire to return to fundamentalism, both cultural and religious. Small wonder that the French periodically go through spasms of policing the purity of their language or that many Islamic cultures see the United States as "the Great Satan." American exports are teaching French and Muslim children the same disrespect for their cultures that American children are learning for their own.

And the process of the homogenization of global culture exacerbates another trend: we are losing the symbols of our own identities.

FORGETTING WHO WE ARE

My father had a total of three employers over his entire career. My father-in-law had two. Today, the phrase "job security" seems as archaic as phrenology or alchemy. People expect to have to change careers anywhere from five to seven times, and may change the companies they work for even more frequently, either because they are pushed or because they jump ship. In the repulsive words of one Wall Street whiz, "Loyalty is for losers."

We have paid a terrible price for the improvements in our life-style. As society has changed, we have systematically been destroying the psychological symbols of who we are. If you don't identify yourself by where you live, who your family is, where you work, what your culture is, and who your friends are, then who are you? Such symbols have, throughout history, been the benchmarks that gave us identity and told us where we belonged. Without them, we may wind up identifying with our purchasing power, and our creed may become "You are what you own." In these perilous times, this is shaky ground indeed. If we lose our sense of self, we fall prey to anger, anxiety, and aimlessness, and lash out randomly at others.

I see symptoms of this all around me. I see it in aggressive, abusive drivers on the highway, in the increase in senseless violence, in the "swarming" of teenagers, and the hostility between cultural groups. I see it in the "networks" of "contacts" that are replacing circles of friends. And I see it most chillingly in the increasingly insensitive and violent way that our children behave towards each other and towards their parents and teachers.

Without intending it to happen, we are being isolated in smaller and smaller, and often mutually hostile, special interest groups. As the traditional ways of defining ourselves crumble, we had better have other props in place. And to cope with a more difficult and lonelier age, we especially need deep sources of inner strength. But these sources arise from spirituality, and we have also been systematically destroying respect for our various spiritual traditions.

When the German philosopher Friedrich Nietzsche said that God was dead, he was making an observation about the state of humanity rather than the state of God. After all, whether God exists or not, and whether He lives or dies, doesn't depend on what we believe. So Nietzsche's point was that our belief in God is dying, and when the belief in God disappears, it is we ourselves who are affected. This century has seen an enormous decline in spiritual practice in Canada and in Western civilization as a whole. If God is dead, we miss Him terribly, for without Him to act as a beacon to give us direction, we are in danger of losing our way and are stumbling into darkness. Worse, we are doing it of our own free will.

Which brings me, finally, to religion.

WHY SHOOT THE MESSAGE FOR THE SINS OF THE MESSENGER?

This century has been hell on spiritual practices. In the name of truth, we have systematically been destroying goodness. The apparent debunking of spiritually based religion by value-free science may well turn out to be the thing for which the twentieth century is longest remembered. When Yuri Gagarin, the first human into space, returned to Earth, he was interviewed on Soviet television and was asked by Nikita Khrushchev whether he had seen God while in space. Of course the answer was no.

We laugh at such a foolish image — a cosmonaut waving to God through the viewport of his space capsule — yet privately our culture has been just as dismissive of the central message of our various religious traditions. Turning the old saying around, we have rejected the message because of the failings of the messenger.

Religious practice is based on much more than a belief in a big man with a long white beard who lives in the clouds. It is rooted in centuries, even millennia, of people who lived, thought about life, and preserved their thoughts for their descendants. The practice of religion contains more than the supernatural. It contains much of the distilled wisdom about the nature of humanity, and how humans can and should get along with one another. In short, you don't need to believe in God to live a godly life. It is, however, more difficult without God.

At the beginning of this chapter, I quoted sociologist Reginald Bibby on the importance of religion. He had more to say on the subject:

> It's clear that the number of Canadians who are in the market for the meeting of their spiritual needs easily exceeds the number who are participating in organized religion. For example, while only 18 percent of 15-to-19-year-olds are attending services regularly . . . no fewer than 60 percent explicitly acknowledge that they "have spiritual needs." . . . Numbers of Canadians well in excess of the country's 4.5 million weekly attenders also indicate they are trying to resolve questions of meaning and purpose.

> Observers assume, in a naive, matter-of-fact manner, that if increasing numbers of Canadians are not having their spiritual needs met by the country's religious groups, they are having them met in other ways. Academics, for example, have presumptuously spoken of "privatized faith," while the media have given considerable attention since the 1950s to a variety of new religious expressions.
>
> My research, however, has found little evidence that Canadians who are no longer turning to the churches with their spiritual needs are automatically turning elsewhere. . . . As a result, it appears that a large number of people are failing to have their spiritual needs met. One of the great ironies of our time is that Canada's religious groups are going broke at a time when the population is going [spiritually] hungry.[19]

Our religious traditions are not mere fairy tales prattling on about a hereafter that never comes. Their roots run deep, and they carry messages of wisdom and strength to those willing to listen. It's unfortunate that many of those who deliver these messages have feet of clay, but the messages themselves are true. The fact that we live in a technological age doesn't mean we must live in spiritual poverty. We turn away from spirituality and religious tradition at our peril, for if we persist in the way we have been going, we will be rudderless, without a sense of right or wrong. Cultural relativism is fine for cocktail parties. It's worthless in real life.

WHAT CAN YOU DO ABOUT ALL THIS?

Human beings depend on community. Indeed, research now being done on animal behaviour and human psychology indicates that the way our brains work makes us social animals who help and are helped by others on a "tit-for-tat" basis. But we no longer live in small, stable, tight-knit communities. So how are we to survive the shattering of society? I believe there are several concrete things that we can do:

• Be involved in the lives of those around you. While you should of course be concerned about the poor and starving in distant lands, you should first be concerned with the homeless of your own community. As well, look for opportunities to help the people whose lives you touch: your friends, your co-workers, your neighbours. Get involved. Even more important: care. There will be a time when you need others, too.

• If you are a parent, start living up to your responsibilities. Parenting is a tough and often thankless job, but it's one you let yourself in for, so stop shirking your duties. This means providing consistent and clear boundaries of conduct that are based on your children's need to learn civilized behaviour, not on your need for comfort or convenience. It means making sure that along with "quality time" there is enough quantity time; "quality time" without quantity is a lie, a cop-out.

Parenting also means recognizing that your children must be taught right from wrong. It means restricting their access to television and video games, and encouraging them to read, especially by reading to them. Their opinion is not as good as yours, nor is it as good as their teachers' opinions. And while your kids may tell you that "you're not the boss of me," you are nevertheless responsible for them and have authority over them.

• You, too, should free yourself from the TV, the VCR, and computer games. Go out and find some people you can learn to like, respect, and admire. Read more books — hell, some people don't read any books. Read an in-depth analysis of a problem that concerns you. Become expert at something outside your work. Specialization is for ants. You're human. Live up to the potential of a human.

• Become a good example. Our society is the sum of its individuals, and from your perspective, that starts with you. If you won't take the lead in your own life, who will? So start by doing good things for others.

• Get to know your political representatives. Politics is not an especially dirty game in Canada, and it's the best way humanity has found for getting along without bashing people over the head. But it only works if good people represent us in government. So get to know the people who speak in your name, who act with your authority, and who help shape the world that you and the people you care about live in. If you like them, work to support them. If not, work to defeat them. But don't just sit on the sidelines. People who aren't active in politics, especially those who don't bother to vote, have no right to bitch. They are the problem, not the politicians.

• Be polite. Remember: "What goes around, comes around." Cutting someone off in traffic, or jumping a queue, or taking something that is not rightfully yours is short-term gain that guarantees long-term pain. Yes, you can probably get away with it; but in doing so you pollute your own society. Even if you wind up personally richer for it, you will find yourself living in a meaner, tougher, and less desirable world, and you will deserve to. You cannot escape the ultimate consequences of your own oafish behaviour.

• Find your spiritual foundations, whether traditional or otherwise, and work at your own wholeness as a spiritual being, whatever brand name that may have. Thousands of years of tradition and experiment in finding what works for human beings should not be rejected without careful consideration of the alternatives. Winston Churchill, himself an avid pursuer of material pleasures, said, "The destiny of mankind is not decided by material computation. When great causes are on the move, we learn that we are spirits, not animals, and that something is going on in space and time, and beyond space and time, which, whether we like it or not, spells duty."[20]

Duty. To oneself. To one's community. To one's family and history and ancestors. Without it, we will suffer, helpless and unloved, in a society that cares nothing for us and will not lift a finger to help us.
    Alone.

Commencement

FOURTEEN

Courage

What lies behind us and what lies before us are tiny matters compared to what lies within us.

– Ralph Waldo Emerson, "Progress of Culture," Phi Beta Kappa address, 1867

There is a tendency to see the future in the same way we view the past: as fixed and beyond our ability to change. But the future has yet to be invented, and we have it within our hands to do much to make it better — or worse.

It is true that there are forces at work in the world that will have a lot to do with how the future will turn out. That, after all, is the central theme of this book. But all the problems I have discussed could in fact be solved and all the opportunities could be explored. There is very little about the future that is inevitable. However, one thing is certain: we cannot act stupidly and continue to prosper as individuals, as a nation, or as members of the human race. The future belongs to those who ride the waves of change with intelligence, persistence, foresight, compassion, and courage. I cannot promise you that it will be a comfortable ride.

For us individuals, the days of one-decision career planning are over. From now on, we will constantly be improvising and looking for opportunities to exploit in order to stay gainfully employed. Many of us will be self-employed, with the result that we will have to re-invent our careers virtually every day. This will be an uncomfortable and often difficult process — quite different from our parents' struggles to nail down job security. We don't need to worry about that issue, because there no longer is any job security to be had.

Our society will struggle to cope with the rising friction between groups, with the needs of shifting workers from one kind of employment to another, and with the problems of intergenerational inequities. We are becoming increasingly reliant on institutional care for the poor, the weak, the infirm, and the elderly, reversing the family and community orientation of our history. Yet our institutions are already under financial pressure and are looking for ways to limit their responsibilities, which adds additional stress. As Joan Green, director of education for the Toronto Board of Education, is fond of saying, "When the waterhole dries up, the animals look at each other differently." Meanwhile, our country of Canada will have to contend with the question of unity for many years ahead, regardless of what Quebec decides to do in the immediate future.

As a race, we humans are outpacing the Earth's ability to cope with our growth. We risk killing ourselves through famine, drought, war, disease, or pollution unless we change the way we live and think. Most importantly, we must stem the growth of humanity, for all the other problems ultimately stem from this.

Once, when I was giving a talk to a group of high school students, one student put up his hand and said, "This is really scary stuff. Is there any good news?"

I looked at him, then nodded and told him the following story.

The United Kingdom experienced a political crisis in the 1860s. Because of the country's prosperity over the previous decade, its population had shot up, and the rising standard of living meant that food consumption had risen with it; in fact, food consumption had risen by more than 25 percent in the decade. If it continued at this rate rate, Britain would soon outstrip its ability to feed its people, and the nation's leaders were worried that this would lead to food riots, political instability, and even the end of democratic government.

However, around 1850 an American doctor named John Gorrie, practising in Apalachicola, Florida, had been looking for a cure for malaria, whose cause was then unknown. Gorrie reasoned that since malaria occurred only in tropical climates, if he could keep his patients cool, it might break the disease cycle leading to death. Accordingly, he used the adiabatic principle, a well-known principle in physics which says that expanding gas cools. He pumped room-temperature air into the chamber of a piston, then pulled the piston down the cylinder, causing the gas to expand and cool. He then expelled the cooled air into the hospital ward, and repeated the process. He thus invented air conditioning. A year later, in 1851, he passed the cooled air over a pan of water, causing it to freeze, and invented refrigeration.

In 1872 two Australian entrepreneurs used Gorrie's refrigeration system to send a shipload of mutton from Australia to the United Kingdom — and Britain was saved; for it could now import food from a distance and thus was no longer dependent on domestic food supplies.[1]

This is serendipity: an American doctor, looking for a cure for malaria, solves a political crisis across the ocean in the United Kingdom. I can't predict when miracles will happen in our future, but I know that they will.

At the outset of this book, I said that my purpose was to help you make better plans for the future (rather than to try to come up with accurate predictions about it). I hope that I have helped you focus your thoughts. Whether you agree with what I've said is of far less importance.

The future will offer us many opportunities to live good and fulfilling lives and do exciting new things, as well as presenting us with many problems that we cannot afford to ignore. We will have to work at it together. The world has become too complex, the forces too strong, for us to dismiss or ignore people who are of a different colour, sex, sexual orientation, religion, or culture — they may possess solutions to problems that might otherwise kill us.

Besides, they are our brothers and sisters.

I believe that all of the problems before us can be solved, if we have the will to do so. But it will take wisdom, compassion, and education — and it will take courage. James Barrie, the Scottish playwright, once said, "When courage fails, all fails." Humanity cannot afford to fail.

Despite all our problems here in Canada, we have so many advantages compared with most of the other countries of the world that if we fail we will have no one to blame but ourselves. Ours should be a prosperous and exciting future — if we have the wit and will to make it so.

There's an old saying that forewarned is forearmed.

You have been warned.

What Did I Miss?

The future is an awfully big subject for one person. Accordingly, I'm sure I've made mistakes, got things wrong, and left things out. There are also undoubtedly things that I don't know. If you are aware of some of these things, write to me (please don't call) care of the following address:

Stoddart Publishing Co. Limited
34 Lesmill Road
Toronto, Canada M3B 2T6

I will reply if I can. As for speaking engagements, if it is to adults, please contact my agent:

The David Lavin Agency, Inc.
77 Mowat Avenue
Suite 406
Toronto, Canada   M6K 3E8
(416) 588-8822   or   (800) 265-4870

If you want me to speak to a group of high school students, I do that free of charge whenever I can. However, I must warn you that I only do so when my travel schedule and other obligations make it possible. Aside from anything else, I am a father, and my children have a higher claim on my time than other people's children. If you'd like to contact me about speaking to your high school, write to me care of my publisher at the address given above.

Notes

One   The Path Ahead of Us
1   Peter W. Schwartz, *The Art of the Long View* (New York: Doubleday Currency Books, 1991), p. 9.

Two   How the Rules Have Changed in the Working World
1   Michael E. Porter, *Canada at the Crossroads,* a study prepared for the Business Council on National Issues and the Government of Canada, October 1991, p. 10.
2   GATT estimates, as reported in the *Economist,* October 16, 1993, p. 104.
3   "Singapore and the Problems of Success," *Economist,* August 22, 1993, p. 25.
4   Lester C. Thurow, "The Need for Strategic Approaches" (speech to the Liberal Party of Canada, Aylmer, Quebec, November 1991).
5   Peter F. Drucker, *The Frontiers of Management* (New York: Harper & Row, 1986), p. 31.
6   The World Bank, as quoted in the *Economist,* July 31, 1993, p. 33.
7   Actually, the term Third World is ethnocentric in origin. It originated with the concept of the Old World, being Europe, the New World, meaning mainly North America, and the Third World being everything else. Nevertheless, the term has become firmly fixed in our language, and today it is used to denote poor and undeveloped countries.
8   Thurow, "The Need for Strategic Approaches."
9   Peter F. Drucker, *Post-Capitalist Society,* (New York: HarperBusiness, 1993), p. 193.
10   "The Wealth of Nations," *Economist,* May 15, 1993, p. 15.
11   Organization for Economic Cooperation and Development.
12   "A Billion Consumers: A Survey of Asia," *Economist,* October 30, 1993, p. 5.
13   Ibid., p. 15.
14   "The Biggest Prize," *Economist,* January 16, 1993, p. 68.
15   "Asia Beckons," *Economist,* May 5, 1992, p. 63.
16   "NAFTA: The Showdown," *Economist,* November 13, 1993, p. 23.
17   Drucker, *Frontiers of Management,* pp. 23–26.
18   Thurow, "The Need for Strategic Approaches."
19   Interview with Lewis F. Jackson, November 1993.
20   Drucker, *Frontiers of Management,* p. 27.
21   Ibid.
22   M. C. Urquhart, editor, *Historical Statistics of Canada* (Toronto: Macmillan, 1965), p. 59.
23   Drucker, *Frontiers of Management,* p. 31.
24   Ibid., p. 32.
25   Drucker, *Post-Capitalist Society,* p. 74.
26   Sebastian Edwards, economic development specialist at the University of California at Los Angeles, as interpreted in "Trade Winds Blowing in Prosperity's Direction," *Globe and Mail,* December 16, 1993.
27   Ibid.
28   "The Foul Smell of Success," *Economist,* October 5, 1991, p. 54.
29   "How GATT May Change the Rules for Everyone," *Toronto Star,* December 11, 1993.
30   "Trade Winds Blowing in Prosperity's Direction," *Globe and Mail,* December 16, 1993.
31   "The Trough," *Economist,* June 27, 1992, p. 22.
32   "How GATT May Change the Rules for Everyone."
33   "The Trough," p. 22.
34   "Protection's Stepchild," *Economist,* May 16, 1992, pp. 97–98.
35   "Aluminum Jobs Costly, Study Finds," *Globe and Mail,* September 3, 1991.

260

36 Richard Worzel, "Floating Exchange Rates Are Hurting Canadian Trade Diversification," *Financial Post,* March 27, 1976.

Three Will Canada Be Rich or Poor?

1 Dr. Michael E. Porter, *Canada at the Crossroads,* a study prepared for the Business Council on National Issues, and the Government of Canada, October 1991, pp. 4–5.
2 Auditor-General Denis Desautels, in his January 1994 report to Parliament, as quoted in "Debt and Other Unnatural Disasters," *Globe and Mail,* January 21, 1994.
3 Eric Malling, CTV's "W5" television program, February 28, 1993.
4 Ibid.
5 Ibid.
6 Ted Carmichael, "Government Revenue Shortfall . . . Tax Avoidance/Evasion May Cost $20 bln," Burns Fry, December 17, 1993.
7 Coopers & Lybrand, *Canadian Tax News,* Sept./Oct. 1993, p. 2.
8 Eric Malling, "W5."
9 Ibid.
10 See, for instance, the example cited by Peter Drucker in *Post-Capitalist Society* (New York: HarperBusiness, 1993), p. 94. This, and related subjects, are dealt with in greater detail in David Osborne and Ted Gaebler's excellent book *Reinventing Government* (Reading, Mass.: Addison-Wesley, 1992).
11 Drucker, *Post-Capitalist Society,* p. 84.
12 "The Mother of All Reformers," *Economist,* October 16, 1993, p. 20.
13 *Economist,* July 31, 1993.
14 Porter, *Canada at the Crossroads,* pp. 49–50.
15 As quoted by Professor Peter H. Pearse of the Department of Forestry Management, University of British Columbia, in the *Globe and Mail,* January 10, 1992.
16 Economic Council of Canada, *A Lot to Learn: Education and Training in Canada,* (Ottawa: Economic Council of Canada, 1992), p. 2.
17 Ibid., p. 13.
18 Richard Worzel, "Dealing with the Brat Factor," *Globe and Mail,* September 15, 1992.
19 Economic Council of Canada, *A Lot to Learn,* p. 58.
20 Porter, *Canada at the Crossroads,* p. 90.
21 Private correspondence with the author, February 1994.
22 Drucker, *Post-Capitalist Society,* pp. 202–3.
23 Correspondence between the author and Premier Frank McKenna, December 21, 1993.
24 Deborah C. Sawyer, "When Creating Jobs Doesn't Work," *Globe and Mail,* January 27, 1993.
25 David Roberts, "The Brew Crew Takes Over," *Globe and Mail,* December 21, 1993.
26 Ibid.
27 "The Wealth of Nations," *Economist,* May 15, 1993, p. 15.
28 Lester C. Thurow, "The Need for Strategic Approaches" (speech to the Liberal Party of Canada, Aylmer, Quebec, November 1991).

Four   Tomorrow's Business

1 Charles Baden-Fuller and John Stopford, *Rejuvenating the Mature Business* (London: Routledge, 1992).
2 From a speech given by Professor Michael Boehlje of Purdue University, Iowa, to the Crop Protection Institute, in Calgary, Alberta, September 9, 1993.
3 Lester C. Thurow, "The Need for Strategic Approaches" (speech to the Liberal Party of Canada, Aylmer, Quebec, November 1991).
4 Joseph Pine, *Mass Customization* (Boston: Harvard University Press, 1993).

5   "The Car Industry," *Economist,*, October 17, 1992, p. 7.
6   Ibid., p. 6.
7   Pine, *Mass Customization.*
8   M. Malone, "If Badger Meter Can Do It . . .," *Forbes Magazine,* December 7, 1992, p. 105.
9   George Stalk, Philip Evans, and Lawrence Shulman of Boston Consulting Group, from an article in the *Harvard Business Review,* as quoted in "The Wal-Mart Advantage? It's All about Inventory," *Globe and Mail,* January 18, 1994.
10 Peter Drucker, *Managing for Results* (New York: Harper & Row, 1986).
11 "The Cracks in Quality," *Economist,* April 18, 1992, p. 67.
12 Ibid.
13 David Pecaut, "Brainstorming," *Globe and Mail,* July 20, 1993.
14 John Banka, interview with the author, November 21, 1993.
15 *Business Week,* January 15, 1991, p. 8.
16 M. Malone and W. Davidow, "The Virtual Corporation," *Forbes Magazine,* December 7, 1992, p. 106.
17 As reported in "Pink Slip Productivity," *Economist,* March 28, 1992, p. 79.
18 John Diebold, "Automation and the 21st Century" (speech in Washington, D.C., June 29, 1993).
19 Carol Kleiman, *The 100 Best Jobs for the 1990s & Beyond* (Chicago: Dearborn Financial Publishing, 1992), p. 23.
20 Max DePree, *Management Is an Art* (New York: Dell, 1989).
21 *Economist,* April 4, 1992, p. 87.
22 From "The 21st Century Corporation," a speech by Alfred West, CEO of the SEI Corporation, delivered June 29, 1993.
23 Based on author's interviews with company management.
24 Malone and Davidow, "The Virtual Corporation," p. 104.
25 "Gone West," *Economist,* July 11, 1992, p. 69.
26 Robert Hicks, "No Service, No Smile, No Sale," *Globe and Mail,* June 8, 1993.

Five   Where Will the Jobs Be?

1   Richard L. Knowdell, "Rights and Responsibilities Regarding Work" (speech delivered July 1, 1993).
2   Author's private correspondence with Premier Frank McKenna, December 1993.
3   Richard Worzel, *From Employee to Entrepreneur* (Toronto: Key Porter, 1989).
4   As cited in Carol Kleiman, *The 100 Best Jobs for the 1990s & Beyond* (Chicago: Dearborn Financial Publishing, 1992).
5   Ibid.
6   S. Norman Feingold and Norma Reno Miller, *Emerging Careers: New Occupations for the Year 2000 and Beyond* (Garrett Park, Md.: Garrett Park Press, 1983).
7   Kleiman, *100 Best Jobs,* p. 17.
8   Based on personal conversations with George Chester, an organizer of Out of the Cold, a program to feed and house the homeless during the winter.
9   I don't have answers for these questions. If you do, I would appreciate hearing from you. Write to me (please don't call) care of the publisher, at the address given at the back of the book.
10 Richard Barnet, as quoted in "World without Jobs," *Globe and Mail,* September 14, 1993.
11 As quoted in *Policy Options,* July 1993.

Six   The Time Boom

1   Statistics Canada, *Population Projections 1990 to 2011 Based on Recent Changes in Fertility Levels and Revised Immigration Targets,* December 1991.
2   Ibid.
3   Ibid.
4   Ibid.

5   This concept was introduced to me by David Pecaut of Canada Consulting/The Boston Consulting Group, and I appreciate his help.

6   Peter F. Drucker, *Post-Capitalist Society* (New York: HarperBusiness, 1993), p. 58.

7   Colleen Hamilton and John Whalley, "Reforming Public Pensions in Canada: Issues and Options," in *Pensions Today and Tomorrow: Background Studies,* edited by David W. Conklin, Jalynn H. Bennett, and Thomas J. Courchene (Toronto: Ontario Economic Council, 1984), p. 125.

8   Ken Dychtwald, Ph.D., and Joe Flower, *Age Wave: The Challenges and Opportunities of an Aging North America* (Los Angeles: Jeremy C. Tarcher, 1989), p. 81.

9   "Canada a Third World Debtor, Think Tank Says," *Globe and Mail,* May 12, 1994.

10 Statistics Canada, *Population Projections 1990 to 2011.*

11 C. Ross Healy, "Pensions and the Capital Markets: Independence or Intervention," in *Pensions Today and Tomorrow: Background Studies,* edited by David W. Conklin, Jalynn H. Bennett, and Thomas J. Courchene (Toronto: Ontario Economic Council, 1984), p. 285.

12 Hamilton and Whalley, "Reforming Public Pensions in Canada," p. 125.

Seven   The Detonation of the Population Bomb

1   Paul R. Ehrlich and Anne H. Ehrlich, *The Population Explosion* (New York: Simon & Schuster, 1990), p. 14.

2   Bryant Robey, Shea O. Rutstein, and Leo Morris, "The Fertility Decline in Developing Countries," *Scientific American,* December 1993, p. 60.

3   Robert Fox, *Population Images* (New York: United Nations Fund for Population Activities, 1987), pp. 10–12.

4   Ehrlich and Erhlich, *The Population Explosion,* p. 20.

5   Edward Goldsmith and Nicholas Hildyard, *The Earth Report: The Essential Guide to Global Ecological Issues* (New York: Price Stern Sloan, 1989), p. 142, based on U.S. Agriculture statistics, as quoted in Ehrlich & Ehrlich, p. 96.

6   Donella H. Meadows, Dennis L. Meadows, and Jrgen Randers, *Beyond the Limits* (Toronto: McClelland & Stewart, 1992), pp. 54–57.

7   Ibid., p. 56.

8   Robert S. McNamara, "The Population Explosion," *Futurist,* November-December 1992, p. 11.

9   Meadows, Meadows, and Randers, *Beyond the Limits,* p. 62.

10 "The Question Rio Forgets," *Economist,* May 30, 1992, p. 11

11 Meadows, Meadows, and Randers, *Beyond the Limits,* p. 67.

12 McNamara, "The Population Explosion," p. 13.

13 Meadows, Meadows, and Randers, *Beyond the Limits,* p. 67.

14 "A Prospect of Growth," *Economist,* July 13, 1991, p. 16.

15 "Rural Indian Can't Bear More Children," *Globe and Mail,* March 3, 1994.

16 One economic refugee said to me, "You Canadians are so naive. Anyone who can find the money to get on a plane to Canada cannot be a true refugee, for the truly poor could not make enough money for the plane ticket in their entire lives. But we wear shabby clothes, and long faces, and act scared, and you let us in. And why should we not? Life here is much better than we had at home."

17 From a statement released by the Club of Earth on September 3, 1988, at the Pugwash Conference on Global Problems and Common Security, Dagomys, USSR, as quoted in Ehrlich and Ehrlich, *The Population Explosion,* p. 18.

18 Ehrlich and Ehrlich, *The Population Explosion,* p. 23.

Eight   The Computer Revolution Finally Begins

1   Based on a conversation with Bill Buxton, scientific director of the Ontario Telepresence Project, who works on the development of this kind of application with the research group at Xerox PARC (Palo Alto Research Center) in California. This work was first pioneered by Olivetti's research laboratory in Cambridge, England. PARC and EuroPARC, the European Rank Xerox counterpart, are pioneering this kind of low-profile, or no-

profile, use of computers.

2 Based on a conversation between the author and Professor Eugene Fiume of the University of Toronto, March 1994.

3 Prototypes are already being worked on. However, such vehicles are not currently capable of operating in the complex and often confusing environment of a normal highway, except in carefully controlled circumstances.

4 Based on a conversation between the author and Dr. Ernest Kornelsen of the Institute of Microstructural Sciences of the National Research Council of Canada, March 23, 1994.

5 "Dark fibre [meaning optical fibre using photonics] will not only mean the end of the telephone industry as we know it but also the end of the telephone industry as they plan it: a vast intelligent fabric of information services" (George Gilder, "Into the Fibresphere," *Forbes Magazine*, December 7, 1992, p. 112).

6 Ibid., p. 115.

7 Ibid., p. 114.

8 "Telepresence: A Model for Collaboration," from the *TRIO Network*, the newsletter of the Telecommunications Research Institute of Ontario, as supplied by Bill Buxton of the University of Toronto.

Nine Creations from Technology's Laboratory

1 I am indebted to Professor Al Miller of the Department of Metallurgy and Materials Science, University of Toronto, and Tony Redpath, communications officer for the Ontario Centre for Materials Research, for their time and assistance in guiding me through an area I know so poorly.

2 "Parallam" is a trade mark of MacMillan Bloedel.

3 *Scientific American*, December 1993, p. 121.

4 Absolute zero is so called because it is the temperature at which all molecular motion ceases — hence, there is no heat at all.

5 "Grow Your Own," *Economist*, August 1, 1992, p. 75.

6 This idea has been proven in pilot projects, but no one has ever put it into production. I got it from Dr. J. Lamar Worzel, the now-retired associate director of the Marine Sciences Institute of the University of Texas. His other claim to fame is that he's my father.

7 Elizabeth Pennisi, "Natureworks: Making Minerals the Biological Way," *Science News*, May 16, 1992, pp. 329–31.

8 Ibid., p. 331.

9 "Hardcore Films," *Economist*, July 25, 1992, p. 81.

10 "Uses to Come," *Economist*, June 1, 1991, p. 82.

11 "Steeling Diamonds," *Economist*, July 25, 1992, p. 81.

12 Based on comments in "Simple Recipe Yields Fullerene Tubules," *Science News*, July 18, 1992, p. 142; and on a conversation with Dr. Ernest Kornelsen of the Institute of Microstructural Sciences, National Research Council of Canada, March 23, 1994.

13 If this seems unbelievable, it is nonetheless a real possibility, although admittedly not likely until well into the next century. See, for instance, Arthur C. Clarke, *The Fountains of Paradise* (New York: Harcourt Brace Jovanovich, 1978). And lest you dismiss Clarke's fiction too quickly, recall that it was he who successfully anticipated and described the communications satellite some thirty years before its reality. Moreover, as Clarke himself acknowledges, he got the idea from a letter which four bona fide scientists (John D. Isaacs, Hugh Bradner, and George E. Backus of Scripps Oceanographic Institute, and Allyn C. Vine of Woods Hole Oceanographic Institute) published in *Science* on February 11, 1966.

14 "What Can We Learn from Apollo?" *Space Studies Institute Update*, March/April 1992, pp. 1–3.

15 Drawn from the testimony of Robert Anson Heinlein before a joint session of the U.S. House of Representatives Committee on Aging and the House Committee on Science and Technology, July 19, 1979.

16 Larry Niven, Jerry Pournelle, and Michael Flynn, *Fallen Angels* (Riverdale, N.Y.: Baen Books, 1991), p. 392.

17 Based on conversations and correspondence between the author and the Space Studies Institute of Princeton, N.J., May 1992.

Ten   The End of Infinity

1   N. Craig Smith and John A. Quelch, "McDonald's and the Environment," *Ethics and Marketing* (Boston: Irwin, 1993), p. 62. This is a case-study book used by the Harvard Graduate School of Business.

2   Ronald Bailey, *Eco-Scam: The False Prophets of Ecological Apocalypse* (New York: St. Martin's, 1993), p. 156.

3   Interview with Dr. R. E. Munn, April 11, 1994.

4   David Suzuki, "Why We Must Act on Global Warming," *Toronto Star,* March 26, 1994.

5   Ibid.

6   Eigil Friis-Christensen and Knud Lassen, "Length of the Solar Cycle: An Indicator of Solar Activity Closely Associated with Climate," *Science,* November 1, 1991, p. 698.

7   Interview with Dr. Munn.

8   Bailey, *Eco-Scam,* p. 159.

9   *Webster's Seventh New Collegiate Dictionary* (Springfield, Mass.: Merriam, 1972).

10   Paul R. Ehrlich and Anne H. Ehrlich, *Healing the Planet* (Reading, Mass.: Addison-Wesley, 1991), p. 7.

11   "A Survey of Energy and the Environment," *Economist,* August 31, 1991, p. 4.

12   Ibid., p. 25.

13   Ibid., p.13.

14   D. S. Mahathir Bin Mohamed, "Eco-imperialism," *New Perspectives Quarterly,* Summer 1992, p. 57.

15   R. E. Munn, "Environmental Prospects for the Next Century: Implications for Long-term Policy and Research Strategies," International Institute for Applied Systems Analysis, Austria, 1987.

16   John Holdren, *Scientific American,* September 1990, p. 162.

17   In fact, there are no zero-pollution cars. For instance, electric cars, which are the most likely result of California's experiment, produce pollution at the generating plant that produces the electricity.

18   However, I'd be willing to bet that if humanity started burning hydrogen in the quantities it currently burns hydrocarbons, we would discover that too much water vapour creates problems too. I suspect, for example, that it might turn out to be a more powerful "greenhouse gas" than carbon dioxide.

19   I am ignoring the possibility of cold fusion. So far, it has been a product of wishful thinking. If it were true, it would solve many of our problems — providing we used cheap energy wisely.

20   For example, when the Government of Ontario implemented a $5-per-tire recycling tax, the money went into general revenues and was not used to recycle tires.

21   "Doing It for Mother Earth," *Business Week,* January 15, 1991, p. 44.

22   Sabuto Okita, former foreign minister of Japan and member of the U.N.'s Brundtland Commission, in his article "Japan: Model of Sustainable Development," *New Perspectives Quarterly,* Summer 1990, p. 15.

23   Gustave Speth, in his article "A Climate of Apocalypse," *New Perspectives Quarterly,* Spring 1989, pp. 12–13.

Eleven   How Much Is Enough?

1   "A Survey of the Future of Medicine," *Economist,* March 19, 1994, p. 1.

2   "Radical Concerns over Drinking Water," *Science News,* April 18, 1992, p. 398.

3   Interview with Dr. Kunov, director, Institute of Biomedical Engineering, University of Toronto, March 16, 1994.

4   "A Survey of the Future of Medicine," p. 5.

5   Note, however, that Sweden is geographically a much smaller country than Canada and much more homogenized in racial and cultural terms, both of which make the centralization of records easier and simpler.

6   "A Survey of the Future of Medicine," p. 7.

7   The animal donor will probably already be dead. But if you are willing to eat bacon or steak, you have implicitly already made the ethical decision about receiving this kind of transplant.

8   "Xeno's Paradox," *Economist,* October 23, 1993, pp. 106–7.

9   Interview with Dr. Ron Worton, Hospital for Sick Children, March 1994. Most of the material on genetic engineering in this chapter comes from this interview.

10   Interview with Dr. Sylvia Bacchetti, professor of molecular biology at McMaster University, May 1994.

11 In view of the ratios of male-to-female babies born in certain countries where male children are highly prized and female children are considered a burden, it is virtually certain that the use of abortion to determine the sex of a child is being practised on a wide scale.

12 Ken Dychtwald, Ph.D., and Joe Flower, *Age Wave: The Challenges and Opportunities of an Aging North America* (Los Angeles: Jeremy C. Tarcher, 1989), p. 42.

13 Helen Henderson, "Trapped between Changing Systems," *Toronto Star,* March 12, 1994.

Twelve   The Fate of Canada

1 Peter F. Drucker, *Post-Capitalist Society* (New York: HarperBusiness, 1993), p. 142.

2 Daniel Bell, in a speech given in Washington, D.C., July, 1993.

3 Richard Rosecrance, "Economic Deterrence," *New Perspectives Quarterly,* Summer 1992, p. 34.

4 In addition, there are two other levels in the separate school boards, which parallel the Metro Toronto and City of Toronto school boards. I don't pay taxes to them, but they duplicate the functions and structure of their public school counterparts.

5 "On the Make," *Economist,* January 22, 1994, pp. 96–97.

6 Sometimes these arguments are not so peaceful, as when right-to-life groups bomb abortion clinics.

7 Arthur M. Schlesinger, Jr, *The Disuniting of America: Reflections on a Multicultural Society* (New York: W. W. Norton, 1992), p. 118.

8 If, for instance, American blacks all lived in one area of the United States, I suspect there would be a strong separatist movement for a black homeland.

Thirteen   Alone

1 Used with the permission of Dr. Reginald Bibby, professor of sociology of the University of Lethbridge, Alberta.

2 "Yours, Mine and Ours: Ontario's Children and Youth," a report by the Ontario Premier's Council on Health, Well-being and Social Justice, May 1994, p. 16.

3 Ibid.

4 Ibid., p. 17.

5 Giles Gherson, "Rebalancing the Price of Divorce, So That Women and Children Pay Less," *Globe and Mail,* May 11, 1994.

6 "The Bargain Breaks," *Economist,* December 26, 1992, p. 38.

7 Ibid.

8 "The Troubled Children of Families of Convenience," *Globe and Mail,* November 3, 1993.

9 Reginald Bibby, "Who Will Teach Our Children Shared Values?" *Globe and Mail,* February 3, 1994.

10 Saul Bellow, "Locking Up the Imagination," *Globe and Mail,* March 15, 1994.

11 Arthur M. Schlesinger, Jr, *The Disuniting of America* (New York: W. W. Norton, 1992), pp. 104, 114.

12 Shelby Steele, "The New Segregation," *Imprimis,* August 1992, pp. 1–3. Reprinted by permission from *Imprimis,* the monthly journal of Hillsdale College.

13 Stacie Bergwerff, "Law Faculty Rethinks 'Discriminatory' Exam Policy," *Ottawa Citizen,* January 26, 1994.

14 As reported by Philip Marchand, "Author Protests No-Whites Conference," *Toronto Star,* May 14, 1994.

15 "I may disagree with what you say, but I will defend to the death your right to say it."

16 Marchand, "Author Protests No-Whites Conference."

17 "Kids Get All the Wrong Signals When TV is the Baby-Sitter," *Toronto Star,* June 12, 1994.

18 Larry Woiwode, "Television: The Cyclops That Eats Books," *Imprimis,* February 1992.

19 Bibby, "Who Will Teach Our Children Shared Values?"

20 From a speech given in Rochester, New York, 1941.

Fourteen   Courage

1 This sequence of events is drawn from the audio recording of James Burke's *Connections* (Los Angeles: Audio Renaissance Tapes, 1990).

Index